OLD EUROPE, NEW ASIA

Strategies, Challenges, Responses

BY THE SAME AUTHOR

Non-fiction

- Tricks of the Trade
- The Rise, Decline and Future of the British Commonwealth
- The Jamdani Revolution
- Towards the New Horizon: World Order in the 21st Century
- Diplomatic Channels
- Europe in Emerging Asia: Opportunities and Obstacles

Fiction

- The Fourth Profile
- Guesswork
- The Eccentric Effect
- The Invisible African

The author acknowledges his debt to the Chairman, Director, colleagues and staff of the Maulana Abul Kalam Azad Institute for Asian Studies, Kolkata; the Swedish Collegium at Uppsala; and Dr. N.G. Satish, Librarian at ASCI, Hyderabad. He also thanks Professor Wang Yiwei for his generous foreword.

OLD EUROPE, NEW ASIA

Strategies, Challenges, Responses

Krishnan Srinivasan

Foreword by

Wang Yiwei

MAULANA ABUL KALAM AZAD INSTITUTE OF ASIAN STUDIES,
KOLKATA

PENTAGON PRESS

Old Europe, New Asia: Strategies, Challenges, Responses

by Krishnan Srinivasan

First Published in 2016

ISBN 978-81-8274-854-5

Published by
PENTAGON PRESS
206, Peacock Lane, Shahpur Jat,
New Delhi-110049
Phones: 011-64706243, 26491568
Telefax: 011-26490600
email: rajan@pentagonpress.in
website: www.pentagonpress.in

Branch Office
Flat No.213, Athena-2,
Clover Acropolis,
Viman Nagar,
Pune-411014

Printed at Avantika Printers Private Limited.

CONTENTS

FOREWORD

Krishnan Srinivasan is a former very senior Indian diplomat and an author and scholar, drawing on his considerable experience of world affairs. In this book, he contrasts the rise of emerging Asia with the relative decline of Europe in terms of its political, strategic and cultural involvement with Asia. His narrative takes him to explore a wide spread of subjects, such as the challenges facing emerging Asia and the European Union respectively, strategic relationships, the eurozone crisis, climate change, the colonial legacy, reform of international institutions and contrasting value systems in approaches to human rights and governance.

It is generally accepted that from a unipolar American-dominated world at the dissolution of the Soviet Union, the international community has now evolved into a more multi-polar system. Europe and the emerging economies of Asia constitute two of those poles, and among the biggest and fastest growing economies in Asia are China and India. Srinivasan provides a candid examination of the economic, cultural and strategic assets and liabilities of both Europe and emerging Asia to closer engagement. While not subscribing to the opinion that the rise of Asia is inevitable, he believes in its strong likelihood despite the gloomy predictions of many western academics and politicians, who have so far proved wrong.

In Asia, with the largest concentration of the world's population, concerns over terrorism, proliferation of weapons of mass destruction, inter-state problems, unacceptable levels of abject poverty and adverse effects of climate change, the phrase 'Asian century' may prove to be a misnomer. And in institutional terms, emerging Asia is much less clearly defined than is Europe. It enjoys neither political nor commercial unity, nor any common security agenda. Its multilateral structures are weak and systems of governance vary from communism to liberal democracy. A coherent Asian vision and meaningful architecture will depend on China, Japan and India working together, but these countries have contrary strategic aspirations and yet offer no impulse for greater integration.

Nevertheless, the world must take close account of the rapid economic growth in certain parts of Asia, with its expanding middle class, growing percentage of intra-regional trade, low cost labour, high savings and investment rates, vast territory and resources, and rapidly growing infrastructure and technology. With increasing confidence, Asian culture and soft power are fast becoming global.

For the first time in centuries, Europe has slipped from centre-stage to the near-periphery in the system of international relations. It came belatedly to appreciate the benefits of cultivating closer ties with emerging Asia and initially only as a defensive reaction to Asian economic competitiveness. But Europe is still one of the leading economic partners for each major Asian economy. This book covers the difficulties encountered in Europe-Asian strategic partnerships, free trade agreements, protectionism and collaborations in security and technology.

Given the centuries of European colonialism and imperialism, Asian nationalism carries the imprint of foreign oppression. Europe is still inclined to take a paternalistic view of emerging Asia, and its efforts to spread western normative agendas, values and civilization meet with increasing resistance. Emerging Asia will affect Europe's future far more than Europe can affect Asia's, and Europe must accommodate emerging Asia's desire for respect and a rightful place in managing the world order from which it feels excluded by the post-World War II arrangements.

The implications of the United States role are examined, including the rebalance of American forces to Asia and Chinese President Xi Jinping's 'new type of great power relationship'. To Asian sceptics, Europe can enhance its image in Asia only through showing it is 'not America' though neither Asia nor Europe can afford to consider the other a proxy in checking the power of the USA. The emergence of a European foreign policy was in part intended to provide a balance to the abrasive aspects of American policy, but that initial optimism has now disappeared. Europe suffers from another handicap, namely, that the USA is unenthusiastic about any greater European role in Asian geopolitics.

For Europe, the benefits of intensive association with emerging Asia are the boost that it gives to trade, manufacture and services, and access to liquidity, investment and skilled manpower. It would help Europe to banish the remnants of the negative imperial mindset and stereotyping, to redress the American influence that prevents it from playing a more active role in Asia, and to reinvent itself as a world player if not a world power. It would then be able to adjust to the evolving international order. For this, Europe would need to make its policies more Asia-friendly and its population more Asia-literate.

For emerging Asia, closer ties with Europe could lead to benefits in trade, investment and the latest technology, and would help in the modernisation of society since Asia generally seeks to modernise along western lines. This would apply, for example, to issues such as equality of gender and equal opportunity. Close association with Europe will be essential for emerging Asia to fulfill its legitimate claim for an improved international voice and a say in global governance commensurate with its new status.

The common history shared by the two continents stretches back several centuries and encompasses trade, culture, legend, myth, literature, imperialism and migration. Expectations of a dynamic 'New' Asia, with high economic growth and the development of a strong consumer class, seem to contrast with a well-respected, technologically and culturally rich 'Old' Europe now struggling with problems of unity and identity, and a sluggish economy. Krishnan Srinivasan holds the view that Europe is not only a representative of the past, and emerging Asia is not the sum total of the future; but both need to make much greater efforts to cooperate to ensure Europe's future and enable Asia to fulfill its potential. Despite its vast canvas, the text is succinct and accessible both to those studying international relations, and the person who takes a general interest in world affairs. I am happy to recommend this book to a wide readership.

Wang Yiwei

* * *

Wang Yiwei is a former Chinese diplomat, presently professor of International Studies at Renmin University, director of the Institute of International Affairs, director of the Centre for European Union studies, and director of the China-Europe Academic Network.

ABBREVIATIONS

AIIB	Asian Infrastructure Investment Bank
ADB	Asian Development Bank
APEC	Asia Pacific Economic Cooperation
ASEAN	Association of Southeast Asian Nations
ASEM	Asia Europe Meeting
BASIC	Brazil, South Africa, India, China
BRICS	Brazil, Russia, India, China, South Africa
BTIA	Bilateral Trade and Investment Agreement
CAP	common agriculture policy
CFSP	Common Foreign and Security Policy
CI	Confucius Institutes
CO_2	carbon dioxide
CPC	Communist Party of China
CTBT	Comprehensive Test-ban Treaty
EAS	East Asia Summit
EC	European Commission or European Communities
ECB	European Central Bank
EEAS	European External Action Service
EFSF	European Financial Stability Facility
EEC	European Economic Community
ESS	European Security Strategy
EU	European Union

FDI	Foreign Direct Investment
FTA	Free Trade Agreement
FTAAP	Free Trade Area of the Asia Pacific
G-2	Group of Two
G-20	Group of Twenty
G-77	Group of 137 developing countries
G-8	Group of Eight
GATT	General Agreement on Tariffs and Trade
GHG	greenhouse gas
GMO	genetically modified organism
GDP	Gross Domestic Product
GPS	Global Positioning System
HAL	Hindustan Aeronautics Limited
HFCs	hydrofluorocarbons
IBRD	International Bank for Reconstruction and Development (World Bank)
ICT	Information and Communications Technology
IMF	International Monetary Fund
IPCC	Intergovernmental Panel on Climate Change
IPR	intellectual property rights
LDC	Least Developed Country
MDGs	Millennium Development Goals
MES	Market Economy Status
NATO	North Atlantic Treaty Organization
NGO	Non-government Organisation
NPT	Non-proliferation Treaty
NTBs	non-tariff barriers
ODA	Official Development Assistance
OECD	Organisation for Economic Cooperation and Development
p.a.	per annum (year)
p.d.	per diem (day)
p.m.	per mensem (month)

P-5	Permanent Members of the UNSC
PPP	purchasing power parity
R&D	Research and Development
R2P	Responsibility to Protect
RCEP	Regional Cooperation Economic Partnership
SAARC	South Asian Association for Regional Cooperation
SCO	Shanghai Cooperation Organisation
TPP	Trans-Pacific Partnership
TRIPS	Trade-related Intellectual Property Rights
TTIP	Transatlantic Trade and Investment Partnership
UK	United Kingdom
UN	United Nations
UNFCCC	United Nations Framework Convention on Climate Change
UNGA	United Nations General Assembly
UNSC	United Nations Security Council
USA	United States of America
WTO	World Trade Organization

1

EUROPE AND THE GLOBALISED WORLD

Europe is a continent difficult to define. Philip Johan von Strahlenburg, an eighteenth century Swedish mercenary fighting in Russia, said that Europe began at the Urals, which has been hotly debated ever since, and creates perennial problems for intermediate countries like Ukraine. Europe has no centre of authority and no fixed territory; and its geographical, administrative, economic and cultural borders diverge. Europeans have always questioned Europe's political borders: Europe's identity is built on common interest, peace and freedom, economy, welfare, global responsibility and transnational pluralism.

Europe, the European Union (EU)[1] and the eurozone[2] are used interchangeably in nearly all works about that continent, and the same is the case in this book, but the scope of reference here is mainly to the European Union, which excludes Iceland, Norway, Switzerland and some Balkan nations. And the emerging economies of Asia are generally understood to be China, India, Indonesia, South Korea, Singapore and Taiwan. Japan, a leading Asian economy, cannot be called emerging, since it joined the ranks of the developed countries in the Organisation for Economic Cooperation and Development (OECD) as early as 1964.

Some centuries ago, when more than half the world's product was estimated to have been generated by China under the Mings (1368-1644) and India under the Moghuls (1526-1858), Europe in the pre-Renaissance period was seen from an Indian and Chinese viewpoint as a little-considered outpost abutting the vast Asian continent. In 1411, when the Forbidden City in Ming-dynasty Beijing was being built, Europe was an unhappy backwater recuperating from the Black Death, and in 1500, the biggest city in the world was Beijing with 600,000 people.[3] In 1820, China's share of world GDP was 32.4 per cent; by 1952 it was only 5 per cent . In 1700 India's was 23 per cent, and in 1820 16 per cent, but by 1978 had fallen to 3.4 per cent.[4] By 1913, and after three centuries of European expansion, western empires controlled 3/5ths of the world's territory and population, and nearly 80 per cent of the global economic output.[5]

In a few decades from now, come the middle of the 21st century, could it be a case of back to the future? That is to be avoided for the sake of both Europe and Asia. The American National Intelligence Council predicted in 2008 that in four years' time the EU would be "a hobbled giant, distracted by internal bickering and competing national agendas". That forecast was to be largely accurate. The same council's latest survey in 2012[6] states that, taking into account the variables of population, GDP, military spending and investment in technology, Asia will wield more "overall" global power than USA and Europe combined by 2030, and within 20 years China would overtake the USA as the world's biggest economy.

Europe's relative decline has been both economic and political. Can Europe re-join the future world as a global force or will it be consigned to the margins? Mark Eyskens, one-time foreign minister of Belgium, had called the EU an "economic giant, political dwarf and military worm".[7] Europe's success was in the binary world of the Cold War and the monist world of American supremacy; it now has to accommodate itself to a very different multi-polar environment, and when, in most respects, it is the worst of times for Europe.

The EU as a Foreign Actor

A group of European states, including two permanent members of the United Nations (UN) Security Council and the economic powerhouse Germany, step by step abdicated vital aspects of their sovereignty to hand them over to a still weak, democratically poorly legitimised and hardly transparent central power in Brussels. The EU's legal status does not augur well for its ambition to act as a strong international player. Both its own member states and third parties are reluctant to accept the EU as a member of international organisations, which is a position they want to retain only for themselves. The EU cannot rid itself of this dichotomy; on one hand it represents itself, and on the other its constituent parts. The EU is a minor player, outranked in terms of influence by the foreign policies of its member states.

The Common Foreign and Security Policy (CFSP) of the EU originated in 1993 with the Treaty of Maastricht. Institutional inconsistency is built into the EU system. Considering the complexity of the system of multiple controls, competences, voting procedures, decision making and financing, the number of states, the breadth of issues, competing agendas, the limits of intervention and turf wars, it is amazing that the EU claims to have a common foreign policy at all.[8] Internal functionality makes the EU an introspective and ineffective international actor. Collectively, it has the tools—capabilities, technology, finances, population—of a great power but lacks the consensus to go down that path. Suffice it to say it is a *sui generis* political actor. Members like the notion of the weight of 28 states with one agenda but they baulk at allowing their own interest, even on normative issues, defined by the other twenty-seven. So they end up by being double-minded; they favour a greater role for the EU in global politics, but are reluctant to agree on any common policy. Countries in the EU may have changed from nation states to member states, but are still far from being a unified super-state. Accordingly, the more important the issue, the more parochial the policy making remains. National interest is well and alive in Europe: there is no EU policy unless the big European nations are on-side, and the consensus requirement makes policy risk-averse and reactive rather than proactive. Many nations were not willing for the EU to do more in crisis management than was useful for their own national policies, the North Atlantic Treaty Organization (NATO) or the transatlantic alliance. Yet the Union has churned out more than a thousand common strategies and positions since 1993 and over 2000 statements from 1995 to 2008; on average, one every 2 and ½ days, in the quest for credibility as a global actor.

The EU has a two-way interactive process between national and European that determines the nature of both. But the division of competencies is not clear even to experts and practitioners, and it is evident that member states retain decisive power in foreign and security policy. As one writer has observed; "for external observers, the plurality and diversity of instruments, mechanisms and strategies under the roof of the EU are not easy to catch".[9] The EU's blend of multipolarity plus multilateralism plus inter-regionalism is hard to understand and accommodate, and "no one outside a tiny group of Euro-actors and Euro-academics understands how the EU works".[10] As an EU insider admitted; "the EU's external representation is absurdly complicated and baffling to outsiders,"[11] while former British Foreign Minister David Milliband was more explicit: "Arrangements are ad hoc, coordination patchy, messages confused, and relationships with the great global powers lacking clarity, strategy or purpose. So the choice is simple…make the EU a leader on the world stage, or become spectators in a G-2 world shaped by the US and China. .. We can lead a strong European foreign policy or, lost in hubris, nostalgia or xenophobia, watch our influence in the world wane. .. people are starting to talk about an Age of Continents....The EU and China could drive a surge in new investment delivering energy, economic and environmental security…The trouble is that at the moment the European whole is less than the sum of its parts. Outside Europe, people are confused about what we care about and what we are willing to do. Inside Europe it is not much better; there is not sufficient common purpose."[12]

The EU External Action Service (EEAS) that was established in 2010 under the High Representative of the Union for foreign affairs and security policy (foreign minister) has already come in for severe criticism. A European Parliament expert group report's issued in March 2013 suggests that the external action service was guilty of wasteful duplication, confusion, poor management and lack of elementary diplomatic skills. Morale was falling due to a lack of trust, internal quarrels, clashes with other European institutions and national diplomatic services, and an opaque chain of command. The individuals lacked political expertise, linguistic skills and country-specific knowledge, while the High Representative herself has an "impossible combination of tasks".[13] The

EU has had personnel deployed in peacekeeping in Aceh, Sudan, Democratic Republic of Congo and Kosovo, but the goals were poorly articulated in regard to why the EU should intervene outside its borders, where, and with what criteria. At a deeper level, most European countries have long ceased to be modern states provided with the complete toolkit of classical statecraft and the will for using it. The few states that still possess elements of both, such as the United Kingdom and France, are no longer big enough for the world's premier league, and Germany remains reluctant to take any lead, still immobilised by the nightmares of its own past. In reality, the EU is taking its place in the emerging multipolar order as a small power. It did not figure even once in the 90-minute foreign affairs debate during the United States presidential campaign in October 2012.

It is doubtful that the EU has any soft power, or even normative power, other than through that bestowed on it by its constituent members. "Europe did not exist as a focus of loyalty or even as a meaningful category for most inhabitants of the continent",[14] and the individual European citizen remains culturally affiliated to a specific nation. We do not speak of European cuisine but French cuisine, of European discipline but German discipline, of the European but the British stiff upper lip. The abundance of national soft power at the member state level is impossible to replicate at the pan-EU level. In addition, Europe's soft power wanes the further it is projected from Europe. Nor is the EU a 'smart power', combining both soft and hard power.

By curbing bellicose competition for power and promoting international cooperation, it was possible for Europe to establish supranational procedures and institutions for decision making and political negotiation. But can the European Union without a UN seat, nor participating as one nation in the Olympic Games, make any claim to an international personality or identity, or even a foreign policy? Its status in international law is ambiguous despite the adoption of a flag, the anthem and the euro currency. Its strongest foreign policy asset was enlargement, that is, expansion of membership, which has now weakened. Turkey was the first country to apply for membership in 1963, but now has lost interest, though it was always seen as both Europe's problem and solution—the problem was for European identity, ethnicity and territory, and the solution to declining population, trade space and global actorship. During the eurozone crisis, Turkey began showing it could turn its back on Europe, and the world saw Turkey growing faster than most European economies. If the EU club was a popular idea with 75 per cent of Turks until recently, the figure has now dropped to below 20 per cent. The Turks see the Europeans as racially and culturally prejudiced, while the EU is appalled that the Ankara government has become authoritarian and intolerant. All this despite the fact that Turkey's European identity suits almost everyone in the region rather than the neo-Ottoman demeanor it has lately presumed to adopt. The EU now fears it may have pushed too hard, because if Turkey permanently crosses over to the Eurasia camp, Europe is diminished. With Croatia being admitted in 2013, there is no credible candidate country on the waiting list of the EU. Iceland informed the European Commission in March 2015 that the country was no longer seeking EU membership though—or perhaps because—it already has free trade arrangements with the EU and is part of the Schengen visa-free travel arrangement. It had made an application for membership in 2009 and suspended it in 2013. That year Euro-sceptic parties won the national elections which caused the withdrawal of the application in 2015.

In its own self-estimate, the EU is a major, capable power, with global concerns and a sense of responsibility beyond narrow self-interest, and "Europe's hybrid confederacy is in effect a highly mature evolution of the nation state, a genuinely new political form".[15] As Europe's 17th century nation state became the world's political formula, the 20th century hybrid confederacy, it was hoped, could become the model for new regional systems. The EU is the largest integrated economic area, with a GDP and foreign investments comparable to the USA, with a population 50 per cent higher, 25 per cent of the world GDP, 7 per cent of the population, 50 per cent of its welfare spending, 17 per cent of trade (compared to the US with 15 per cent and China with 11 per cent), the world's largest development aid budget, the biggest services importer and exporter, 28 votes in the UN, two permanent United Nations Security Council (UNSC) members, two nuclear weapon states, a High Representative for Foreign Affairs and an external action service. As late as 2009, Perry Anderson was writing about "the unique role and prestige of the EU on the world stage that now has pride of place".[16]

The EU has three purposes: collective economic interests in the global economy; reshaping the regional milieu including by coercive conditionality clauses for aid and trade; and as a repository for human rights concerns and tackling poverty. Its transformative power is based on economic clout, fear of exclusion from its markets, and promise of future membership—all hard power aspects. The objectives of its foreign policy are the capacity to project power independently outside Europe, inculcate European strategic culture and institutionalise security cooperation in Europe. European foreign policy sees itself as regional pacifier, global intervener, mediator of conflicts, bridge between rich and poor and supervisor of the world economy.[17] It takes as its mandate global challenges like terror, weapons of mass destruction, failed states, a multilateral world order, a global security regime, conflict prevention and civil cooperation, an international legal order, promotion of human rights and democratic regimes, poverty reduction, control of climate change, development assistance, promoting peace, addressing instability and root causes of conflict, regional cooperation, trade links and access to natural resources. Europe's size and economy as the world's largest exporter and importer of goods makes it globally relevant. And without doubt, it is a life-style super power, having as many as 19 of the top 30 in the UN Human Development Report Index for 2013.

Its wider goals are the prevention of protectionism and economic nationalism and restrictions to free trade. Markets must reward hard work and initiative, not speculation. In development, there had to be a transition from fighting poverty to sustainable development. Climate change and energy security are intertwined; environment needs to be factored into national energy policies. Other objectives are to restore trust and confidence in the financial system, reform of international financial institutions, moving ahead with the Doha Round and commitment to the third world. As former French President Jacques Chirac said, "Europe is, and certainly will be in the future, here to stay as a major power". Yet, a multitude of EU actors share fragments of political authority and Kosovo in 1999 found the Europeans woefully unprepared for collective political or military action. Therefore the impression is that "the EU has no buck, at least no buck that stops".[18]

The EU is not a full-fledged actor at the United Nations, and its effort at utilising the General Assembly to enhance its international status has largely failed. First the rotating presidency spoke for the EU, and then the EU sought special status for the High Representative for Foreign and Security Policy. The result of this was 'enhanced observer status'. But this will not be a stepping stone to greater recognition because of opposition from other regional groupings. The French and the United Kingdom (UK) prioritise their Security Council membership over their EU membership, and do not speak for the EU, and so at the Security Council the EU has no special status. There are internal divisions on specific issues like the State of Palestine and UN reform. Voting with the emerging Asian nations is not congruent because of interpretations of sovereignty. The primary driver for the Asians is national interest and domestic stability and the principle of non-intervention, apart from innate suspicion of the EU due to the colonial legacy.

The past decade has seen displacement of power and authority from the West, and the West-inspired financial system imploded between 2008 and 2013. Views such as Mark Leonard's in 2006 *"Why Europe will run the 21st century"*; Paul Hockenos' in 2008 that *"The EU will write the rules for the new global order"*,[19] and Stephen Hill's description of Europe as the "new city on the hill" and can only be regarded today as absurd examples of wishful thinking.

A Globalised World

For the first time in centuries, Europe is not a fulcrum in the global system of international relations. The end of systemic Cold War confrontation between the West and East and the emergence of new Asian countries in the global political and economic arena push the European theatre to the relative periphery of international life. Europe still plays a major role in the world economy, but its ability to influence the global political and economic marketplace is steadily waning. Nothing in the past two decades has changed the global economy like the rise of China, which, with the industrialisation and modernisation of certain parts of Asia, is the cause of the re-orientation of the global economy. Malaysia's former deputy Prime Minister Anwar Ibrahim states that Asia "is in the process of coming into being. The long and intense process of self-definition and self-understanding is just beginning".[20]

The characteristics of power in the twenty first century will include physical size, a large working-age population with total factor productivity, (meaning the value added from all forms of production including labour and capital), a strong national identity, the size of the economy, modern technology, military prowess, a stable and strong currency, knowledge-based and capital exports, access to resources including energy, attractiveness to investable funds, a cultural endowment that will radiate beyond its borders, and the ability to withstand environmental degradation and climate change.

A set of core factors is usually needed for growth: macroeconomic stability (low inflation, tight monetary policy and fiscal deficit reduction), institutional capacity (legal, financial, health, bureaucratic systems), openness (to trade and foreign direct investment, new technology and larger markets) and education (skills). The emerging Asian economies will have to possess these characteristics to a varying degree, along with a range of economic, technological, military and political power assets, a capacity to contribute to international order regionally and globally, a degree of internal cohesion and a capacity for effective state action.

In next 30 years, intra-Asian trade will resemble transatlantic growth between USA/Europe and USA/Pacific in the 20th Century. As gravity shifts towards Asia, trade flows, finance, investment, consumption and movements of labour of high and low value will also shift. Between 1995 and 2005, European trade with China followed the classical pattern between a high-wage, highly-developed economy and an emerging country with cheap labour—evidenced by the fact that 65-70 per cent of the exports from Europe were of hi-technology content. With the growing sophistication of industrial manufacture in Asia, this trend is not likely to continue in future. In trade, the degree of complementarity between China and Europe is diminishing; from 85 per cent in 2000 to 65 per cent in 2010.[21] So as China makes the transition from efficiency-driven to innovation-driven manufacture, it and Europe will soon be competing at nearly the same level.

NOTES

1. The EU comprises 28 members states: Austria, Belgium, Bulgaria, Croatia, Cyprus, Czech Rep, Denmark, Estonia, Finland, France, Germany, Greece, Hungary,

Ireland, Italy, Latvia, Lithuania, Luxembourg, Malta, Netherlands, Poland, Portugal, Romania, Slovakia, Slovenia, Spain, Sweden, UK

2. The 19 countries of the eurozone are: Austria, Belgium, Cyprus, Estonia, Finland, France, Germany, Greece, Ireland, Italy, Latvia, Lithuania, Luxembourg, Malta, Netherlands, Portugal, Slovakia, Slovenia, and Spain.
3. Niall Ferguson, *Civilization.*
4. Dambisa Moyo, *How the West was Lost,* 16-18.
5. Niall Ferguson, *The West and the Rest,* table.
6. U.S. National Intelligence Council, Global Trends 2030.
7. Quoted by Craig R. Whitney, 'War in The Gulf', *New York Times,* 25 January 1991.
8. S. Keukeleire and J. MacNaughtan, *The Foreign Policy of the EU.*
9. www.anjamihr.com/resources/European +Union+and+Asia.pdf
10. David Marquand, books.google.co.in/books?isbn=1400838053
11. Fraser Cameron, *An Introduction to European Foreign Policy,* http://www.ies.be/files/documents/JMCdepository/Cameron,per cent20Fraser,per cent20Anper cent20Introductionper cent20toper cent20Europeanper cent20Foreignper cent20Policy,per cent20Aper cent20Strangeper cent20Superpower.pdf
12. David Milliband, *Independent,* 27 October 2009.
13. *Sunday Times,* UK, 3 March 2013, 31.
14. Bernard Wasserstein, *Barbarism and Civilization,* viii.
15. David P. Calleo, *Rethinking Europe's Future,* 373.
16. Perry Anderson, *London Review of Books,* Vol 29, No 18, 20 September 2007.
17. R. Seiledmann and A. Vasilache, *EU and Asia.*
18. David Marquand, *The End of the West,* 133.
19. Paul Hockenos, *USA and Europe,* 122.
20. Anwar Ibrahim of Malaysia, quoted by Pankaj Mishra *The Great Clamour,* 240.
21. Thomas Christiansen, Emil Kirchner & Philomena Murray, *The Palgrave Handbook of EU-Asia Relations,* Palgrave, Basingstoke, 2013, 500.

2

EMERGING ASIA

Asia remains the home of every conceivable strategic instability despite the economic spurt of the 21st century. There are unresolved disputes of a territorial nature, and the Korean peninsula is the most heavily armed region in the world. North Korea is potentially a nuclear weapon state, and India and Pakistan both possess nuclear weapons. The strategic rebalancing exercise of the USA to the Asia-Pacific, in whatever form it takes, is seen by China as unhealthy containment. If there is any outbreak of fighting in Asia, the impact on the global economy would be immense, with exports, investment, and shipment through the Malacca Straits and South China Sea all being affected. Despite the flashpoints of Kashmir, Tibet, East and South China Sea, Korea, tensions over the Taiwan Strait and the rise of Islamist terrorism, the emerging countries of the East Asian hemisphere have nevertheless enjoyed four decades of stability, security and rapidly rising prosperity.

Taiwan, South Korea and Singapore and some others show that with right interventions, developing countries can catch up in innovation and technology. Emphasis must be placed on enriching human capital, innovation (not adaptation) and technology and hitech exports as a percentage of manufactures, which in the case of China touches 30 per cent in electronics and semiconductor devices, ICT for India, and automobiles for South Korea, China and India. The Asian emerging economies, including China, are likely to focus on their economic growth without external forays. Societal transformation is work in progress and their best years may still lie ahead. They account for half the global economic growth, with high savings and investment rates, and China has invested nearly 50 per cent of its GDP, compared to 15 per cent in the US and 20 per cent in Europe. The importance of growth in the emerging economies, with foreign exchange reserves of over $2.3 trillion in 2009 and $7.29 trillion[1] today, and especially in China, is paramount for European markets and essential for the eurozone's recovery from crisis. Asian economies are strongly linked to the western economies, so the downstream impact of any slowdown in trade, investment, equity markets and employment will be in evidence. China and India invest abroad in manufactures and commodity producing assets, and both nations are essential to absorb the marketing surpluses of the industrialised countries. With a certain fragility in the US recovery, if neither of the world hubs generated any impetus, the eurozone's woes would deepen and precipitate a long-lasting malaise.

China

China has emerged as the world's factory and India as the back office. China's share of global manufactures has risen in 20 years from 4 per cent to 17 per cent. Huawei claims its products service 1/3rd of the world's population in telecommunications: an attempt anywhere in the world to live without anything made in China would find it hard going indeed. At least five hundred million Asians enjoy middle class standards; in 10 years this number could be 1.5 billion or more. By 2030 there will be more middle class Indians and Chinese than in USA and Europe combined, perhaps as many as two billion compared to 780 million.[2] And in a short time, India and China will transit from being aid receivers to aid donors.

In today's world, China dominates markets for many products worldwide and has become wealthy on a world scale, with one million US dollar millionaires. It is the largest trading partner with every country in the Asia Pacific area and its trade and investment weight in Africa and South America is growing apace. It has been the largest buyer of United States treasury bills, and the Chinese rich are investing abroad, even in real estate, especially in Canada and USA.

To be ultracompetitive for the past 15 years, China has kept wages and exchange rates artificially low, transferring real income from workers to consumers and absorbing global inflation for the sake of market share and foreign reserves. China is a volume maximiser, not a profit maximiser; volume drives employment and maintains political and social stability. China has emphasised savings over consumption and productive investment over global policing in contrast to the West whose economic costs of strategy in terms of wars, ideology and interventionism are mounting.

The USA and China face mutually assured monetary destruction if they change their policies from the present arrangement, whereby US is a strong market for Chinese goods, and China keeps prices down and provides cheap cash. The two countries are each other's second largest trading partner, after Canada in the case of the USA, and the EU in the case of China. China is America's largest lender and owns more than $1.2 trillion dollars of US Treasury securities. Chinese direct investment in USA was $12 billion last year, topping $10 billion for the second year running, and exceeds US investment in China. The Chinese companies are coming to USA because they face higher costs at home in land and labour, and also to acquire technological skills and innovation since China wants to move up the value chain. The United States in turn is the third largest investor in China. About 200,000 Chinese study in the US and more than 20,000 Americans work or study in China. This reveals an unprecedented degree of mutual interdependence between the world's leading power and its leading competitor. The US' former rival, the Soviet Union, had never tried to compete in world markets, unlike China.

As it reaches the middle income *per capita* level, or the 'middle-income trap', China's growth may drop from 10 per cent to six per cent or seven per cent, but even at that rate, the size of its economy means that it will be the main single contributor to global growth. China counts on its rising productivity to offset any drop in exports due to competition from cheaper Asian exporters. It has plenty of room to grow even at a slower pace as it fulfils the need to rebalance its economy with less reliance on exports and to stimulate consumption growth within China itself.

The continuation of the economic boom is essential for the authority of the Communist Party of China (CPC), and has led to the most remarkable transformation in human history in just 30 years. Most Chinese know that this is the best time for them to live in. The Confucius tradition urges one to behave with others as they should to one, rulers to pursue benevolence, and subjects to show filial piety to fathers and all in authority.[3] The extent to which China has opened its society and economy to the world, and the way in which it has managed economic progress with stability and sense of purpose is remarkable indeed. And while China is communist, it is very different from Soviet communism or North Korean communism. The CPC had about 76 million members in 2009, about 1 in 12 Chinese adults. It is in control of government personnel, the army and propaganda. From large cities to small villages there are local security departments that protect the party's rule. The party has eliminated political rivals, the autonomy of the courts and media, restricted religion and civil society and thwarted rival versions of nationhood. China today has three classes; the aging remnants of the Long March and the Peasants Revolution, the middle aged of the Cultural Revolution and the Red Guards, and the new Internet generation which is idealistic and challenges the *status quo*. This last is the group that will need very careful handling by the Communist party. The party's response is to encourage party functionaries and officials to use the social media sites to communicate and interact with the public.For the period ahead, China's paramount national objective will be to complete the economic modernisation task for its nation and for its people, and the centrality of this task governs much of China's foreign policy behaviour. There is no sense of triumphalism in China; that feeling has not taken hold. Chinese leaders speak of their country as developing and call their own economy unstable and unbalanced. We are likely to see future decades of cautious and pragmatic rule in China.

For big European manufacturers, the application of know-how to cheap labour, tax breaks, and land on favourable terms offer the prospect of big profits if they can sell to a $1.7 trillion market—well below the American $3 trillion market but growing fast. China is the biggest market for ABB, the Swiss/Swedish energy and technology group, and Siemens is building the biggest digital factory in China, the first such plant outside Germany. Kone of Finland won orders of 226 escalators and 178 lifts in 2011 for 46 railway stations. Pharmaceutical companies will note that

China has 20 per cent p.a. growth in medicine consumption, and a $100 billion plan for hospitals and clinics by 2020. Reactor manufacturers will observe that the Chinese nuclear power station capacity is due to rise from the present 17 to 80 GW by 2020 and then to 150 GW. China now operates 20 reactors and another 28 are in construction. It will become the second nuclear power generator after the US. France and Russia are strong competitors in this field but so far, USA is the leading foreign vendor of nuclear power stations to China.

In a study by Pew research centre in 2009, 44 per cent of American respondents named China as the world's leading economic power, and only 27 chose USA. In a Chamber of Commerce survey in 2011, nearly 80 per cent of European firms operating in China said they had 50 per cent increase in sales in 2009 and significant rise of 40 per cent in average profits in 2011. In a study by the *China Daily*, 90 per cent of 69 multinational firms interviewed said they would increase investment in China by 2015. The EU chambers say, nevertheless, that the Chinese regulatory environment is tilted against their firms in favour of local state owned companies. In 2010, European firms drew up a list of Chinese obstructions that included regulatory problems, obstacles to market access and discriminatory procurement policies. Siemens and BASF of Germany complained to the Chinese about these restrictions, enforced technology transfer and the business climate, but despite such complaints, the same firms have increased their investments in China. Inward investment flows continue to rise, topping $4,100 billion in 2010, whereas Chinese outward investment in the same period was $59 billion.

Seventy million Chinese tourists each year travel abroad,[4] mainly to China's 'near abroad' like Hong Kong, Taiwan, Macau and Singapore. France is the most popular European destination, attracting one million Chinese, and a less obvious city destination is Trier, the birthplace of Karl Marx. Chinese tourists are known for conspicuous consumption, especially among women. With gender equality as state policy, the conditions of Chinese women have been hugely enhanced and they constitute 46 per cent of the labour force. China has 25 per cent of the global luxury goods market from which Europe benefits; Swiss watch sales are highest in China and Porsche sales in China rose 47 per cent in six months in 2011 and have a waiting list of 15 months. Luxury brands in Europe have found an excellent market in exports to China and China has reinvigorated Europe's luxury goods makers like Louis Vuitton and Hermes, whose products are *de rigueur* in China's status-obsessed and gift-giving culture. And China is transforming prestige wine sales—China now imports more Bordeaux wine than Germany.

China will make a cultural as well as an economic global impact. Beijing is acutely aware of Chinese limitations in 'soft power' and promotes it through Confucius Institutes (CI) that started in 2004 and festivals that celebrate its civilisation. The largest number of CIs in Europe are in UK, France and Germany, but fewer than in the USA. There are now approximately 400 Institutes in 108 countries with 600,000 students. Seventy of the world's top 200 universities have CIs, with 400 more in 76 countries on the waiting list. Indian government foreign cultural centres are 39 in number, seven being in the EU, but there are dozens of Indian cultural, religious and region-based civil society organisations in many countries. In contrast, there is no European centre as such in China or India. The main European cultural centres are the French Alliance Francaise, the German Goethe or Max Muller Institutes and the British Council units, each operating in their own soft power interest.

In USA, as of 1999, Chinese and Indian born students were about 35 and 25 per cent respectively. Foreign students get 50 per cent of the PhDs in engineering, mathematics and computer science, and 35 per cent of the PhDs in natural science.[5] Nearly 300,000 Chinese go to study abroad each year.[6] Around one in ten science and engineering degrees in USA go to Chinese, Korean and Taiwanese students. In 2010 Shanghai schools were rated number one by the OECD in reading, mathematics and science. Chinese universities are climbing the league table, with Peking University rising in one year from 109th to 11th position. The cultural legacy of emphasis on education and personal achievement has been highly instrumental in Chinese growth. The Chinese save to send children to the best possible schools and to excel at examinations. They are willing to learn from foreign experiences and adopt them when found useful. Cultural attitudes towards science, learning and innovation explain why China is doing so well.

Chinese research is increasing; it is innovating more, and since 1995, its new patents have increased by 25 times. Critics claim that most of the patents filed in China's patent office represent trivial changes on existing designs or attempts to claim credit for foreign ideas when China does not recognise foreign patents. In American, European and Japanese patent offices, China gets only one out of 30 approved and the other applicants secure the rest. China has indicated that its expenditure on science and technology would be 2.5 per cent of GDP by 2020 and on annual Research and Development (R&D) would be $110 billion—similar to that of advanced countries.[7] China is already the highest spender on R&D among developing countries, and has about 3.5 million people working in this sphere, making it second after USA. China is also second to the US in the fastest computer, number of patent applications and number of published scientific papers. China is 29th in the global innovation index of the Economist Intelligence Unit—virtually at OECD levels, while India is 62nd.The Chinese had a moon probe in 2013 and plan to place a man on the moon by 2020.

Political power invariably follows from economic power and, over time, foreign and security policy power should follow suit. What will China want to do with that accrued power? China has become concerned about the weakness of the global economy given its experience with the US-inspired global financial crisis and now the euro crisis. But open trade and investment flows remain important for China's medium-term economic future. China has a national interest in becoming a respected power with shared global interests like cyber crime, food security, climate change and freedom of navigation. This goes to the core of China's contributions to the stability of the global order. It is likely to become a more active participant in a full range of global institutions—social, economic, humanitarian and environmental. It is the biggest force contributor among the Security Council P-5 to UN peace-keeping operations, having sent 17,000 troops to 19 operations since 1990. China will also become a more prominent player in aid relationships across the developing world and the Chinese are the preferred partners of many African countries and the biggest trading partner of many developing nations. Without articulating it specifically, the 'Beijing Development Model', whereby successful economic growth through market reforms can be achieved without adopting full-scale political liberalisation of the type seen in western liberal democracies, is already attracting some attention in parts of the third world. While the western tradition emphasises democracy, the Chinese attach equivalent importance to state competence, which is closely linked to the idea of meritocracy. Given that state competence is a major weakness and a seriously neglected issue in the West, it may not be impossible to imagine this aspect of Chinese governance influencing some western thinking in the future. But with the deep roots of democracy in the West—and its absence in the Chinese tradition—the overall influence of Chinese governance in the western world will remain very limited.

The situation is, however, different in the developing world. There is an underlying affinity between China and the developing world because, unlike the West, they share, in broad terms, a similar stage of development. And China is indubitably the outstanding example of a rapidly developing country, having grown at around 10 per cent a year for over 30 years and lifted an estimated 600 million persons out of poverty. These achievements have brought China considerable prestige in the third world. China possesses a sovereign wealth fund with $200 billion in assets. In one month, it invested nearly $2.5 billion in 75 countries, nearly all of it in Asia and Africa. Its overseas investment rose 10 times to $26.5 billion between 2003 and 2007, and in 2014 China invested more abroad then foreigners invested in China. Resource-rich countries love Chinese business orders; "it is the cow that gives us milk," exclaimed a Zambian minister.[8]

China is already a financial powerhouse. Within some decades, the renminbi could replace the dollar as the world's major currency, and transform the architecture of the international economic and financial system. Either the International Monetary Fund (IMF) adjusts to the reality of Chinese power—together with that of other major developing countries like India—by becoming something very different from what it is now, or it will in the course of time be replaced. The prospects for the World Bank remaining the main source of aid and lending for the developing world are poor. In 2009 and 2010, two Chinese banks, the China Development Bank and the China Export-Import Bank, lent more to the developing world than the World Bank. In short, the present American-inspired Bretton Woods international economic system might not survive the relative decline of the United States, even though certain features may persist.

The Asian Infrastructure Investment Bank (AIIB) is the latest in a steady stream of Chinese initiatives in trying to create a regional environment appropriate to its interests. It is no longer keen to operate in an international scenario organised by others to reflect their values and interests. Apart from the AIIB there is the BRICS Development Bank, the Regional Cooperation Economic Partnership (RCEP), China-ASEAN Free Trade Agreement (FTA) of 2002, the Shanghai Cooperation Organisation (SCO) in 2001, and the Conference on Integration and Confidence Building Measures in Asia (CICA) where it is the chairman from 2014-17 which includes countries from Egypt and Turkey to South Korea. China wants to be at the centre of a regional order marked by its values of sovereignty, non-interference and maintaining existing borders as understood by China.

While the BRICS bank is to be based in Shanghai, the AIIB is based in Beijing, and will open at the end of 2015 with capital of $50 billion, with 20 initial members, all 10 ASEAN plus India, Pakistan, Bangladesh, Sri Lanka and Nepal; Kazakhstan and Uzbekistan and three from the Gulf—Qatar, Oman, Kuwait. Despite pressure from US/Japan not to join, many pro-western countries sought primary membership just before the deadline of 31 March 2015, and these include Britain, France and Germany, Australia and South Korea. The bank will not have the conditionalities of the Japanese-dominated Asian Development Bank (ADB), IMF and World Bank, namely questions of child labour, human rights and environment. This is what the US harboured concerns about, namely, that the AIIB would follow less scrupulous lending methods, such as clean government and environmental standards, than the ADB. But the real reason of course was one of the exercise of control. The ADB has $175 billion with 67 members, while Asia is reckoned to need $8 trillion by 2020 for infrastructure development. It also takes seven years on average for a project in the ADB to go from proposal to approval to completion stage. So with new rules of governance, the AIIB should also encourage rapid reform of old institutions.

The United States opposed the AIIB to counter a trend towards 'constant accommodation of China'[9] but the lemming-type rush to join the bank moderated its stand and Treasury Secretary Jacob Lew assured China of US cooperation and hoped the bank would formulate a quality management structure. The hopes for the new bank are that China would use its vast investible funds to support infrastructure, including along the two Chinese proposals for a new Silk Road and a maritime Silk Road, which are projected as win-win propositions. At the heart of the struggle for influence in Asia between China and USA is economic power. Despite American military might, and its security treaties with Japan, Australia, Philippines and South Korea, all these countries have more trade with China than with the US. For example, China imports more than 25 per cent of South Korean exports compared to USA with 12 per cent. The applications of the European nations to the AIIB also suggest that the Europe-Asia side of the strategic and economic Europe-USA-Asia triangle will be strengthened and the Silk Road proposals would provide a tool to open a new dialogue between Europe and Asia.

In 2009 China-Africa trade was worth $90 billion, Africa's leading trade partner. The Chinese are pumping oil from Sudan to Angola, logging from Liberia to Gabon, mining from Zambia to Ghana, and farming from Kenya to Zimbabwe. They build roads from Equatorial Guinea to Ethiopia, dams from Congo to the Nile, hospitals, schools, sports stadiums and presidential palaces. They have a $5.5 billion stake in South Africa's Standard Bank and $14 million in a mobile phone company in Somalia. They have invested $23 billion to rebuild Nigeria's refining capacity. China has changed the image of Africa from one of charity to one of business, and has made its direct investment to Africa even greater than aid flows. It is the biggest investor in Africa, and is taking the continent's focus away from the US and Europe. China is investing and is clearly there for the long haul.

Emerging Asia sees opportunities in Africa that were long hidden behind a veil of western 'Africa pessimism'. Emerging Asia needs resources and export markets; Africa needs affordable consumer goods, infrastructure and capital. The EU in Africa is confronted with this shift from charity-based development to an equal partnership, and the share of official development assistance (ODA) in financial transfers to developing countries declined from 70 per cent to 15 per cent from 2001 to 2011.[10] The China/India approach is seen as pragmatic and not promoting any new model, whereas the rights-based approach and focus on the poorest is regarded as a product of western liberalism.

Combined with China's extensive trading and financial ties with many developing countries, which are viewed very positively overall by the partner countries, this has fostered an increasingly close relationship between China and the developing world. As a consequence, there is great interest in many developing countries in how China is governed, in the competence of its state and what they might learn from it. In the West, the Chinese model of governance is not seen as any alternative to the western liberal political order, but when China overtakes the United States to become the largest economy and pulls ahead over the next decades, then growing attention will be paid to the Chinese system of governance.

Sometimes it appears that one has to be either a Sinophobe or a Sinophile: there is no middle ground for agnosticism about China's rise, or credit gained for attempts at a balanced approach. Predictions of the demise of China have been a constant feature in western analyses after the Tiananmen Square incidents of 1989, but the Chinese economy has kept growing. The dire western predictions, mainly from the Americans, have thus far proved wrong—China is overheating, it is over-cooling, it is facing a middle income trap, manufacturing is slowing, corruption is all-pervasive, investment in fixed assets is too high, consumer demand is down, there is excess capacity in products like steel, real estate is a bubble, there are bad loans to be found everywhere and runaway inflation looms.

China indeed has weaknesses that are all too apparent: domestic red tape, economic institutions that are weak and business costs high. The economy is protected by domestic barriers defended by entrenched insider élites, the public sector and state monopolies. Forty-two Chinese companies are in the Fortune 500 list but only three of those are outside the public sector. The bulk of profit in joint ventures comes from organisation, sales and marketing, and not in actual manufacture; thus, for example, only 3.6 per cent of profit in Apple goes to China. So 'Made in China' may often mean made in China by Japan or the USA. Export-driven growth and top-down decision making may not yield good results indefinitely. Around three thousand Chinese families constitute the apex of politics, economics, social position and connections with the security apparatus, so contacts known as *guanxi* are essential. This is actually a commonplace situation in Asia and is to be encountered and carefully navigated in all the emerging economies.

China is still a poor country, with about 6 per cent of the population in absolute poverty. The flow of internal migration from rural to urban life is slowing. Today 40 per cent of China is in cities; in 1949, only 12 per cent was. Around half the population still lives in the countryside. The China one child policy has led to 5 million between 35 and 54 joining the labour force this decade compared to 90 million in the last decade. The demographic time bomb will explode in the next decade, when workers from ages 20 to 29 will drop by a quarter by 2026, and 20 per cent of the population will be over 60 by 2020, total 300 million by 2030, and by 2050, there will be 100 million Chinese over 80.There is unrest due to inflation, centrifugal tendencies in Tibet and Xinjiang, debt-burdened banks and public sector, and over-dependence on exports. There is a non-objective legal system, health standards are poor, there are human rights abuses, and a general trust deficit, especially of the local bureaucracy.

Therefore China has serious, even existential, political and economic transitions and demographic and environmental challenges to overcome. The famous artist, now famous dissident, Ai Weiwei, notes that China is like a runner going very fast but suffering from a heart condition.[11]

China lives in a dangerous neighbourhood, with the US re-balance to Asia, Japan/China and Japan/Korea, India/China and India/Pakistan tensions, North Korean unpredictability and the East and South China Seas maritime boundary disputes. China, Japan and India, the Asian big three, have contrary strategic policies and show no leadership in international organisations. There is no Asian strategic architecture in the making. China has neither an universal message nor any rules-based vision for Asia. It is as yet ill equipped for the exercise of power politics other than the power of negation already seen in climate change negotiations, the World Trade Organization (WTO) and occasionally in the UNSC; in the last forum, never alone, but on the coat-tails of the Russians.

Given all that, Communist China has risen in the most extraordinary circumstances. It has not fought any major wars, and none on its own territory. It has risen with remarkable speed. It has risen despite lack of allies other than the widely discredited Pakistan and without international understanding or sympathy. It has had little say in international organisations, and there is no Chinese person at the head of any international organisation so far. It has no cultural or soft-power outreach, and all its neighbours are wary of it. These are some of the reasons why its rise is still inscrutable. A non-English speaking, non-western, non-democratic state will become the world's biggest economy. As yet, the world still seems unprepared for this dramatic development though it has had plenty of advance notice. In many countries in the world, they might harbour fears of a new type of tributary relationship with dominant China because, despite the rapid westernisation of its society, China's approach to world politics remains the old-school imperial model.

For a century before the Second World War, China endured dislocation and humiliation. Thirty years after 1949, China was the worst performing country; in the succeeding thirty years it became the best. So China has entered a new phase and has to play a completely new role. It will sustain high growth for decades to come as it continues to enjoy the core advantages of a rising developing country. The post-18th Party Congress leadership wants to keep the growth path on track and places high store on political stability in the short term. Domestic policy occupies much more attention than foreign affairs, and the idea of a G-2 with the USA does not attract much interest. The maintenance of the internal political system is the highest priority, and China sees instability in other countries as a negative example to be avoided. Chinese citizens have a social contract with their government and have no wish to destabilise it. In return, there has been a gradual liberalisation of personal space that has gone largely unnoticed. China has managed the complex transition from the centralised state-planned economy to a dynamic one with great competence. It can take complex decisions quickly, and can bring immense domestic resources to bear on clearly defined national goals. The biggest challenge may come in the next few years and these attributes may be needed soon.

China's economy is slowing because of reduced exports, slow investment growth, rising labour costs, its strengthening currency, and its manufacturing sector inevitably losing some competitive edge. State owned enterprises' share of the economy has declined because of poor performance and reliance on subsidies; now they are fewer but bigger in size, and enjoy monopoly privileges. They constitute special-interest groups with strong resistance to reform. There is mounting local government debt and bad loans in state banks because the economy has become addicted to government controls and state credit. China has been providing liquidity to the world, and if it gets into fiscal difficulties, the global consequences would be unimaginable. The next 10-15 years may be crucial. China's budget deficit is 12 per cent of GDP, and national debt 25 per cent of GDP. China's total debt is only around 60 per cent of GDP, so China has plenty of margin for fiscal stimulus, but the government does not prefer to use that method. Exports are 38 per cent, and China will adjust its export-led growth model and increase domestic consumption where they have enough leeway with a high savings rate and foreign exchange reserve, and low budget deficit, public debt, and *per capita* income.

President Xi Jinping and Prime Minister Li Keqiang are alive to the current problems. Xi has been hinting that meritocracy in administration, and avoiding a US-type nexus between administration, politics, money, wealth and influence, will be China's answer to corruption and save the Communist Party from decline. China will be a cautious liberaliser. Xi is not a dominant figure in the way that Mao, or even Deng, was, and will not be able to take big risks. The party does not want another Mao, and the removal of Bo Xilai was a case to illustrate that point. So the great policy lurches that took place under Mao are things of the past. Xi will have to proceed cautiously, keeping the party behind him, because there is resistance to even minor reform within the party itself.

Social and economic reforms have been considered, ranging from a loosening of government approval procedures and a break up of state sector monopolies and more controversial land reforms to making the yuan fully convertible within 10 years. There is relaxation in the one child policy that will apply to 75 per cent of Chinese to reduce gender imbalance. There will be elimination of re-education through the labour system that started in 1957,[12] allowing farmers to own land, education reform to stress entrepreneurial skills, accessibility to health and hygiene and reform of the judicial system.

China plans to reduce the state's role in the economy, giving market competition and private business a bigger say in investment and setting prices. Foreign investors will be allowed into finance, healthcare and other sectors, but no break-up of the huge public sector, or privatising banking, telecom or energy is contemplated. The government plans to loosen foreign exchange controls and liberalise interest rates. In a slimmer role for the government, making prices of energy, interest rates and exchange rates more market-driven would improve the economy, encourage private consumption and innovation. A technological upgrade will also be necessary instead of relying on low cost labour. Pro-market bureaucrats are to be inducted, with more delegation of power, and easing burdens on business. Shanghai's much-heralded new free trade zone was launched in late 2013, being touted as the most important economic reform since China began opening up in the 1980s. Banks and businesses inside the pilot zone will enjoy greater freedom in trade, investment and currency exchange.

The nature of Chinese growth is changing. Private companies are creating nearly all the new jobs. The potential of the services sector needs to be unleashed and the public sector monopolies broken. As China moves towards a knowledge economy and its demographic profile changes, its growth is slowing down, but is not unexpected given the restructuring under way with less emphasis on government-led investment, openness to the private sector, application of new technologies, switch from traditional business to e-commerce and shift from large projects to smaller enterprises. Privatisation is only one aspect of public sector reform; the Singapore model of a capital investment holding company, like the China Investment Corporation, to maximise shareholder value is also mentioned. It is challenging to execute this transition from an economy powered by investment to one driven by consumption: there is a risk that as investment falls, consumption—currently 36 per cent of GDP—will take time to catch up. Double digit growth can no longer be the yardstick to assess China's performance. But even then resilience is being shown; more than ten million jobs were created in 2014, real income also increased and the income gap between rich and poor narrowed. Given a successful handling of the potential financial crisis, China will move with more certainty towards great power status with the backing of the people of China for the Communist Party. China has suffered huge and spasmodic upheavals—the Taiping rebellion, the Boxer Uprising, four decades of warlordism, the Great Leap Forward, the Great Famine, the Cultural Revolution and Tiananmen and it is hardly surprising that the Chinese people, despite what grievances they may harbour, support the stability and predictability of the present system.

China must invest more abroad for technology and brand names, and move into the knowledge economy. Its currency must appreciate to its proper purchasing power level. China's economic ties with East Asia will bring prosperity to those countries, create an upwardly mobile middle class and a market for Chinese goods and services. The percentage of intra-East Asian regional trade will exceed the European Union's to become the highest in the world. China says it will work to provide stability in the international financial market and the eurozone, but would not shoulder the same responsibility as those directly responsible for the crisis. It takes the same attitude towards climate change—namely, common but differentiated responsibility. In a cash-starved and shrinking export environment, the belief that the free market is always more efficient than regulation and public ownership may have to be revisited.

China's GDP growth rate for the first three months of 2015 slowed to 7 per cent, which was the target for the year. Consumption was more than investment, services outpacing manufacturing, and domestic demand rather than exports. Taking the data for March and the full year picture for 2014, this shows that China's growth drivers are changing. Consumption contributed 3.8 percentage points to 2014's 7.4 per cent growth rate, which is more than investment, which accounted for 3.6 percentage points. Net exports, exports minus imports, contributed nothing. Consumption has risen to account for more than 50 per cent of GDP, which is a sizeable increase from 2009's 35 per cent, and places China in the realm of market economies where consumption is between half to two-thirds of GDP. It mirrors the rise of the services part of the economy, which includes non-tradables like haircuts, becoming larger than manufacturing that included many exported goods.

Industrial production expanded by 5.6 per cent in March 2015, the slowest on record, and was significantly outpaced by retail sales – a measure of consumption—which grew at over 10 per cent. This is what China has been trying to achieve, a re-balancing of its economy away from excessive reliance on exports and investment and more on its own middle class consumers and expanding services, as part of its aim to overcome the middle income country trap by improving the quality of the growth drivers in the economy. Growing more through consumption and services is similar to the growth drivers of developed economies such as the USA and Europe. So China's re-balancing also marks the beginning of the end of a period of rapid growth based on industrialisation. Manufacturing and catching up launched China from a poor to a middle income country in the past 35 years. The next stage is growing as a middle income economy, which will be slower than the initial phase.

Five per cent growth for an emerging market looks slow while three per cent for a developed one would be considered fast. Yet, a slowdown poses risks. For China, it is real estate and investment which may be slowing too quickly and pose a risk for banks. It is why the government has introduced measures to support the housing market and cut interest rates to stimulate lending. China is likely to spend to support the economy if job growth slows, but so far, a slower growth rate has not meant fewer jobs since the services economy is labour-intensive and last year saw 13 million plus jobs created against a 10 million target. The unemployment rate is 5.1 per cent, though that is likely to be mis-measured since rural area employment is not well captured.

The IMF downgraded China's growth to below seven per cent in 2015 and 2016. If growth slows down considerably, even if planned as part of restructuring the economy, will lower demand affect the ability to repay loans? Commercial developers are leveraged and there are reported difficulties in leasing office space. House prices have fallen across the country and requirements have been loosened for mortgages. These are questions that will be raised as China seeks to do what no other country has done, which is to overcome the middle income trap for a billion-plus population. What the rest of the world also has never experienced is its second largest economy undertaking such a dramatic structural transformation that is likely to entail volatility.

The strengths of the China model are threefold: its ability to think strategically, its infrastructural prowess and the competence of its government. For its part, though, China does not see itself as a model for others. Unlike the West, or the Soviet Union earlier, it does not proselytize about its own arrangements or seek to persuade other nations to copy it. The underlying reason for this mentality is that China has for many centuries regarded itself as separate and distinct from others, and in view of its deep historical roots, it seems highly unlikely that this attitude will change. The Chinese leadership is extremely cautious and not given to acting in a rash fashion: it will avoid anything that might be seen as provocative or unnecessarily divisive.

Since the beginning of the reform period in 1978, China's attitude towards the international system has been shaped by the overwhelming priority it has attached to its own economic growth and reduction of poverty. China is acutely aware, given its dependence on both exports and imports, of the importance of maintaining good relations with the rest of the world. To this end, it was essential that China gain access to foreign markets and admission to the World Trade Organization. Adaptation to and acquiescence with the existing international economic order has informed the Chinese strategy. The present international system has served China well, having played a crucial and indispensable role in its economic transformation. There has, so far at least, been no substantial change in this underlying approach in the past 35 years.

Will China project its values to reshape the international system? Its rise has been so closely bound to the process of modernisation along western lines that the result may be modernising without westernising, or more likely, a western world order without western leadership. Any common Asian vision will depend on China, Japan and India acting together, but they have different and often conflicting and confrontational approaches. So the prospect is of China acting alone and unilaterally, like the USA, but without any formal allies. This does not appear to worry China, though even its 'all weather' friend Pakistan cannot be considered a valuable asset. North Korea was once regarded as a close ally but has by its unpredictability distanced itself from China.

The 18th Chinese Communist Party Congress in 2012 warned about hegemony, neo-interventionism and power politics, with obvious reference to the USA. It urged China to go out to seek new markets and project an increased international voice without abandoning its essential core interests. China's paramount objective is to complete the economic modernisation task for its nation. The centrality of this task governs much of China's foreign policy behaviour. For centuries, foreign policy in China has meant border-state management. That China should tower over its geographical sphere was taken for granted and did not necessarily imply an adversarial relationship with neighbours. China thought it commanded a special position, but it confined itself to controlling the barbarians at the gates. It did not export ideas but let others come to it. This is the first time in history that China has been in the international system, and the first time ever that others have had to deal with such a rapidly rising non-west country. But there will be no new Cold War involving China because China's rise is not ideological. Ideological approaches like political idealism and democratic liberalism are considered impractical, and the political organisation of the Chinese state has not changed.

The Chinese military is a powerful force. If there was a financial crisis which the party could not handle, the rural areas would see tumult and only the military could step in to save the party, or organise a take-over. But this is hardly a likely scenario as of now. The army sees itself as poorly trained and poorly equipped: hence the present emphasis on its modernisation. China's People's Liberation Army is the world's largest, at three million strong, and its budget is rising. Its first aircraft carrier has just gone into service and it is believed to be investing heavily in stealth technology, space warfare and cyber security. These are natural developments for a country of its size and influence, China argues, and do not signal any basic strategic change. Attitudes in the military are also probably responsible for the more aggressive assertion of 'core interests', which it felt was not pursued energetically enough by former President Hu Jintao.

In foreign affairs, it is taken as a given in China that China will be strong, united and recognised as a great power. Xi has adopted the party's *dicta*, and has tweaked the old Five Principles of Peaceful Coexistence to call for a 'new type of great power relations'. In introducing respect for core interests into this concept, China seems to want to determine the nature and intensity of bilateral ties as the final arbiter. We may expect China to become more assertive and less deferential. It will resist external intrusion or interference in its affairs and its rise may challenge the liberal solidarist view of international society. We can expect a future China to emphasise non-interference on the lines of Article 2.4 and 2.7 of the UN Charter, to be sceptical of the West-inspired Responsibility to Protect (R2P) doctrine, to de-emphasise the Doha Round in favour of greater regionalism, place more emphasis on second and third generation human rights, especially the right to development and poverty reduction, and seek reform of international organisations, beginning with the IMF and International Bank for Reconstruction and Development (IBRD), to win more parity.

China wants a stable periphery; the 18th Party Congress stated "Chinese people are peaceful who fear turmoil". It sees stability with neighbours as important for its development, and the USA as having the biggest potential to support or disrupt its rise. It is not enthusiastic that regional Asian states should strike coalitions with the USA, and it will respond to medium powers asserting their own interests in China's periphery, but too strong a response will lead to counterbalancing efforts, and so it will try to avoid stimulating threat perceptions among its neighbours. It must delicately balance the need to show that its rise is peaceful while underlining its existing sovereignty and territorial claims. China will avoid military confrontation with the USA or even with American allies in the region, if there is any fear that the US will intervene on their behalf.

Domestically, can one party rule co-exist with a private enterprise economy and is state capitalism possible in post-revolutionary times? The received wisdom is that economic freedom must spill over into political freedom. Once property rights are granted, certain liberalising tendencies must follow—neither buyer nor seller can be above the law, which means law courts, lawyers, free speech, free association, group interests and political parties. As income and education rise, human rights, property rights and civil liberties should normally follow. Can China defy this historical logic? But the Chinese Communist Party will see economic growth as an endorsement and not as a threat. If China follows the received theory, it will be forced to a new politics, but the result may not be a western model but a Sino-government like Taiwan, Hong Kong or Singapore. The Communist Party shows no sign of relinquishing power; quite the contrary—it recently warned against the adoption of western values that were designed to "westernise and disintegrate".

The subliminal message in all China's actions is that China wants to be a world leader, whether in trade, education, technology, military matters or eventually, politics. In issues relating to Asia, the international community already cannot operate without China's support. As for the

West, the majority of the world's population cannot be governed by an international system designed to benefit the 12 per cent minority in the global population. And a China containment policy will not work. The time has come for the West to treat China as an equal partner. But the Chinese do not help this process with any clarity; by defining its role and identity in world, or by defining modernity with Chinese characteristics. Perhaps they have to set their house in order first before any clear formulation emerges.

The more the USA and China cooperate, the better the chance of crisis situations not spinning out of control. They should not undercut each other in world issues: they should resist the historic trend of rising powers clashing militarily with the established powers. The rest of the world should not have to choose between two contrasting models. If the USA and China can find a *modus vivendi* the world will be a safer place for the coming decades. American and European attitudes to China's rise have thus far been comparatively benign, facilitating its access to the WTO and open markets. With the financial problems now besetting the West, this openness has become politically and economically more difficult, and China is regarded more as a threat than an opportunity. This view may prove short-sighted and counter-productive.

Europe should make its citizens, and especially its business community, more Asia-literate. It should show emerging Asia that Europe has much to offer in terms of world-class institutions, a skilled work-force, a multi-cultural environment and an open economy ready to transfer technology and accept controlled immigration. It should cede space gracefully to emerging Asia in regard to quota and voting rights in the IMF and IBRD—the indebted can no longer be allowed to manage these organisations. It should regard China's rise not only as an economic and commercial opportunity, but as a strategic event. But Europe does not have a strategic policy in East Asia and its Asian 'strategic partnerships' with China, Japan, India and South Korea are void of substance. Despite the USA's obvious reluctance to see Europe engaged in any geo-political issues in East Asia, the EU should bring some its vaunted qualities like diplomacy, best practice and persuasion to bear in the region. To appear 'less American' will win credit in Asia and create a space in the strategic theatre, but with Europe in its present disarray, this may be asking for too much too soon. Finally, Europe should stop lecturing China on human rights and good governance, especially when these issues are used as conditionalities. Such tutorials do not have a receptive audience, only prove counter-productive, and sit uncomfortably on the European continent that has been responsible for the colonial era that ended only recently.

India

India is a free country, with the most amazing diversity of human talent, originality, personality and spirituality. It has the use of English as a *lingua franca* and is accessible to the outside world. India has the best demographics of all the large economies. The average age today in China is 38 and in India only 28. By 2020 the average Chinese person will be 37, Indian 29, and European 49. India has 65 per cent of its population under age 35 and 560 million under age 25, of whom 225 million are between 10 and 19. It has the world's biggest student population of 315 million.[13] In a decade, India will have a work force surplus of 56 million against a shortage of 47 million in western countries.

India is a high savings and investment country; 35 per cent of the national income is invested. Foreign inward investment in 2011-12 was $47 billion, and in investment abroad, Indian companies in net overseas purchases rank fifth—after USA, Canada, China and Japan. In India's freewheeling democracy, and due to its youthful profile, there is entrepreneurial energy which has found expression abroad in investments in the developed world. In Britain, 700 Indian-owned businesses employ 90,000 people, and an Indian firm is the biggest corporate employer.

Apart from ICT exports of $10 billion a year, there are cutting edge technologies like Moser-Baer selling data storage products. Hero Honda is the world's largest producer of motorcycles in the world. Low cost is obviously a factor—in supplies, design, by-pass surgery, nursing and care for elderly, editing, printing, binding and accountancy. India has launched satellites for UK, Germany and Belgium. In India 10,000 motorbikes and half a million mobile phones are sold daily. It is able at short notice to organise mega events like the *Kumbh Mela* every 12 years for 55 days duration for 30 million people on a particular day and 100 million during the whole period, which means building a temporary megacity with roads, sanitation and drinking water. Its general elections every five years involve an electorate of more than 800 million people eligible to vote, despite persisting poverty, illiteracy and inequality.

India is home to 270 million absolutely poor people but both India and China have contributed to large reductions in world poverty. The UN states on the Millennium Development Goals (MDGs) that poverty is declining, especially extreme poverty cases in China and India. In both countries these declined by 455 million from 1990 to 2005, and 320 million more will do so by 2015. In China the absolute poor (at $1.25 a day) has dropped from 20 per cent ten years ago to 6 per cent now; in India these will fall from 51 per cent to 22 per cent in 2015. Backward states in India are making gains; in Uttar Pradesh, Bihar, Assam and Odissa; and backward castes and dalits are less poor. In India, the National Rural Employment Guarantee Act has raised rural incomes, especially among women.

Association of Southeast Asian Nations (ASEAN)

In 2017 ASEAN will celebrate its golden (50th) anniversary, and in 2015 the countries will head towards an ASEAN Economic Community. The association is the world's seventh largest economy, accounts for seven per cent of world exports and surpasses all Asian economies bar China and Japan. With a $2.4 trillion GDP and 620 million people, it has the world's third largest labour force of which 50 per cent are below 30 years.

Singapore

Singapore is a city-state with a population of five million of diverse ethnicity. It is the world's fourth financial centre and one of the top five ports. It has an export-oriented economy and has the third highest *per capita* income in purchasing power parity. It has a tradition of being highly assertive in policy matters, rather like the Venice of the 16th century Mediterranean, and aspires to be an academic and learning hub for the whole of emerging Asia. But its growth has slowed due to the global macroeconomic scenario, and it has a debt/GDP ratio of 110 per cent and high consumer debt levels.

Among Singapore's assets are: exceptional leadership, few prime ministers since independence, good governance, meritocracy, pragmatism, and honesty. Also noted are its multiculturalism, English use, rule of law, open and globalised trade, a green environment, soft power, the best of east and west in a modern Asian city.

Indonesia

Indonesia is the world's fourth most populous nation, with a 250 million population, and more than half will be in the middle class by 2020. Sixty per cent of the population is under 30. Indonesia has around 40 per cent of the total population of ASEAN and 36 per cent of ASEAN's GDP but does not seek to impose its agenda. With an impressive growth since 2008, labour costs are only a quarter of China's and it is the best run commodity (oil, gas, coal, palm oil, nickel) economy, with a public debt of only 27 per cent of GDP. It grows at around 6 per cent, foreign investment is 33 per cent of GDP, and the per capita income is expected to quadruple by 2020. With a GDP of $1 trillion, making it the 16th in the world in 2012, the 2015 growth forecast was 5.2 per cent [14] and domestic consumption accounts for more than 50 per cent of the economic growth. The main investment is in mining, chemicals, pharmaceuticals, transport, storage, and telecommunications. It attracts investors through its political stability, and expects that foreign direct investment (FDI) will rise to 33 per cent of GDP by 2014. It can no longer rely on cheap labour, but can count on better government services. It has a plan of strong infrastructure investment for 750 projects to boost GDP to $4.5 trillion by 2025 and the *per capita* income to $15,000.

As elsewhere in ASEAN, Indonesia suffers from wide disparities in income levels with about half the population living on less than $2 a day. Older élites are still dominant in the deep rooted structures of power. There is inflation, corruption and a three-way axis of military, business and government. There is a massive religious revival of both Islam and Christianity, and all parties claim to be following some kind of Muslim agenda in order to gain votes.

Indonesia accounts for only one per cent of EU imports and 0.5 per cent of EU exports. But the EU is Indonesia's fourth trade partner and Indonesia is the EU's 32nd. Athough it has been a democracy since 1997-98, it attracts little interest from the EU. A Framework Agreement on Comprehensive Partnership however was signed in 2009 and came into effect in 2012. There have been low expectations from both sides of the Europe/Indonesia relationship. The EU contested Indonesia in East Timor and Aceh, the latter in 2005-6 when the EU brokered peace with the Aceh separatists which led to the withdrawal of Indonesian troops. The EU regards this as the high-water mark of its peace-building efforts in Asia, but seems to have little interest in Indonesia otherwise and the relations are essentially economic. No EU member gives Indonesia priority, and there are no civil society advocacy groups or media attention, even when the humble-origin Joko Widodo defeated an army general to the presidency in 2014 and introduced a massive welfare programme for the poor, including health care, through electronic cards, and has cut subsidies on fuel, increasing its cost by 30 per cent. Indonesia's transition to democracy has always been underestimated in Europe.

Republic of Korea

South Korea is one of most open world economies. The existing four per cent growth is good for a rich economy which is the 15th biggest in the world. It has a sizeable share of the world's manufacturing exports, comprising 31 per cent of its economy, with new growth industries like robotics, biotechnology, aerospace and material science. It spends 3.7 per cent of GDP, has a vast number of persons engaged in research and development, and is one of the top five nations for international patents. It has global brands and high-end manufacturing including shipbuilding. Exports grow twice as fast as the economy and comprise 53 per cent of GDP. It is an egalitarian society with a population of 50 million, but it has a rapidly aging population below the replacement rate of 2.1 and no service industries.

The Korean economy swung up with the export demand created by the US war in Vietnam and has never looked back. Its backbone has been the '*Chaebols*' that are large business conglomerates patterned on the Japanese '*Zaibatsus*' business houses. To outdo the Japanese has been Korea's biggest driving incentive. This is a reaction to Japan's occupation of, and atrocities in, Korea during the Second World War. Korean workers are among the most disciplined and industrious: symbolic strikes only take place to facilitate negotiations; a worker can cut a finger in protest and then go quietly back to work. Production managers are workaholics and devoted for life to their *Chaebol*.

From 1987, South Korea has been democratic. Back in 2005, OECD marked South Korea as a frontrunner for academic attainment, and Italy and Britain at the bottom. Its *per capita* income at $32,100, is only just behind the EU average of $34,500. The EU supported South Korea joining the OECD in 1996 in order to secure liberalisation of its domestic market. Relations are largely economic, with issues of anti-dumping, subsidies, pricing, IPR and patent protection. South Korea is the 10th largest trade partner for the EU, and the EU is its largest source of investment. The EU ranks above the USA both in trade and investment with Korea. It has a 'strategic partnership' with the EU—which to South Korea was a symbol of its international status as part of the western world – and an FTA begun in 2007, signed in 2010 and ratified in 2011, the first in the 'deep integration' series of the EU that started in 2007 and the first that any Asian country has concluded so far with the EU. The negotiation was eased by structural complementarity, but there are large market access gains for the EU in services like banking. For South Korea that FTA was an escape from over-dependence on the USA, China and Japan. It also has a framework agreement with the EU that covers about 40 areas of discussion. There are however differences between the EU and South Korea on human rights in third countries, commitments on carbon dioxide (CO_2) emissions, emissions from aircraft, national sovereignty and non-interference.

China is now South Korea's biggest trade partner and biggest export market for hi-tech goods. South Korea's moves to China are explained partly by Seoul being discomfited by attempts by Japan under Prime Minister Shinzo Abe to whitewash its wartime past and by US deliberately strengthening Japan's military and regional influence to counter China that South Korea feels is buttressing Japan's historical revisionism.

The EU has a limited role in Korea and endorses the US position. It successfully pressed to be a part of the Korean Energy Development Corporation in 1997, created to denuclearise Korea and build two reactors in North Korea. This was not welcome to South Korea, USA or Japan who were the main partners, who saw Europe as buying into the project for commercial reasons once the North Korean 1994 crisis was over. The Energy Development Corporation was to construct two light water reactors and give heavy fuel oil supplies in return for Pyongyang dismantling its nuclear programme, which did not happen. The EU had internal differences on recognition of North Korea in 2001, and there was only one heads of government dialogue with North Korea in 2001[15] though since 2000 the EU and most of its members have diplomatic relations with Pyongyang. The EU was not admitted to the 6-power talks in 2003 on North Korean nuclear matters, though it showed an interest in joining, and none of the present six members[16] are enthusiastic about the EU presence.

The strong outflow of South Korean popular culture in TV, dramas and films has to be particularly noted, especially in its Asian neighbourhood. But direct cultural exchanges with the EU are still rudimentary.

Taiwan

Taiwan with 23 million people is one of the EU's top trading nations. It is an export intensive capitalist economy with a stable GDP growth and a leading investor in assembly factories that export to the EU. It has been a full democracy since 1996. Its trade surplus is substantial and in foreign exchange holdings the fourth world-wide. It is an innovation hub in electronics and an indispensable partner in the chains of the global electronics industry. It is dependent on exports especially of semi-conductors, laptops and mobiles. While most of Taiwan's exports to China are electronic items such as television displays and cellphone chips, there is also a big upsurge in agricultural sales from southern Taiwan. Taiwan is the EU's fourth largest market in Asia and the EU is Taiwan's largest source of investment. Taiwan citizens have 90 day visa free travel to the Schengen countries.

Taiwan is caught between autonomy and independence. It has switched from agriculture to industry and become a world leader. It has trade surpluses which give it a healthy foreign exchange reserve and it possesses a vibrant media and popular culture. All EU countries have non-official ties with Taiwan. From the end of the 1970s, Taiwan's economic dynamism offered commercial opportunities and a network of offices with various designations was set up in Europe and Taiwan. For the EU, trade with Taiwan was never as important as it was for Taiwan, which traditionally favoured US or Japanese firms when it came to politically motivated commercial decisions, and was concerned about EU's strict labour laws and costs and cultural differences.

The EU position on China/Taiwan is to support the peaceful resolution of disputes on a mutually acceptable basis with reference also to the wishes of the Taiwanese population. The EU believes in China's peaceful reunification and resolution through dialogue, and opposes any unilateral change in the status quo (undefined) in the Taiwan Strait. It is curious that in regard to Taiwan the European Parliament has set the pace for the EU's other organs. Taiwan has strong lobbies in the EU based on its democracy and individual freedoms which effectively found an ear in the European Parliament which openly supports Taiwan's democratic system over China's authoritarian regime. China's reaction to the European Parliament has been mild because it knows its power is only symbolic. China focuses on the European Commission, while Taiwan cultivates the parliament.

Ministerial talks between Taiwan and the EU began in 1992, but Europe was frustrated with nationalist governments seeking referenda on full independence. The EU has focused on the economic and functional, and not the geostrategic aspects, so the USA has been left to define EU policy in regard to China and Taiwan. Through its economic diplomacy Taiwan has established dialogue, bilateral committees, direct flights, cultural, scientific and academic exchange, and visits of officials and parliamentarians with Europe. The first EU-Taiwan official agreement was in 1998 on WTO accession. Taiwan entered WTO in 2002 and an EU office opened in Taipei in 2003. The European Commission has an annual consultation with Taiwan. The EU Council approved a one-China policy in 2006, and this tense period passed after 2008 and détente in the Straits. There are commercial interests, inter-parliamentary dialogue, and shared values, but Taiwan wants an FTA, a seat on the UN Framework Convention on Climate Change (UNFCCC) and the International Civil Aviation Organisation (ICAO), and there are disputes on price manipulation, government procurement, technical barriers, preferences for American agricultural produce, the death penalty and climate change issues.

Culturally and politically, Taiwan is well ahead of China, and its pop music and films are appreciated all over east Asia. It has a large and well educated middle class, and is very prosperous *per capita*, with little inequality and few environmental problems. Taiwan has become a repository of Chinese culture due to the Nationalists under Chiang Kaishek fleeing the mainland with much of China's material heritage. Its present culture is more influenced by USA than Japan, which had ruled it from 1895 to 1945. Taiwan has helped China with Taiwanese investments routed through Hong Kong to China in the 1980s and 1990s and has thereby helped China into globalisation in trade and investment.

The Emerging Asian Middle Class

Five hundred million Asians are middle class by European standards. The Asian emerging economies constitute about 25 per cent of the global middle class. That could double by 2025 and rise to 1.5 billion or more, with half the world middle class being in Asia and accounting for 40 per cent of global middle class consumption. Estimates of the size of China's middle class vary depending on the definition used, but one thing is certain: it was virtually non-existent three decades ago and is now growing exponentially. The consultancy firm McKinsey says that what it calls the 'upper middle class'—a segment of the population with annual household incomes of between $17,350 and $37,500—accounted for 14 per cent of urban Chinese households last year, but will account for 54 per cent of households in less than a decade's time.

Chinese consumers are already catching up with their counterparts in the wealthier countries. Total consumer spend in China is less than half of USA's but more than Japan's, and closing in on the EU. Already China is the world's biggest consumer in many things, such as beer and mobile phones. A few decades ago, there were unisex baggy Mao suits and pork-pie Kim Jong-un-style haircuts; now there is a vast grooming industry for hair, nails and faces. 150 million or 13 per cent can afford luxury goods, and China wants to raise the average consumption rate from the present 33 per cent of GDP to 70-80 per cent like USA. Then China's consumers will become the motor of global economic growth and demand, and create world-wide jobs by purchasing foreign goods.

At a time in emerging Asia when big is beautiful—big markets, big populations, big militaries, and big ambitions, the *per capita* income of the Asian emerging nations will remain smaller than that of the industrialised countries, but in terms of spending, their expenditures will be many times higher. About 150 million in India with an aggregate purchasing power equivalent to about the whole of the European Union watch televised cricket matches. China and India will make up 2/3rds of the increase (China 52 per cent, India 12 per cent) in the global middle class by 2030, and the purchasing power of India and China together will far exceed the combined consumer class populations of the European Union and the USA by mid-century although their *per capita* income will still only be a fraction of what it is in the developed countries.

The dominance of the West will continue in the areas of technology and human skills but the engine of new demand growth and spending power will shift to the emerging economies, especially in Asia, with their higher growth rate. Their share in global investment portfolios and foreign direct investment will rise sharply. The *per capita* disparity will mean there will be extreme price sensitivity in the Asian market. The implications of this development on production, out-sourcing, investment, pricing, sales, advertising and marketing in this century will obviously require urgent research and analysis, and will have a bearing on the future shape of European industry and manufacture, but has so far been strangely neglected.

The material rise of Asia is easier to document but the mental and spiritual resurgence is harder to track. There has been an undeniable explosion of the cultural confidence of the emerging Asians. There is a pan-Asian cosmopolitanism, with popular culture, cinema, rock music, variety shows and TV sitcoms crossing Asia. Diasporic communities play their part in creating this pan-Asian middle class life style, which has become global with South Korean films like *Old Boy* and pop music like Psy's *Gangam Style.*

NOTES

1. http://www.imf.org/external/pubs/ft/ar/2013/eng/pdf/a1.pdf
2. India has (according to the Credit Suisse Global Wealth report) 3 per cent of global middle class or 160 million people and China's has doubled since 2000 and has 33 per cent. But the bank's criteria is very high; $10,000 to $100,000.
3. Jonathan Fenby, *Tiger Head Snake Tails,* chapter 11.
4. www.scmp.com/business/.../97-million-chinese-tourists-went-abroad-2013ý

5. Dambisa Moyo, *How the West was Lost*, 100.
6. Angus Foster, *BBC News*, 15 October 2012.
7. In 2011 Chinese R&D expenditure was 1.9 per cent of GDP at PPP with $297 billion. USA was 2.7 per cent with $403 billion. (UN Innovation Capability Index)
8. Jonathan Fenby, *Tiger Head Snake Tails*, chapter 12.
9. Kishore Mahbubani, *The World Post*, 17 March 2015
10. T. Christiansen, E. Kirchner and P. Murray, *Palgrave Handbook of EU-Asian Relations*, 438
11. Jonathan Fenby, *Tiger Head Snake Tails*.
12. A UN 2009 report said 190,000 persons were in these camps
13. Indian Census 2011.
14. www.reuters.com/.../us-indonesia-economy-gdp-idUSKBN0JM0D82014...
15. The dialogue was short-lived due to North Korea's clandestine nuclear programme.
16. China, USA, Russia, Japan, South Korea, North Korea.

3

Problems for Emerging Asia

Pan Asianism was dealt a deathblow in the first half of the 20th century by the Japanese who turned it into a pretext for imperialism, and again by the India-China conflict in 1962. India drifted away from Indonesia after 1955, from Japan from 1960 and ASEAN from 1967. War with China accentuated its withdrawal from Asia, and it became a marginal player from 1962-92, but it became in 2005 a founder member of the East Asia Summit (EAS). Today's Asia lacks any impetus towards political integration as nation states have proved to be the potent and enduring model. Regional markets are badly integrated, and Asia has too many disparities in government policy, security perceptions and levels of economic advancement, with the history and hostility between China and Japan obstructing any move towards a political, economic, social or monetary union like the EU. This neglect in the emerging Asian region is due to interests of individual states, lack of political will, resource constraints, geopolitical factors, lack of leadership and weak institutional frameworks. Regional solidarity for China is secondary to bilateral and multilateral activities, and India's desire to encourage any norms-based multilateralism is weak or non-existent.

Any Asian integration will depend on relations between China, Japan and India who are the big three on which a new Asian architecture would have to be based. They have a special role to lead the effort for stability, integration and projection of common interests, but they are too domestically preoccupied and have too little say in global economic institutions. Different Asians have different expectations from a future Asian Community—some nations like Singapore and South Korea want to limit confidence building to concerns only with their own security.[1] The USA described the EAS after it had joined the group as representing the premier institution for political and strategic issues, the "capstone of an increasingly mature and effective regional architecture",[2] but this judgement is likely to have been premature.[3]

Regional integration in Asia has some new initiatives: in 2009 Japan proposed an East Asian Community and Australia an Asia Pacific Community. China prefers the ASEAN 10 plus 3 (China, Japan, Korea) whereas Japan wants ASEAN 10 plus 6 (China, Japan, Australia, New Zealand, India and Korea). Intraregional trade in East Asia was 55 per cent in 2006, less than the EU at 66 per cent but more than NAFTA at 44 per cent. In South Asia, intraregional trade is 10 per cent of total trade and 5 per cent of GDP, and India is at about the worst level, with only 3 per cent of its total trade in its own sub-continent. Most trade is now governed by regional and preferential trade agreements but Asia's FTAs are trade light. Many criticise FTAs as creating a spaghetti bowl of market preferences—"an unholy mess of arbitrary, tailor made regulations for politically influential companies, moving ever further away from the simplicity, transparency and predictability of non-discriminatory multilateral rules".[4] They are limited to tariff cuts but do not deal with Non-Tariff Barriers (NTBs), Foreign Direct Investment (FDI), government procurement, red tape, corruption, complex rules of origin or trade restricting product standards. The consequence therefore will be unilateral liberalisation and breaking regulatory barriers. Two problems with such FTAs is that (1) they take up political and financial resources that could be used in reenergising WTO and (2) they do not address global economy issues like agriculture subsidies and anti-dumping. China, USA and others need to re-engage in WTO and make the post-Bali trade facilitation programme work.

In the biggest emerging economies such as China and India, reforms have stalled and not moved much beyond first generation reforms that have not unlocked competition or boosted productivity. Domestic red tape continues, economic institutions remain weak and business costs are high, stifling entrepreneurship, innovation and consumption. These economies still have considerable domestic protection with internal barriers to enterprise defended by entrenched insider élites, the public sector and state monopolies. In Asia, all the emerging economies must consume more, import more, open the capital account and float the currency to be more market determined.

The anticipation is that there will be a decline in the productivity growth in emerging Asia as the *per capita* income level (the 'middle-income trap') approaches that of the advanced economies, along with the decline in output in Japan and the eurozone due to demography. As the developed markets buy less, emerging Asia will have to rethink its export-led growth model and must reduce its dependency on exports. Growth strategies relying primarily on exports must sooner or later reach their limits when many countries pursue them simultaneously. The Asian Development Bank has singled out slowing growth in China and India, the ongoing sovereign debt crisis in the euro area, and the recurring fiscal cliff in the US as posing major risks to the world economic outlook.

The export-oriented emerging Asian countries need to take a longer-term perspective, entailing a shift in strategies that accord greater emphasis to domestic demand as an engine of growth. Accelerating domestic demand growth could be highly beneficial, because output growth and industrialisation make producers of goods and services more willing to invest. A domestic demand-oriented strategy would focus on the income aspect of wages, as it is based on household spending as the largest component of effective demand. If wage growth follows the path of productivity growth, it will create sufficient domestic demand to employ fully the growing productive capacities of the economy without having to rely on continued export growth.

Emerging economies must be open to bigger volumes of imports. Excessive foreign exchange reserves in Asia are themselves one cause of the crisis, and saving too much is as bad as saving too little. South and East Asia may become bigger players in global finance than USA and the EU, and these changes will bring a perception shift about global security and questions about who polices the world. Any economic cooling in China and India will mean that the wider Asian region is affected. Beijing has slashed its growth estimate and the economy is burdened with excess capacity and rising debt with unsold goods piled up. The IMF forecast in January 2015 for China was 6.8 per cent in 2015 and 6.3 per cent in 2016. Indian GDP was at 5.3 per cent in January–March 2012, the lowest for nine years but with the new Narendra Modi government in 2014, the IMF forecast rose to 6.3 per cent in 2015 and 6.5 per cent in 2016.

China and India

The Indians have never been able to forge any long term strategy for dealing with the Chinese; it is always ad hoc. India has no real bargaining leverage. Between India and China, greater strategic balance is needed and India should carefully cultivate the other nations on China's periphery. The simultaneous rise of India and China cause Asian uncertainties, and will require careful navigation. China easily outperforms India in economic indicators. India has all of China's faults and none of its strengths. For years, FDI faced almost insuperable obstacles; technology imports were controlled, royalties were low, bureaucratic approvals were many and time wasting. But India scores higher than China in human and societal values, in domestic institutional maturity, governance, personal freedom and social capital—a measure of how the individual and communities support each other. India and China will prove to be cautious liberalisers; both need to reform the financial sectors. On capital account controls, both are among the most restrictive of Asia, reflecting a history of closed markets and state-led growth. The inadequate domestic absorption of foreign capital has weakened the contribution of foreign capital towards growth.

India and China show little interest in each other. With China, there are Indian restrictions in visas, permits and licences; labour conditions inhibit investment; there is mutual distrust and reserve. In bilateral relations, the Indian grievances are (1) India's one China policy is not reciprocated in Jammu and Kashmir or Arunachal Pradesh; (2) China's military ties with Pakistan; (3) China sees Pakistan-occupied Kashmir as Pakistan's, but Indian Kashmir as disputed; (4) China occupies large parts of India; (5) lack of support to India's claim for a permanent seat on the UNSC. On the other hand, China rightly accuses India of trade protection—with high duties on power equipment and discouraging foreign investment in infrastructure. India also blocks purchases of telecom equipment from China on security grounds. China considers India as 'western' because of its democracy, and blames the democratic political system for India's ills. It can be argued that democracy has been a drag on development because it opens the way to dissent and opposition to land use and environmental concerns, when no effort was made to curb misuse by vested corrupt interests. Democracy created a sentiment where failures, bad governance and weak institutions have thrived on fatalism, and India has become regarded as unpredictable, unreliable, uncompetitive and difficult for business activity. Successful democracies, according to China, adopt capitalism and development first and then democracy but in India it was other way round. India, for its part, thinks Beijing will eventually come to a point where authoritarianism does not work. As Shashi Tharoor has written, "in the information age, it is not the side with the bigger army, but the side with the better story that wins".[5] In India, the opinion is that if India fixes its governance before China fixes its politics, it will win. Indian corporate spokesman Gurcharan Das observed that India has a weak state and a strong civil society, while China has a strong state and weak civil society. India will become a strong state when the best of society joins the government, and China will get a strong society when best of society joins the private sector.

China papers over its lack of transparency and regulatory clarity much better than does India. Compared to China, India comes out poorly in the yardsticks of consistent gross domestic product growth, low inflation, current account surplus and infrastructure. China has grown primarily because it was such an attractive destination for FDI with low wages, productive labour and practically non-existent labour legislation that made it a manufacturing success. From hosting only assembly units, China had moved over the years to producing important manufactures of basic industrial goods without restrictions on technology imports or royalties, though a significant amount of foreign investment was money belonging to Chinese residents sent illegally abroad and brought back as foreign investment. Another tranche was from overseas Chinese in Taiwan, Hong Kong, USA and elsewhere, but investments also came from Japan, South Korea and Europe, and most of the foreign investment was direct. In recent years, as stock markets developed in China, investment has also come in as portfolio investment. However, return on FDI has been rather poor in China and intellectual property and patent protection are weak.

India and China receive one third of all annual global remittances—India gets $71 billion p.a., China $60 billion. None of the other emerging Asian countries are among the leading recipients. Thanks to inward remittances rather than export earnings, Indian foreign reserves showed the following trend: $252 billion (2008-09), 279 (09-10), 305 (10-11). 294 (11-12), 293 (12-13) and $340 in February 2015.

Some contrasting features may be revealing: China has a small fiscal deficit—2 per cent in 2010 but India is the only major country in Asia with both a current account deficit and a fiscal deficit of about 10 per cent. The rupee has fallen in value by 20 per cent in one year, which should mean bigger exports, though this did not happen.

Both India and China are using their Buddhist traditions to finance religious sites, display relics and sponsor conferences. In 2011, China sent a Buddha tooth to Myanmar and its use of Buddha to promote its culture is recent—partly designed to counter adverse propaganda on Tibet. China helps Nepal to develop Lumbini. India has organised a Global Buddhist Congregation attended by the Dalai Lama and sent the Kapilvastu relics to Sri Lanka. But even in the cultural field, and even on Buddha, India and China find it hard to work together, and all this is a far cry from much desired joint action by both to promote the Asian cultural heritage.

China

China's top leaders have warned that growth may slow further before rebounding. China is a poor country—only 86th in *per capita* income. At $1.25 there are 100 million poor in China, 150 million are on less than $1.5 a day; at less than $2 a day, there are 240 million. China's Gini coefficient has touched 0.47 in 2009, which is above the 0.4 United Nations warning level. (The UN usually draws the line for alarm at 0.4:[6] above that number indicates a high potential for social instability.) Inequality has increased to a point when social unrest is a potential threat, and where 0.5 per cent households own 60 per cent of the national wealth.[7] The regime enjoys legitimacy in the eyes of its people though there is concern in some other parts of Asia—such as Vietnam, India and Japan. China does not obstruct India's cooperation with its neighbours, but as it did with Japan in Southeast Asia, China may leapfrog India to overtake India's pre-eminence in South Asia.

China has abundant capacity for growth; its *per capita* income is only what Japan was in 1963, but Chinese productivity is less than USA's. It has to turn an export-driven economy to services and domestic consumption. Chinese banks lent money to sustain growth in a stimulus that resulted in a property boom, though China took some steps to curb speculation and bring down prices. Housing is a crucial driver of growth but has to be kept stable. There has been too high a fixed asset investment in construction—50 per cent of growth in 2010, and 70 per cent of GDP. Property is 13 per cent of Chinese economic activity and fuels 40 industries.

China has ballooning private debt at 230 per cent of GDP. But China's advantages include huge foreign exchange reserves of $3.8 trillion, a current account surplus, low need for foreign capital flows, high savings and low loan to deposit ratios. But Taiwan suffered a banking crisis in 1995 despite having a reserve of 45 per cent of GDP, and other countries like Japan (1970s) and Malaysia (1990s) had bank crises despite high domestic savings of around 40 per cent.

Over the past few years China has built a skyscraper every five days and 30 airports, 25 city metros, 3 longest bridges in the world, 6000 high speed railway tracks, 26,000 miles of motorway and commercial and residential property. It was the modernisation necessary for a rapidly urbanising economy. But this could herald the third financial crisis after the USA and the eurozone. During the US crisis China had unleashed a stimulus of $600 billion of direct government spending which was investment at a faster rate than any big country in history. Investment pre-US financial crisis was about 40 per cent of GDP; after it, it was 50 per cent, much of which will never generate an economic return. Debt to GDP has increased from 125 per cent in 2008 to 200 per cent now, the banking sector went from $10 trillion to $25 trillion, and the boom has to be deflated in a controlled way and the economy reconstructed.

Any economic slowdown is likely to affect China's manufacturing industry, given this sector's share in the total economy. China suffers from high inflation in food, energy and basic commodities, and social unrest due to inflation worries Beijing. For this, the government is using the tools of higher interest rates and increases in the reserve ratios that banks need to hold. Chinese financial institutions are backward. There is overweight in bank finance (80 per cent) and inadequacy in budget finance (15 per cent) and securities finance (4 per cent). China's state companies hide credit risks and bad loans, and there are too many unprofitable enterprises.

China favours domestically created intellectual property. Eighty per cent of the counterfeit goods seized by the EU customs originate in China. China attacks Google's privacy and indulges in cyber espionage, with Baidu as Google's main rival. For China to be a dominant and influential power, it must invest abroad more and innovate more by moving into the knowledge economy. By consuming more, it will reduce its trade surplus and help other emerging markets as well. China lacks private enterprise, a free market, inclusive political institutions and a free media. There is a property bubble and inflation. When there is a threat to political power, the party élites close ranks to form a barrier to innovation. As incomes and education rise, democracy, human rights, civil liberties and property rights could follow, but autocratic governments tend to see economic growth as an endorsement and not as a threat. The bottom third of the population is far from happy despite a four-fold improvement in material conditions. The transition to a semi-private economy has led to layoffs, decline in health, and worries about provisions for children and the elderly. Migrants from the countryside have taken urban jobs with no benefits, and only 30 per cent of urban Chinese have pensions.

There seem to be five possible future scenarios for China: 1. The *status quo* where CPC protects its legitimacy, keeps the military in its place, and a lid on popular dissent. 2. Implosion. (Both 1 and 2 are unlikely: the authorities are ready to impose repression to protect the one-party rule and subdue the minorities. The Chinese state has a strong institutional capacity, a layered federal structure, and a sophisticated security system—relaxed on the outside but vigilant inside.) 3. A slow process of reform like Myanmar, though the new 'princeling' leaders of the 18th Communist Party Congress do not look like radical reformers. 4. A new cultural revolution to weed out dissent inside and outside the party, since ruthlessness and corruption are endemic in China's oligarchy. 5. The People's Liberation Army (PLA) calls the shots increasingly to rule with a civilian facade.

China's main challenges are corruption, ecological degradation and demographic imbalances. There is wastage of scarce resources like water and energy, along with excess capacity in steel, cement, cars, aluminium and hotels. There is inflation, a slowing of exports, huge credit expansion that produced bad debts and rising wages that affect smaller firms. Annual disturbances now amount to about 180,000, on widely varied issues. These are reactions to local events and do not constitute a challenge to the political system. They take place to bring local abuses to the attention of supposedly benign rulers in the far off capital. Beijing's task is complicated by its weak hold on local governments—the provinces respect the emperor, provided he keeps on the other side of the mountain.[8]

How long can the Communist Party survive in China? In a few years' time, the Chinese Communist Party will challenge the Soviet Union (69 or 74 years in power depending on how one calculates it) and Mexico's Institutional Revolutionary Party (71 years until 2000) for the longest unbroken rule by any political party. Modernisation theory holds that authoritarian systems tend to democratise as incomes rise, that the creation of a large middle class hastens the process, and that economic slowdown following a long period of rapid growth makes that transition more likely. Serious and worsening inequality coupled with high levels of corruption can add to the impetus for change.

All these factors exist in China, but some political theorists, including many at the Beijing Central Party School, argue that the country is culturally and politically exceptional. Others, including some influential Chinese intellectuals, distinguished western sinologists and liberal-minded senior party members, believe these are the final days of the communist era and the party could be washed away if it does not launch serious political reforms soon. Chen Shu, a professor of party history, party-building and Mao Zedong Thought at the Central Party School, is already contemplating the party celebrating its centenary in power in 2049. "Those theories about a China crisis or China collapse are all completely western," he says. "The more pressure placed on Chinese culture and the

Communist Party, the more united and cohesive they become and the more capable they are of producing miracles."[9]

The opposing camp cites the signs that include a hollow state ideology that society does not believe in but ritualistically feigns compliance with; worsening corruption, failure to provide the public with adequate social welfare and a pervasive public sense of insecurity and frustration: "people join the party these days to make connections and get ahead rather than for any kind of socialist ideals."[10] Other negative signs include increasing social and ethnic unrest, élite factionalism, over-taxation with the proceeds mostly going into officials' pockets, serious and worsening income inequality and no reliable rule of law, especially in a growing middle class that cares more about clean air, clean water, clean government and safe food than GDP growth rates.

Probably the most important stimulus for cynicism and questioning of authority has been the rise of mass internet communication. Since his ascension, Xi has shown no sign that he is the covert political reformer that some had hoped for. 'Document Number Nine',[11] a secret memo that was distributed to cadres in April 2013 and leaked in August through overseas Chinese media, shows how worried the new leadership is about perceived threats to party rule. "Western hostile forces and domestic dissidents are constantly infiltrating the ideological sphere," the document says. "In order to preserve the party's grip on power, attention should be paid to the mistaken ways of thinking, positions and actions." Seven perils were enumerated in Document No. 9; the first was "western constitutional democracy"; others included promoting the "universal values" of human rights, western-inspired notions of media independence and civic participation, pro-market "neo-liberalism," and "nihilist" criticisms of the CPC's traumatic past. It went on to say "western forces hostile to China and dissidents within the country are still constantly infiltrating the ideological sphere". No doubt the pro-democracy movement in Hong Kong would only have added to the CPC's fears.

In short, it is too early to tell whether China will prove or disprove modernisation theory, but in the medium term, the latter looks more likely.

Pollution and Consumption

China is now the second biggest energy consumer after USA. In 2009 it used 46 per cent of global coal. It has been a net energy importer from 1993, and by 2020 its imports will double compared to 2005. China emits more greenhouse gas than any country, overtaking the USA in 2007. Seven of the world's most polluted cities are in China.[12] Acid rain from coal burning affects 2/3rds of China. The natural resource degradation and biodiversity loss is sobering, 20 per cent of plant and animal species are in danger, and China is blamed for fuelling the poaching of endangered species. Deforestation, overgrazing and over cultivation have led to soil erosion and local climate change. 40 per cent of soil is affected by erosion and 10 per cent contaminated by heavy metals. Water scarcity and water pollution have degraded 75 per cent of the rivers.

The US embassy in Beijing records an air quality index, where a reading of level 500 toxicity is supposed to be the top of the scale and 301 to 500 is considered hazardous. On 13 January 2013, it reached 755, the highest level since recording started in 2008. This infuriated the Chinese authorities who in 2009 told the US that the data was "not only confusing but also insulting" and could lead to "social consequences." A former health minister later admitted that air pollution in China was causing as many as half a million deaths a year. From 2001-11, lung cancer cases nearly doubled in Beijing and at national level nearly quadrupled, being the fourth biggest health threat in China. In 2010 the World Health Organization (WHO) stated that there were 1.2 million premature deaths due to air pollution.

China seeks to feed 21 per cent of the world population with only 9 per cent of its cultivated land.[13] As the saying goes, the Chinese may soon consume everyone else's breakfast, lunch and dinner. Some experts believe the world will have to get used to higher food prices and to Chinese farmers buying up more and more overseas land. China's voracious consumers are importing up to 60 per cent of the world's soya bean exports, pushing up prices for everyone else and raising real fears over the consumption's environmental impact. And there are spikes in prices for commodities like copper – needed by China to cable up rapidly growing cities and infrastructure.

Foreign Policy

If and when the USA loses its position of leadership, China yet seems ill equipped and unready to take over. It seems to have no interest in global responsibilities nor a G-2, nor any interest in standard-setting for Asia. But Beijing shows extreme sensitivity when it feels it has not been shown due respect and this makes it a volatile player that may lurch alarmingly when its vaguely defined 'core interests' are at stake. China's cooperative relationship with the highly volatile Pakistan is probably the most stable element in China's foreign policy.

Chinese foreign policy is a synthesis of historically conditioned values and contemporary influences. It is practical, goal-oriented, and materially motivated with long term objectives rooted in its historical and psychological experience. It is taken as a given that central policy is aimed at a strong powerful united China, and that it is recognised as a great power, but the Chinese regard ideological approaches like democratic liberalism or idealism as impractical, so there is a state-directed market economy. The opening to international trade has given rise to growth in the private sector and a commercial banking system, but the political organisation of the state has changed little in nature.

China feels its soft power is not commensurate with its international status, but soft power is generated from civil society and not by a government diktat. China repudiates western standards, but has nothing to replace them with except recently reinstated traditional Confucian values. Heavy-handed censorship does not help its overseas image and cases of brute power and a biased legal system against dissidents and nonconformists give China a bad image abroad. China likes to present itself as a model for modern development, a trading partner and fraternal exemplar, but China has a problem with any universal message or any vision for Asia. This comes from the lack of any commonly shared experience with its neighbours in attaining the goal of political independence and economic development. China's challenge is to redefine the role of the state while accelerating economic growth and curbing corruption.

India's Problems

India is in the *per capita* league table at around 162 out of 215.[14] It is the only low-income country in G-20 but suffered from an onset of premature over-confidence in this century, even though India has not yet entered the ranks of important trading nations and its trade and investment are not at levels that ensure critical interdependence with major powers. Ever since independence, India has been trying to cope with several revolutions taking place at the same time—a democratic revolution, an urban revolution, an industrial revolution, the communications revolution and the social revolution. Military defeat by the Chinese in 1962 made India a marginal strategic player in Asia for the rest of the Cold War and now it is getting increasingly hyphenated with Pakistan due to Islamic militancy across the border and the endless tensions in Afghanistan. India is a land of a million mutinies, dysfunctional governance, and a soft state. India spends much time just dealing with the challenges of its diversity in freedom. It is a commonwealth, a continent, without any uniting narrative, but multiple competing narratives, many of which are highly divisive. To stay stable and peaceful, India is obliged to be a muddle and a mess. India has evolved a brand of democracy in its own chaotic image; to have a stable, efficient, predictable central government is a utopia that will probably never come about.

India has many more domestic impediments than China and they are all quite evident. The state does not work well for those without the financial and other resources to become part of the marketplace. Nearly 160 million women, or 45 per cent of the working age population between 15 and 59 do not work.[15] There is Maoist violence in about 165 out of 625 districts, generated by persons who have not benefitted from growth opportunities and have been abandoned in the economic backwaters. Indian rigid social structure limits intergenerational and inter-social economic mobility and fosters acceptance of vast disparities, though it must be said that urbanisation dilutes some adverse effects of caste that coexist with other monstrous inequalities among more than half the urban population who live in slums.

"India's fatal growth handicap is non-performing political governance bereft of ideology, commitment or competence," wrote one commentator.[16] Is India to continue in the manner it has been accustomed to since 1950? Is its economic ambition out of step with the current system of political governance that includes coalitions, influence of regional parties, fringe sectarian elements of a Hindu revanchist character, and local conflicts and aspirations? Does India need more decentralisation, more states with more powers such as direct income taxation like the USA? How could the central bureaucracy be reduced in numbers and powers? How could there be more governance and less government? These are among the many pertinent questions that arise.

The governance agenda in India has run aground with dysfunctional politics, an ineffectual bureaucracy that gets worse at each descending tier, denial of justice in legal systems through delays,[17] underdeveloped financial systems not mobilising savings, financing corporate or private investment in infrastructure or development, unproductive state ownership, state intrusion, a poor public education system, resistance to change across the board, misguided development strategies and misunderstanding of the role of government in a modern economy.

Among the many democratic deficiencies in India are the influence of money in elections, paid news in the media, corruption, criminal elements in parliament, the low status and treatment of women, misuse of office, understaffed and underpaid lower judiciary, misbehavour of lawyers, and an unaccountable military protected by a highly controversial but central government-backed Armed Forces Special Powers Act. India thus has some of the forms but not the full content of democracy. Even in freedom of expression, Reporters Without Borders lists India at 140 out of about 180 positions, in part because censorship is imposed both by the government and non-official civil society agents of suppression citing religious, cultural or community sentiment. However, India also has a Right to Information Act, an Employment Guarantee Scheme that has improved the life of rural households, a Panchayati Raj that has brought many women into public life, and a degree of obedience by the executive to judicial orders, though even these favourable aspects are subject to subversion and corruption.

There is a bloated government and official leaning towards graft and crony capitalism. Land labourers stay on farms with no mass migration to production centres, so the urban population grows too slowly. Companies go abroad to avoid problems in India, and investment at home has dropped from 17 per cent of GDP to 13 per cent. Over half the earnings of the top Indian companies are outward-facing, dependent on exports, global commodity prices or international acquisitions. Despite growing demand for aspirational goods like mobile phones, there is gross inequality. The top 10 per cent own 40 per cent of the total wealth and the Indian Gini coefficient is 0.65 in urban India, well over the World Bank's danger mark of 0.4. The government increases handouts instead of widening business and job opportunities, of which eight to ten million need to be added each year, and for the past five years government spending is up by 20 per cent p.a. which is higher than economic growth. The current account and fiscal deficits are high and the total public debt is 85 per cent of GDP.

Indian *per capita* income lags at one quarter of China's but the top segment may own cell phones, colour TVs and mechanised transport in the next five years. This would be at best 25 per cent of the population. Indian income inequality doubled from 1991 to 2011, and 10 per cent of GDP vests with 55 individuals.[18] When India slips from 9 per cent growth rate to 5 or 6 per cent, it is like a recession because India is in the poor low income group of countries. Indian authorities show a lack of urgency while India needs to create new wealth in technology rather than in politically-connected sectors like extraction of natural resources and real estate.

India is rated one of the worst countries to do business in and for delays in getting permissions. It takes 117 approvals and 7-10 years to build a power plant. Both in the ease of doing business and in global competitiveness, India lags far behind China and other major economies. In the 2013 World Bank report 'Doing Business' India ranks 134th out of 183. Thirty-four permits are needed before construction of an office as opposed to 14 in an advanced economy, and seven to 20 years are needed to wind up a failed business.[19]

India is home to 25 per cent of the world's hungry—210 out of 842 million according to Global Hunger Index 2011-13.[20] In the first three decades of independence, India saw no decline in poverty at all. The Tendulkar report of 2009 says that 37 per cent of the population is below the poverty line (42 per cent in rural areas) using criteria such as calorie intake, health and education. The Saxena committee report (with criteria of Rs 1000 p.m. urban and Rs 700 p.m. rural) says 50 per cent, with 23 per cent of the poor not having ration cards at all, and the Sengupta report says 77 per cent have under Rs 20 p.d. or Rs 600 p.m. The Rangarajan Panel of 2014, using a cut-off figure of Rs 32 a day for rural and Rs 47 a day in towns, estimated 363 million, or nearly 30 per cent, to be below the poverty line in 2010-11.[21] The Planning Commission, with criteria of Rs 539 p.m. in urban and Rs 356 in rural areas, says 28 per cent and other specialists put it as even lower at 22 per cent. Whether one accepts the Tendulkar report or the government statistics, it is clear that unprecedented poverty alleviation has happened in the past twenty years.[22]

India's size and big population make its GDP look big, but it also means the largest number of poor, infant deaths, maternal deaths in childbirth and child malnutrition. It is a laggard in the annual UN Human Development Index and the MDGs determined in 2000; namely in eradicating extreme poverty and hunger, universal primary education, gender equality, reducing child mortality, improving maternal health, combating HIV/AIDS, malaria and other diseases. Progress in non-income aspects of poverty is weak, skilled health personnel attend to only 48 per cent of births, maternal mortality is 301 per 100,000, and India accounts for one in five child deaths world-wide. 79 per cent of children between 6 and 35 months and 58 per cent of pregnant women are anaemic. 38 per cent of children under three are stunted and 46 per cent underweight, and 33 per cent women and 28 per cent men are also underweight. Annual health spending by the Indian government during the Congress-led government until 2014 was only 1.37 per cent of GDP, (out of all social welfare at eight per cent) and urban and rural sanitation are poor. An Indian man cannot expect to be healthy after 54, compared to a Chinese after 65. Government expenditure is 24 per cent of budget on social services (10.8 per cent on education and 5.1 per cent on health) but these outlays need to increase.

The government has not yet cut waste and theft in social programmes and subsidies. The vaunted Employment Guarantee Scheme has started failing due to corruption, with delayed wages, lower wages than legally permitted and corruption by panchayats. Though 100 days of employment or unemployment allowance has to be paid, the average number of days paid for dropped from 54 in 2009/10 to 44 in 2013/4, and children from 8 to 14 years are working allegedly on job cards issued to adults. Reforms in agriculture, administration, bureaucracy and transparency are not yet on the agenda. Infrastructure and natural resources are plagued by opaque allotments of land use, and legislation to allow easier land acquisition and removing restrictions on foreign investment is frustrated by political opposition. There is an inconsistent approach to exports of sugar, cotton and other commodities. Financial facilities that enable money laundering continue. The judiciary is limited in numbers, status and remuneration. All public sector enterprises are inefficient—steel, aluminium, railways, road construction, food procurement and distribution. Government expenditure must be slashed, deficits reduced and the public sector made autonomous or privatised.

With the known liabilities of weak agriculture, manufacturing at only 17 per cent of GDP, poor bank finances, inefficient state enterprises and weak infrastructure, the 2015 budget was hoped to address all these problems. The budget is still cluttered with dozens of populist schemes for people young and old, male and female, rural and urban, and people divided into interest groups. Removing subsidies could be done when fuel prices were low and inflation under control, though there is no really optimum time, because subsidies have been embedded in the system for so long. Welcome were the movements towards Direct Benefits Transfer with the opening of millions of new bank accounts, allocating more money to states and proposing to amend the Agriculture Produce Marketing Act, but criticisms of the 2015 budget were manifold; reductions in allocations for backward castes and tribes, education, health, rural development, women, children and AIDS control, the lack as yet of a comprehensive bankruptcy code, and a delay till 2016 of the uniform Goods and Services Tax. There is also doubt that even with the new methodology announced by the government on estimating GDP growth, the targets of 6.9 per cent in 2014-15 and 7.4 per cent in 2015-16 can be achieved, leading the chief economic adviser Arvind Subramaniam delphically to say that these figures were "statistical and not a real number"—whatever that might mean. He went on to add, however, that the revised methodology followed international best practice. More fundamentally, the government has to consider the matter of the execution of its programmes and overhaul the political and administrative structures without which delivery will be impossible. The existing apparatus is unused and resistant to the detail-oriented robust style of supervision of Prime Minister Narendra Modi. Devolution of financial authority to states is conceptually good but the government will be even more dependent on a machinery that it has little control over.

India has 2.4 per cent of the world's land, 4 per cent of the water resources and supports 17 per cent of population. The World Bank says environmental damage accounts for 5.7 per cent of GDP; in other words, economic growth is wiped out by environmental loss. India has the third largest ecological footprint, using twice its biological capacity. Agriculture employs 50 per cent of the population and comprises 15 per cent of the GDP. India's priority is to shift agriculture to higher productivity because agricultural output in every crop is lower than in many Asian countries. The June to September monsoon, the life blood of Asia's third largest economy, is critical because two-thirds of Indians depend on farm income and nearly 60 per cent of the country's cultivable land does not have any other source of irrigation. Subsidies and support prices prevent crop diversification, environmental issues receive insufficient funds, low investment in agricultural supply chain results in wastage and farmers are faced with low prices by middle men. Free or below cost power has led to groundwater depletion and salinity due to a shift to water-intensive crops. Ninety million farming and another 28 million agriculture labour households exist in India. Forty per cent of farm families do not own their land and average land holdings have halved over the past 30 years.

Indians consume only 3.7 per cent of world energy supply. Five hundred and fifty million Indians have no access to electricity, several million others have only primary sources like sunshine and biomass—wood crop residue and animal droppings that meet 80 per cent of household needs. India now has 234,000 MW installed capacity of power, but 40 per cent of the population has no access to commercial power and power generation is always behind planned output. Going by *per capita* consumption, population and economic growth, India needs as much as 850,000 MW by 2030, and 12-15 per cent needs to be nuclear, which is clean, gives energy independence and lower energy bills. India aims to have 20,000 MW from nuclear in 2020, 60,000 MW by 2032 and 25 per cent of its requirement by 2050. Seventeen nuclear plants (4000 MW) exist and six are under construction (3000 MW). India plans to build 16 more heavy water reactors and produce 63,000 MW by 2032. Sixty-eight per cent of energy generated is coal-based and coal cannot meet demand. Indian state owned power companies are in the red to the extent of $54 billion. Due to protectionist domestic interests, India imposes high tariffs on power equipment, preventing Chinese investment in this infrastructure. Neither coal nor gas are transparently regulated and India will become totally import-dependent; 90 per cent of oil, 66 per cent of coal and 60 per cent of natural gas will be imported by 2030.

Only an industrial revolution can make a poor country prosperous. India has only about 25 per cent of GDP in industry compared to 50 per cent in China. It needs revised labour laws, an end to reservations for small scale industry and new bankruptcy laws and tariffs comparable to East Asia. For inward FDI India needs a robust legal and supervisory mechanism, low corruption, transparency and good corporate governance. India's debt to GDP needs reduction to about 40 per cent by 2020 if it is to be attractive to foreign investment. Land acquisition delays, slow bureaucratic, environmental and forest clearances, honest investigative practices and slow court judgments, to name a few reasons, have deterred investment. The Indian government should concentrate on making India a manufacturing nation, reforming the rigid labour laws, investing in power, roads and ports, and cutting red tape. Instead past governments introduced retrospective taxes, stopped hundreds of projects in red or green tape, imposed arbitrary penalties on companies and placed various conditions on foreign investment. Existing law implied that acquiring agricultural land for industry was inherently bad or coercive. It assumed 2/3rds of the population were hungry; so India would have to provide 800 million people with grain at 10 per cent of the market price – although less than two per cent claim to be hungry according to other authoritative figures. Only ten million people have life insurance, and the average bank account is only Rs 40,000. Banks are saddled with bad loans and overstaffing, with non-performing assets. Tax laws are archaic and untaxed money is estimated at about 50 per cent of GDP.

More than 20 per cent in the 15 to 24 age group are jobless; this would represent about 47 million, of which 26 million are male and 21 million female. These figures include the unemployed and marginal workers who get work for up to six months of the year. In the overall 15 to 59 age segment, 14.5 per cent are unemployed. 4.3 million children between the ages of 5 and 14 are forced to work as labourers.[23] There is large scale underemployment in the unorganised sector, which accounts for 90 per cent of the total employment, with the organised sector contributing a meagre 9 per cent. A large sector of the potential labour force is unemployable due to illiteracy and lack of skills. Desirable jobs are not easy to come by, so these people have little or no incentive to acquire skills. Indian industry can never create enough jobs for the unskilled, barely literate and illiterate majority of the work force. An annual growth of 7 per cent is necessary to absorb the new entrants in the job market and only 8 per cent growth over a sustained period to create 200 million jobs over two decades would bring the unemployment rate to acceptable levels. India has the largest youth bulge the world has ever seen. Informal casual labour is the bane of manufacturing and its contribution to the formal economy is in excess of 50 per cent. Whereas knowledge-based industry will be the hallmark of the 21st century, in India only 1.3 million are employed in IT out of a working population of 400 million.

The Indian government assumed that its strong investment and savings rates would maintain growth, and dismissed inflation as a natural price for prosperity, but managers of the Indian economy now face the challenge of the collapse of growth. The main factors responsible are fears of inflation, fiscal deficit, declining investment and the current account deficit. Low growth is related to poor investment which is sluggish due to high interest rates and the declining exchange value of the rupee. Cuts in expenditures and subsidies and improved tax collection can reduce the deficit, but an unwillingness to slash social welfare expenditures and improve administrative efficiencies remains. Apart from unaffordable doles and subsidies, regulatory uncertainty for investors in telecom, mining, real estate and pharma, inaction on corruption and unprecedented judicial activism affect coal production and power generation, while natural gas, telecom and road projects are in a state of constant uncertainty. More fundamentally, India has liberalised its product market but not yet its factor market of land, labour and capital.

The current account deficit is caused by crude oil, coal and gold imports. Nationalised coal mining has been inefficient and exports are depressed not only due to the sluggish world economy but corruption scandals that have affected commodity exports like iron ore. The suspicions, lately proven by Ranbaxy and Wockhardt, about falsification of trial results also affect pharmaceutical exports.

Foreign investment is only two per cent of Indian GDP. It can restore the balance of payments and stimulate the economy, and rising domestic investment, both private and public, would be an economic stimulus, but domestic investment is currently going abroad. India categorises foreign investment into direct and portfolio investments. Direct investment is in equity or debt and recently has been defined to include foreigners holding above 10 per cent in any venture. Portfolio investment which is in debt and securities through the foreign direct investment route, is up to 10 per cent of the securities traded in both primary and secondary capital markets including shares, debentures, warrants, and units of mutual funds, government securities and derivative instruments. Between 2000-01 and 2011-12, direct investment rose from $3 billion to $22 billion; and portfolio investment from $2.5 billion to $17 billion. Indian dependence on the latter is too high though it is volatile and inflows and outflows seesaw the stock market and rupee exchange rates.

Foreign direct investment in building new manufacturing has been low for several years, more in buying existing businesses rather than adding fresh industrial capacities. There has been too little foreign investment in infrastructure except for some minor power projects. India has ramshackle infrastructure, cities and towns are poorly governed, and utilities are neglected. India needs massive foreign investment in physical infrastructure; roads, power, ports, railways and airports. There is little coordination and agreement between central and state governments. Complex bureaucratic procedures add to costs and the government does not compensate for these losses.

Genuine foreign investment of late has been hurt by the downturn in European economies and the preference of investors for the safety of the dollar for investment, in spite of the tribulations of the US economy, because there is innate confidence in the dollar as a reserve currency and in the innovative ability of the US economy. This is compounded by the fact that foreign investment is still considered suspect by many Indian political and other influential circles. Decades of hostility to private investment, private profit and foreign investment have fostered a negative mindset. The Indian public has been led to believe that essential services like water, electricity and road transport must be free or cross-subsidised by the suppliers, which has led to unbridled increases in deficits of state-owned enterprises whereas infrastructure investments must produce adequate returns for maintenance and further investment.

Indian big business sectors like land, mining, and infrastructure are among the most corrupt. Corruption in India slows down the system and does not speed it up. In the 2014 Transparency Corruption Index, among the emerging Asian economies, Singapore was at position seven, Taiwan at number 35, Korea 43, India 85, China 100 and Indonesia 107. India has done much to stimulate foreign investment into equities, debt and other financial instruments, encouraged by politicians and bureaucrats as well as businessmen, because this has helped 'black' money to exit and return to be laundered in Indian stock markets. A genuine investigation will probably show that much of the foreign institutional investment to India is unaccounted Indian money coming back by these routes.

To become an important investment destination and build a current account surplus India should remove nearly all restrictions on foreign investment including in defence industries. There should be no compulsory ceiling or compulsion to have local investment participation. Clearances must be simplified, taxation should be stable, clear, and consistent. The bureaucracy should be made responsible and accountable for timebound clearances. Land acquisition should be made easier. Inflation must be cut and for this, government deficits must come down by pruning misspending and theft of wasteful social welfare, much of it stolen or reaches people who are not among the defined poor for whom such schemes were designed.

Investor-friendly policies should have been introduced in the years of high growth, low inflation, low current account and fiscal deficits. Today, India must get foreign money into its reserves by any means, and there must be a clear vision of what must be done to increase foreign investment significantly.

Indian Solutions

What India needs are low inflation, stable growth, export growth, increase of manufactures in GDP, a balanced current account and decline in debt and deficit. India needs to cancel subsidies for all but the poorest, change the pension scheme and reduce the budget deficit to three per cent. Reforms that have so far been "in homeopathic doses",[24] must be completed with agriculture decontrol, taxes simplified, more FDI allowed in retail, defence and insurance, land and labour reforms, and supply side constraints like weak infrastructure removed.

India must give up the present stress on government ownership, eliminate reservations for the small scale sector, end protection to organised labour, encourage foreign investment, incentivize agriculture production by scrapping agriculture marketing boards which are cartels, discarding minimum support price, introducing genetically modified organisms (GMOs), and creating predictable trade regimes for farm products. Efficiency must be brought to social expenditure, and uncompetitive state owned companies privatised.

India's wounds are self inflicted. A high fiscal deficit has become politically addictive. Food inflation is due to supply chain constraints, slow productivity growth, and unreformed agriculture. There is capital flow volatility when the need is for expenditure reduction, policy reform strategy, and reduction in government consumption and subsidies. India needs to revive the corporate sector, to dismantle the coal monopoly and monopolies in infrastructure, railways, airports, ports and electricity distribution, and to introduce the Goods and Services Tax and a Direct Tax Code speedily to make India a national market. India must renegotiate stranded projects, revive public-private schemes with immediate clearances, set up a states reorganisation commission, institute police reform, fill judicial vacancies, and enact electoral reform to eliminate criminals posing as representatives of the people.

NOTES

1. Asian regional institutions as in early 2015: Asia Pacific Economic Cooperation APEC(1989) Australia, Brunei, Canada, Chile, China, Hong Kong, Indonesia, Japan, Korea, Malaysia, Mexico, New Zealand, PNG, Peru, Philippines, Russia, Singapore, Taiwan, Thailand, USA, Vietnam. Asian Regional Forum ARF (1994)

ASEAN 10+3 (China, Korea, Japan) + 3 (India, Australia, New Zealand) + EU, Bangladesh, Canada, DPRK, Mongolia, Pakistan, Russia, PNG, Sri Lanka, Timor, USA=27. Asia Europe Meeting ASEM (1996)=53 members, 51 members plus EU Commission and ASEAN Secretariat. East Asia Summit EAS (2005) ASEAN 10 +3+3+Russia, USA=18. Trans-Pacific Partnership TPP (2005), USA, Canada, Chile, Peru, Mexico, New Zealand, Australia, Vietnam, Singapore, Malaysia, Japan, Brunei=12. Regional Comprehensive Economic Cooperation RCEP(2012), ASEAN 10+3+3=16.

2. Hillary Clinton, www.state.gov/secretary/rm/2012/07/194988.htm
3. USA and Russia were included in the East Asia Summit in 2011.
4. Razeen Sally, *Free Trade Agreements*, ECIPE 2007.
5. Shashi Tharoor, *Pax Indica*, 312.
6. International Institute for Urban Development, Blue Book on China's Social Management.14 September 2012.
7. www.deloitte.com/.../ch_en_POV_wealthper cent20mgtper cent20inper cent20china_1020...ý
8. Jonathan Fenby, *Tiger Head Snake Tails*, chapters 15 & 17.
9. *FT Magazine*, 20 September 2013 'How Long Can the Communist Party Survive in China?'
10. *FT Magazine*, 20 September 2013 'How Long can the Communist Party Survive in China?'
11. www.nytimes.com/.../chinas-new-leadership-takes-hard-line-in-secret-mem... 19 August 2013.
12. Angus Foster, *BBC News*, 15 October 2012.
13. Angus Foster, *BBC News*, 15 October 2012.
14. http://databank.worldbank.org/data/download/GNIPC.pdf.
15. Indian Census 2011.
16. N.J. Jhavari, *Business Standard*, 23 August 2002.
17. 31 million cases are pending in the judicial system, 4 million in the upper courts and 60,000 in the Supreme Court. The backlog will take 320 years to clear.
18. Sunil Khilnani in *Times of India* 31 January 2014, 14.
19. In the IBRD '*Doing Business in India*' report 2013, India is rated overall at 134, for starting business 177, construction permits 183, and sanctity of contract 186.
20. *Times of India*, 16 October 2013.
21. *PTI*, New Delhi, 7 July 2014.
22. In India poverty figures are always contested. The World Bank has two definitions: \$1.25 p.d. for extreme poverty and \$2 p.d. for moderate poverty.
23. Indian Census 2011.
24. *Times of India*, 7 August 2013.

4

THE EUROPEAN UNION

The EU aspires to be an innovative and dynamic economy, but this requires the ability to pursue internal economic reforms and build decision-making structures to implement policies which support innovation at a time when the EU is beset by multiple preoccupations: aging populations, fiscal problems, the future of the euro, economic slowdown, ailing health services, failing pension schemes, and endless debate on the vaguely defined European social model as opposed to so-called Anglo-Saxon forms of global competitive capitalism. Among other challenges facing the EU are the need for coherent internal governance, the Ukraine crisis, financial solidarity in an asymmetric economy, the political and military profile, immigration issues and management of diversity, the use of biofuels, and normative and moral issues like biotechnology. When the current economic crisis is over, these concerns will remain; together with the debates over a proposed banking union and increased European centralisation.

Despite being the most powerful and choate political and economic association of states in the world, it is the political dimension that will define the European Union as a meaningful international player. Europe is increasingly turning away from power into a self-contained world of laws, rules, transnational negotiation and cooperation. Its external relations are based on normative values such as democracy, the rule of law and pluralism. It seeks partnerships, cooperation and engagement on a wide range of global issues like globalisation, terrorism, proliferation, energy and environment. It is respected for conflict resolution and nation-building, especially within Europe, and peaceful consensual politics, but not as an actual or potential political and military force with geo-strategic capacities. The European experience in Iraq and Afghanistan is not likely to alter that perception. Internationally, the EU's voice is often contradicted by its internal dynamics. It has few common foreign and defence policy attitudes, which is hardly surprising in an entity that is not a state but a transnational, decentralised, confederal construct. Europe's divisions are nothing new. Differences of opinion on the best way forward to arrive at a goal pursued, peace through trade or trade as consolidation of peace, have always been vexatious problems for its leaders, as indeed have the current concerns about the direction of powers, subsidiarity, and maintaining national identities.

The EU makes its budget only once in seven years and the latest argument was over a trillion euros for 2014 to 2020—one hundredth of its GDP over the seven year period. And 30-40 per cent of the budget goes on the Common Agriculture Policy (CAP) which is the most important EU policy. But governments have made promises to their people, including the unemployed, pensioners and students, and these are financed by taxes, so giving one euro more to Brussels is politically unpopular.

The EU is "a process that is attempting a construct where the fundamentals are constantly under debate, in which there is no consensus on the organising principle, and fundamental divisions persist about the importance to be attached to the federal principle, and ...the idea of subsidiarity."[1] It is "an enlarged Europe fatigued by the influx of labour, by its antiquated health, pension and welfare systems, and by the inertia of a population more inclined to enjoy the fruits of life than to strive to compete with foreign workers, but one buoyed by a balanced response that encourages a more long term and a patient approach to international relations".[2] Europe thought it was with the tide of history when in fact it had started to turn. Bilateralism has gained over multilateralism as power has gained over idealism. Currently, observers have scaled down their expectations, and admit that the EU's place in the multipolar order would be as a subordinate transatlantic partner dependent on the United States, despite misgivings, for strategic leadership.

From 1914 to 2007 Europe's percentage of world population declined from 27 to 11 per cent. In 1913, it produced half the world output; in 2004, 30 per cent. In 1913, its share of foreign investment was 90 per cent; in 2003, 60 per cent. In 1914, its share of merchant shipping was 80 per cent; in 2005, 50 per cent. In 1914, six of eight great powers were European (Russia, Germany, France, UK, Austria-Hungary, Italy) and the other two were USA and Japan. Now there are none. In 1913 inflation and unemployment were almost unknown; now unemployment is a seemingly ineradicable phenomenon. The shifts over the past three decades from production to finance, and labour to capital, have aggravated economic inequality. In 1914 Europe led all universities in science and technology; now European universities and laboratories have fallen behind the USA. In 1914, life expectancy was between 40 and 50; by 2005 it was 70 for males and 80 for females, and 19 of the 20 top countries with highest percentage over 65 are European. Europeans work less than ever before and the average retirement age is below 60. The response to demographic imbalance was immigration and Europe went from emigration to immigration in 100 years.[3]

Europeans believe in early retirement, free healthcare and unemployment benefits as fundamental human rights. There is a smaller share of the population available for work, and of that work force there are more persons unemployed than elsewhere in the developed world, and more strikes and shorter working days. Europeans are the idlers of the world and the heaviest drinkers of alcohol. On average, they work less than Americans and a lot less than Asians; holiday tourism is considered a birthright; religion is not the fount of the value system. They enjoy protracted education and early retirement, leaving a smaller share of the population available for work. With aging populations, Europe will be one third over 65 and one tenth over 80 by 2050. Savings rates are much higher in Asia than Europe, and private debt much lower because consumer credit plays a much smaller role. With high divorce rates and single parents and women's wish to be fully employed, the demand for family services has risen despite fixed resources.

Foreign Policy and Asia

During the 1980s Europe had been slow to take the opportunities of the Asian marketplace. After de-colonisation, relations were predominantly bilateral in nature. Attention to Asia began with Japan, then covered South Korea, the Asian 'tigers' and then China, but ties with Asia were not pushed by any important member of the EU. Only in the 1990s did the EU give attention to South Korea because producers put pressure on governments to control imports from the new industrialising countries. In return EU sought access to the Korean market and pressed for IPR and NTBs. In fact, Europe was more important to the export-oriented Asian economies than *vice versa* as they tried to reduce their dependence on USA and Japan. Europe's 'Asia strategy' document was devised in 1994 and revised in 2001. There was a Korea strategy in 1993, China in 1995, Japan in 1995 and ASEAN in 1996. There was an untoward delay in recognising the dynamics of the emerging countries, but the EU is slowly becoming attuned to the opportunities in the new multipolar global setting. The 'New Asia Strategy' of July 1994 first formulated European policies towards Asia, but the EU's ability to set the political agenda outside the European continent is highly limited because the EU is strongly integrated from an economic point of view but weakly integrated from a political one. The reason that Asia considers Europe as a lower priority is that Europe is not a single entity for transactional purposes in the international arena. Its soft power wanes the further it is projected from Europe; it is a polity without coherent demos, power without identifiable purpose, a geopolitical entity without defined territorial limits.[4] So Germany, Italy, UK and France will try to strike individual bargains with emerging Asia. With its export-oriented economy, investments to and from the USA, dependence on energy imports from the Middle East and Russia, and links through migrant workers and immigrant communities to the Muslim world, the EU has to be outward and not inward looking. It goes without saying that although it may be tempting for the bigger EU member states to forge separate engagements with some powerful Asian counterparts, the EU's unique selling point will be to stay united.

It will be in the EU's obvious interest to cooperate closely with the new fast-growing economies of Asia that now produce about 23 per cent of global GDP, and whose share is rising. Capital and goods move across borders, but not labour, and capital has moved to places in Asia to take advantage of low-cost labour there. European corporate profits are up, but jobs have disappeared. The EU must develop a more comprehensive dialogue as an indispensable partner for peace and economic progress and as an important source of technology. Such partnerships and common understandings are critically needed against the proliferation of weapons of mass destruction seen in the larger Middle East, North Korea and South Asia; and China, though having a huge part in all Asian security issues such as the Korean crisis, has itself a questionable role in proliferation. Likewise, the world-wide defence against terrorism cannot be effective without cooperation between the EU and the countries of Asia where much of this terror originates. The Asia-Europe Meeting (ASEM)[5] framework requires to strengthened considerably.

Development Assistance

The EU has to be content to exercise influence outside Europe mainly through reconstruction and peace-building operations. The present global economic downturn is having a devastating effect on poor developing countries and has become the invisible face of the recession. Therefore the EU must continue to be a leading donor of ODA on concessional terms and show more determination to bring the languishing Doha Development Round to a successful conclusion. The EU thinks of itself as a humanitarian donor and is the biggest provider of development assistance, representing about 40 per cent of global aid. But the size and quality does not match any of the big EU members' bilateral programmes, and members are unwilling to cede any further authority to the EU. The efficacy of development assistance in the emerging Asian economies is diminishing rapidly; the financial outlay is small and of declining importance in China and the rest of Asia, while none of the bigger EU countries will forsake their bilateral aid programmes or their existing contacts on trade, environment, business and technology with countries in Asia.

Of the six Asian emerging economies, the EU provides development assistance to three—India (€260 million for four years 2007-10, mainly on education and health), Indonesia (€248 million mainly on education, trade, law and judiciary) and China (€128 million). These are small amounts and in all cases amount to a 70767small fraction of GDP, and a small percentage of the ODA from individual EU member countries. In China, this assistance is for social and economic reform, sustainable development, promotion of good governance, training such as the Sino-European Business school in Shanghai, development of European studies, AIDS prevention, and the Sino-European Law School Beijing. In Shenyang, (the old Mukden), a EU-Shenyang Cooperation Zone has been started but its website gives no information about its activities or its outcomes. EU ODA to India is in the process of being phased out.

The Eurozone Crisis

When the Treaty of Maastricht was signed in 1992 and endorsed by a number of European countries in referenda, there was a general belief that the world was witnessing a new chapter in international relations. A Europe that had witnessed two bloody wars in the first half of the 20th century and a Cold War in the next four decades had, it seemed, consciously chosen to turn its back on past history. To an outsider, the European Union has often seemed a win-win proposition. A passport from a member country allows free, visa-less travel, the right to live and work in any member state and even benefit from healthcare and other welfare facilities available there to its own citizens. For businesses, there was the great attraction of free movement of goods (though not yet of services) in a common market.

The European Monetary Union project using the euro common currency which led to the creation of a eurozone seemed a great idea for business. But a single currency requires a central bank that can regulate monetary policy. The member states, however, chose to retain a large measure of national monetary sovereignty. The euro was an 'incomplete currency' with a central bank but no treasury. Developed countries that control their own currency have no reason for default: the risk is non-existent because they can always print more money though the currency will depreciate. As Jorg Asmussen, former German deputy finance minister said, "Completing monetary union means four things—a banking union, a fiscal union, an economic union, a democratically legitimised political union. They belong together and depend on one another." Completing the monetary union did not happen and the results were predictable: the thrift that underpinned German monetary policy was offset by fiscal profligacy in countries in southern Europe that viewed their entry into the eurozone as the right time to borrow, leading to the eurozone crisis that came in the wake of the crisis spawned in the USA which shook the world.

The financial crisis originated in the USA, thereby reducing the crisis-resolution ability of the global system. In 2008 governments provided financial stimulus, and central banks liquidity, at very low cost, which placed strain on sovereign budgets. The expansionist fiscal and monetary policies described as stimulus avoided collapse in the financial system and depression, though not recession, and an uneven recovery took place. With system-wide leverage and escalating real estate prices, short term debt was subject to runs in the shadow banking system, with innovations like derivatives, repurchase agreements and collateral debt obligations. "If the acronyms of modern financial life are impenetrable, the issues technically complex, the terminology euphemistic and the sums involved unimaginable, this is not accidental: such factors have functioned to enhance the mystique of the market in whose name these developments occurred, and to obscure its imperfections and asymmetrical opportunities."[6] The crisis crossed the Atlantic at the start of 2010, spreading the crisis of developed countries. Though the epicentre had been in the USA, now the new epicentre was in the eurozone. The crisis of the eurozone is due to under-consumption in the core region of the EU and the lack of export opportunities for others to the core countries.

Europe's economic and monetary integration had run far ahead of its political institutions. According to the 1997 Stability and Growth Pact, the budget deficit and government debt had to be below 3 per cent and 60 per cent respectively of GDP from 1999. There were three No's; no default, no bailout, no exit. The Pact was vulnerable to electoral politics and was in effect suspended in 2003. In deficits the eurozone including Germany is at 4.2 per cent, in public debt, it is at 88 per cent. The Maastricht Treaty ruled out fiscal bailouts and the European Central Bank (ECB), the latest central bank barely 15 years old, was precluded from budget financing, and each nation had its own central bank. European banks have a small amount of equity and large borrowings, in cases debt 50 times their equity. In India 95 per cent of sovereign debt is financed by domestic savings and domestic investors and 75 per cent is held to maturity. In the EU 55 per cent is financed by foreign savers/investors, liquid, and traded frequently. 79 per cent of Greek debt was owned by foreigners, 75 per cent of Portugal's, 71 per cent of Ireland's. All three together contributed only one per cent to global growth and seven per cent to eurozone growth, but any default would impact the global business of the European banks with exposure.

A sovereign default is when a government fails to meet a principal or interest payment on the due date. There have been 21 defaults in Europe from 1900 to 2008. So the European countries have 'form', and Greece has the worst history. To stay in the eurozone means signing up for prolonged austerity, but to leave it is to have a dramatic fall in living standards, potential bankruptcy and hyperinflation. Returning to its national currency by any eurozone member would be post-war Europe's biggest catastrophe and an unmistakable sign of the continent's dwindling power.

European countries have long been using private capital to fund public expenditures, and the 1997 Stability and Growth pact failed to check members spending more than they could finance through taxation. Euro borrowing at cheap interest rates led the weaker economies to run up huge deficits when there was no sovereign backing for the currency other than from the country concerned. The housing bubble forced governments to secure their banks by pledging billions of euros they could not raise in tax. The basic problem is the precarious nature of the euro project, with highly performing economies along with laggards. Interest rates were low to suit the German economy but created housing bubbles in nations like Spain and Ireland. This is the danger of economic integration when massive differentials exist among members. The amortisation of the debt added to the burden of the cost of public services that are already too great a proportion of the total economy. Funding the welfare state at this level will no longer be possible unless the economy grows bigger, while Europe may grow by only two per cent or less over the coming decade.[7] Slender growth will only have a marginal impact on unemployment, whereas confidence in the euro and the wider European project depends on being able to deliver jobs. To make a significant difference to the jobless figures, growth of 1.5 per cent is needed. Some are saying that even by 2018 unemployment in Spain could still be 25 per cent, and France's jobless rate of 10.6 per cent could climb to 11.6 per cent before coming down. High unemployment will therefore continue to act as a brake on the wider economy. The survival of the eurozone requires a fiscal and banking union and controls over members' budgets; alternatively, some nations abandoning the euro.

There is loss of confidence in the eurobonds issued by governments, but average government deficit and the debt situation in the eurozone is no worse than in USA and Japan. The euro area is easier to target because speculators can pick off countries one by one, but the real problem is the credibility of the sovereign debt, where countries have used public and private borrowings to make up for the loss of earning capacity and productiveness. The extreme disparities of the two speed euro economy came into sharp relief: money was centralised in the ECB but political and financial power was atomized among the individual countries. The ECB was given the power of surveillance but not the power to close a bank.

Unemployment in the eurozone currently stands at 12.1 per cent, and the European Commission said it would peak at 12 per cent in 2014. Under 25s youth unemployment is 25 per cent in Spain, Portugal and Italy. UK has 83 unemployed graduates for every job vacancy. Even in Germany the jobless rate has risen to 6.8 per cent. With huge unemployment, the aging population, excessively leveraged banks, and the eurozone debt crisis with flat-line or negative economic growth, a Europe fractured into debtors and creditors will face a long depression and decline in competitiveness. Competitive austerity, even when politically feasible, will restrict prospects of any early solution, and it is far from certain whether the crisis of capitalism can be overcome when the risk-taking, market oriented, minimally regulated market economy is questioned and market self-correction, regulatory bodies, ratings agencies and auditors have all failed. If all major economies cut back expenditure, there will be a fall in global demand which will push weak economies further into negative growth.

The eurozone crisis resulted in a shift in attitudes. Since 50 per cent of German GDP are exports, 70 per cent of German exports are to the European Union, and 60 per cent of German exports go to the eurozone, even if there are fiscal costs for Germany preserving the euro, the benefits are worth it. Anxious to dispel allegations of Berlin's expansionist agenda to create a Fourth Reich by another name, Germany has put its entire political, emotional and entrepreneurial energies behind the construction of a Federal Europe. Of all the EU members, Germany has made the best use of available facilities and has about 20 per cent of the EU's GDP. Chancellor Angela Merkel declared, "The euro is much more than a currency. The monetary union is a community of fate. This is our historic task. If the euro fails, then Europe will fail."[8]

The demands for fiscal prudence in Spain, Greece, Italy and Ireland have resulted in social upheaval and political uncertainty. The vocal electorate of these countries are loath to admit that they were living beyond their means and a punishing bout of belt-tightening was necessary. Instead, they directed their ire at Germany, demanding that the most successful member-state bail out and subsidise the least successful ones. Meanwhile, Merkel has to confront an electorate that is slowly beginning to question the wisdom of abandoning Germany's greatest post-war achievement: the Deutsche Mark. In the common sense logic of popular discourse, Germans are asking why Greece and Spain and even France cannot work harder, live less indulgently and make their own industries more competitive. Of course, Germany is fully aware that the EU has ensured that its own products have found a ready market in eastern Europe, but the anti-German tirade emanating from parts of the Balkans and the Iberian peninsula has meant that there are now Euro-sceptics in the country that once boasted its unflinching commitment to an ever-growing and ever-powerful EU.

If this was the mood in Germany, its fallout in the United Kingdom which embraced the idea of a Common Market, but remained deeply suspicious of a federal Europe, was wholly predictable. The UK has firmly stayed out of the eurozone and has not joined the common visa regime that governs the rest of the EU. Peter Steinbruck, former German deputy finance minister said, "Britain's self-awareness, its identity and its self-definition are not really those of a country that believes it is part of Europe. You see this in its leanings to the US, its permanent search for alternatives outside Europe."[9] Westminster values its residual sovereignty, as befits an institution that fought long and hard to free itself from monarchical absolutism. Successive governments, both Labour and Conservative, have quite openly been hostile to the notion that a European Parliament or a European judicial court can overrule national laws, and prevent undesirable foreigners and convicted terrorists from being deported on the ground that their 'family life' would be affected.

The latest issue that has given a fillip to the UK opposition to continuing membership of the EU is immigration. In the 1960s and 1970s, the steady stream of Asian and Afro-Caribbean immigration from the former colonies in the Commonwealth was the issue. Today, primary immigration from those places has come down to a trickle, and the new fear is that urban Britain will soon be invaded by hordes of Romanians and Bulgarians who take advantage of EU regulations to put a further strain on Britain's already beleaguered welfare state. The EU stands for free movement of labor and immigration, which was a core principle, and denial of welfare payments is a major issue. There is no anti-EU sentiment in Germany, but even there immigration is a debated topic. Britain is hostile to free movement of labour with the support of 70 per cent of its population, though statistics suggest that drain on welfare services is less from immigrants than from the British themselves, and also does not take into account that British are big emigrants to other countries.

Meanwhile, the UK used the Eurozone debt crisis to advocate a two-tier EU, demanding a *quid pro quo* for assent to treaty change providing for a looser UK relationship while emphasising the value of the EU single market. EU officials claim the UK must stick to the social terms of the single market; otherwise it would gain competitive advantage. UK has stayed out of the banking union, as have other countries like Sweden. They feel that the EU might become an extension of the eurozone at the expense of the internal market, and the eurozone will then write the rules for the rest because they are in the majority and non-eurozone countries may become second class EU members.

If the UK left, the single market would shrink by 15 per cent, and about £16 billion would disappear from the EU budget and would increase the others' contributions. The EU would become more protectionist and legitimacy would be reduced with one UNSC member going out: EU's influence on world peace and security would be reduced. But the EU must change if it is to be competitive and retain the confidence of voters. There has to be a reconciliation of joint decisions in the euro area with the opinion of others that the EU interferes too much. When there is a case for the EU to do less, it should roll power back to member states. It cannot be a one way street from which members cannot return; for example, working hours are best managed locally and not from Brussels. There are discords on regional subsidies and agriculture subsidies. The CAP needs an overhaul. The EU should continue with maximising free trade, free movement of goods, people, services and capital, and cannot any longer behave like the quondam centralised model of the 1950s for six similar economies.

In a Eurobarometer poll in April 2013, the EU's polling organisation found that over 50 per cent of those polled in Italy, France, Germany, UK and Spain had 'no confidence' in the EU. "The damage is so deep that it does not matter whether you come from a creditor, debtor country, euro would-be member or the UK: everybody is worse off," said José Ignacio Torreblanca, head of the European Council on Foreign Relations Madrid office. "Citizens now think that their national democracy is being subverted by the way the euro crisis is conducted."

The seven countries that joined the eurozone since 2007[10] added only 1.5 per cent to its economic size. In the Cyprus bailout, the sum was $22 billion whereas the Cypriot GDP was only $18 billion. In Croatia, the newest EU member with corruption, organised crime, weak rule of law, a public sector employing about 1/3rd of the work force and youth unemployment at 40 per cent, its credit rating was reduced by Standard and Poor to junk status. With excruciating speed, the atmosphere surrounding the eurozone has turned negative. Germany has avoided leading Europe from the front because of anti-German feeling in Greece, Italy, Spain and Portugal. Politically difficult compromises have to be made and money spent and promised in the face of growing German voter discontent. The Germans regard the woes of the Mediterranean and far-west periphery as negative examples of moral degeneration and self-discipline; fiscal rectitude and strict discipline are to be the order of the day. How Germany reacts to the vulnerability and fragmentation in the eurozone is of great significance. It could act further to consolidate the eurozone under its *de facto* control or it could progressively withdraw from the responsibility for upholding continent-wide policy, which would lead to the entire or partial disintegration of the eurozone.

There are four basic weaknesses in the eurozone: firstly, the Stability and Growth Pact is not respected, which was for fiscal governance in absence of a federal state. Second, there is no surveillance of external imbalances. Third, there is no banking union. Fourth, there is no stabilisation mechanism to cope with crisis. Globalisation has increased the crisis, with the over-large banking sector, uncompetitive economies, current account deficits, a bloated state sector and high unemployment in the private sector.

Countries like India and China are competing in markets that advanced economies once monopolised, with goods produced with technologies developed in the west, but with costs much less than the west. The loss of markets should have resulted in lower standards of living, but borrowing took place either directly by households or through governments. China, that is winning markets from the West, lent profits back to the West at cheap interest rates. There has to be a long term agenda to rebuild capacity to produce goods and services at prices the world will pay: there is no entitlement to prosperity. Tertiary education cannot be an undemanding free rite of passage. There has to be an innovative system for people of all ages, especially the unemployed, to readapt themselves to a changed world. Cutting costs should mean an end to restrictive practices and padded prices, postponing increases in living standards, and paying more tax, with fewer benefits. Germany did this when faced with the huge costs of reunification. It kept costs down, by using part-time workers rather than causing unemployment, and focused on exports. Germany now needs to save to protect its aging population and is determined to make fiscal discipline the price of German credit. To the extent that the European Central Bank and European Financial Stability Fund buy bonds, it increases money supply more than economic activity justifies, and will cause inflation which hits the elderly and their savings. That is why Germany insisted that ECB be first concerned with keeping inflation in check.

The eurozone is now working towards a fiscal compact, and monitoring through the Macroeconomic Imbalance Procedure. In 2010 a eurozone summit set up the European Financial Stability Mechanism (EFSM) with €60 billion and the European Financial Stability Facility (EFSF) with €440 billion at its disposal. It was also agreed in 2012 to set up a European Stability Mechanism (ESM), a permanent fund with €500 billion to replace both the EFSM and the EFSF by 2013. This has helped to alleviate tensions, along with a renewed commitment of members to preserve the euro. Now it needs education, creativity, innovation and research for EU growth, structural reforms and the 2020 endeavour of the Lisbon agenda of 2009. Eurozone leaders have taken an important step towards setting up a banking union but it is unclear when this will be fully operational. They have agreed to set up a single supervisor for banks in countries that use the euro, because eurozone countries could not be persuaded to dismantle their own central banks. The European Commission (EC) had hoped the supervisor would be in place by January 2013 but that was unrealistic, and only when a banking supervisor is in place can the zone's rescue fund inject cash directly into ailing banks. EU leaders are playing for time, hoping the worst is over, five years after the crisis broke out. The ECB president, Mario Draghi, in 2012 introduced a new policy of unlimited bond buying, albeit tied to stringent conditions, which relieved pressure on Italy and Spain. With bail-out funding, there should be no departure from the euro. The ESM bailout fund, an embryo EU monetary fund, is operative, and can rescue failing banks without adding to government debt.

During the years of the eurozone crisis, governments are believed to have spent some $2 trillion in support of ailing banks. After the German elections returned Merkel in late 2013, European governments are driving forward a more centralised European Union by agreeing on a pact on dealing with failing banks. Financed by the banking industry, the new plan is to raise $75 billion over the next 10 years to create a fund that will be managed by a new agency. This is part of a wider effort by the eurozone economies to avoid future taxpayer-funded bank bail-outs and to build a banking union, whose purpose is to stabilise the European currency as the basis for the return to growth. The proposed banking union will comprise three elements—a common banking supervisor will be created in the form of the European Central Bank, which will, together with the national supervisory authorities, monitor the health of all the major banks in the eurozone. If a bank gets into trouble, the decision to bail it out, or let it sink, would be taken by a common resolution authority. A common deposit guarantee will be established by which a bank account holder in the eurozone will have a deposit guaranteed up to a maximum of $138,000.

During the Great Depression 25 per cent of the economy was the financial sector; it is 75 per cent now. It does not generate jobs, it has destroyed public institutions and any change of politicians makes no difference. The financial sector has not been regulated and the weaknesses continue. It will be as strong as before when money is injected but the question is whether Europe can grow or only protect what it once had. Institutions like care for the aged are breaking down. Can economies based on imported raw materials develop into a knowledge economy? Nationalism has not disappeared, but has even been strengthened by globalisation. Religion has also not disappeared, and it is opposed at times to national identity, as in Islamic fundamentalism.

At this time of writing, the eurozone has eased out of recession, but six EU nations, all members of the eurozone, are considered to have unsustainable debt burdens. There are Croatia, Cyprus, Greece, Ireland, Spain and Portugal.[11] The signs are that not only is investor confidence returning but consumers are spending again, particularly on cars and household appliances. Germany very much remains the engine of the European economy. Surveys of manufacturers have shown increased optimism because industrial production has grown at the fastest rate for three years, and some countries, like Spain, have seen a surge in exports. Although some of the economies in southern Europe are still shrinking, the rate of decline is slowing. But there are grounds to be cautious.

The Greek economy has shrunk, with unemployment at around 25 per cent, youth unemployment at around 50 per cent and a growing national debt-to-GDP ratio approaching 175 per cent. In Greece, more social misery and political extremism seem inevitable. Elsewhere, in Spain and Ireland for example, painful reforms are beginning to show some slow if uncertain results. But Greece remains a problem unsolved. There are some green shoots, but its economy has declined 25 per cent since 2008, unprecedented in the modern era. The recession is predicted to moderate, but the country is currently not meeting its targets for raising tax revenue and the debt target agreed by the IMF—120 per cent of GDP by 2020—is out of reach. Greece headed for an election in 2015 with austerity as the main issue, and the election of Syriza, the first genuinely left-wing government in Europe for long decades, has plunged Greece into conflict with its creditors. The German-driven austerity conditions attached to the loans to Greece have reduced it to second-world status. Trade unions are neutered, public resources sold at distress prices, wages lowered and social security reduced. Suicides and prostitution increased by 150 per cent and the homeless and hungry have increased manifold. Greece owes $240 billion or 175 per cent of its GDP, of which debt 60 per cent is from the eurozone, 10 per cent from the IMF, 6 per cent from the ECB and 3 per cent from the Greek banking system. Among Syriza's election promises are free electricity, food and medical care to the most needy, more jobs, a new minimum wage and restoration of public sector employment. Syriza has ruled out taking more loans and wants to negotiate a debt write-off, moratorium, and new repayment terms linked to economic growth and export surpluses. The indignant German reaction was predictable; its finance minister said "Elections change nothing. There are rules." There is great bitterness in Greece against north Europeans punishing them for voting against the bitter medicine imposed on them in return for bail-out loans, and this has taken the form of demanding a debt write-off similar to the one that cut fifty per cent of Germany's debt after World War II, and for Berlin to pay war reparations to Greece and repay a forced loan taken during the occupation.

Syriza has declared, perhaps prematurely, it will no longer deal with the IMF, the EU and the ECB, the trio that was supervising the bail-out implementation, and the refusal of the ECB to lend to Greek banks against the collateral of Greek government bonds has raised the stakes. Without new credit, it is hard to see how the economy can grow. At the same time, the situation is worsening with savers and depositors withdrawing billions of euros and sending them to safer havens to hedge against a return to the drachma and its inevitable devaluation. Syriza's success had ramifications elsewhere. The Spanish Podemos party has the same aims as Syriza and leads in the polls. The tension between the Greeks and the EU has implications for the eurozone and the future of the European Union project itself. The Europeans will not want Greece to leave the 19-member eurozone or the EU, because that could be the start of unpredictable consequences that could unravel both institutions. Despite testy exchanges between the Greek government and EU leaders, all European policy-makers know that the Greeks cannot repay their debts, and compromise on both sides will be necessary.

In Spain and Italy, small and medium-sized businesses are still struggling with tight credit and both economies remain weak. Many of these southern European countries are still having to reduce their deficits, even though austerity has morphed into austerity-lite, but spending cuts are still proving to be a drag on demand. It is claimed that austerity in Southern Europe has delayed recovery and at huge social and economic cost. Any rise in GDP is meaningless when average real wages are less than in 2010, while the wealth of the richest is increasing, public services are being cut and low-paid insecure jobs have become the norm.

The eurozone crisis may be ebbing slowly and some confidence is returning, but the recovery is fragile. The eurozone is just a step away from deflation, when prices are cut and consumer buying and investment are postponed. Germany still wants France to get to grips with austerity, saying that "hiding the unemployed in government offices is not a healthy solution" (Hans-Werner Sinn, president of Germany's Institute for Economic Research). In 2015, the ECB will have to consider quantitative easing because both Germany and France are faring worse than expected. Mario Draghi called the recovery "weak, fragile and uneven". What is unclear is whether the eurozone will be able to discover significant growth or whether it will flat-line and stagnate. More important is the question whether unemployment will start falling significantly or whether this will be a jobless recovery. Also to be noted is that economic pressures have resulted in a sudden and strong surge of nationalism and right wing tendencies in politics, seen in various countries like UK, France and Hungary. There are three reasons for European Union pessimism; first, the design was wrong and so was the membership, with too many diverse economies in a common currency without a common treasury. Then matters were exacerbated by Germany's austerity policies. Second, Europe is disillusioned with the political élites, despite direct elections and more powers to the European Parliament. There is no sense of popular representation, and third, no proposals are forthcoming from the young.

Eurozone Solutions

Europe's core problem is lack of growth; with high wages, large subsidies, high taxes, an aging demography, increasing unemployment and globalisation that has moved manufacture and services across the world. Current account deficits are likely to continue; the options available are to increase competitiveness, increase savings levels to reduce budget deficits, and change consumption habits.

Given the diversity of countries, policies, cultures and financial systems, any uniform approach of good governance is unlikely to emerge. The shortcomings of the EU as a confederation of neighbours has been highlighted by the crisis; members have to forego more sovereignty to ensure fiscal discipline and stability. The trilemma is to manage inflation, the financial system and the public debt, and the tension between national politics and global markets. The survival of the eurozone would require a fiscal as well as a monetary union and controls over the budgets of members. The eurozone needs to gain control of budgets by forging political consensus in national jurisdictions, fiscal consolidation and management of public finances, debt management through elongation of the maturity period, and in the medium term, labour reforms and efficiency gains. The crisis is part of a process of global transition to a new cultural, economic, technological and geopolitical era. Today Europe sees a trend from manufacture to services; the reasons being greater productivity and globalisation trends like outsourcing. Europe needs massive public investment in infrastructure, Internet and biotechnology, basic research for new innovation, cleaner and more efficient energy production, education, technology and real productivity. Small and medium companies are the source of job creation. Banks must stop speculating and start lending.

Faced with the challenges from the Asian emerging economies, Europe's high-cost economies need to adapt if they are to grow. The EU needs to liberalise and integrate its market and reform the CAP, simplify technical standards on industrial goods, open the services market, including utilities and public sector activities, stop efforts to block takeovers of so-called inalienable family jewels, and deregulate rigid labour markets. The average tariff for agriculture in the CAP is 55 per cent, the EU services market has higher protection than trade in goods, and these tariff and non-tariff barriers bear down on exporters with cheap labour. More international competition would benefit developing countries in addition to the European consumers and efficient producers. The survival of the euro is also important for emerging Asia, as an alternative outlet for savings and another reserve currency to reduce the monopoly of the US dollar, and the recovery of Europe matters since it has the largest number of rich consumers in the world.

European Competitiveness

The EU has been living on borrowed money with governments borrowing large percentages of national GDP. Despite stringent rules, fiscal discipline has not always been met even in good times, and the next generation of governments will have to face their electorates with these realities. The Europeans must spend less, consume less, borrow less, save more, stimulate production and stop printing excess money to support their addiction to consumption. They have to invest in their inherent vitality, adaptability and creativity, concentrate on public education, science and basic research, rein in the deficit, and maximise the resources of advanced technology. Europe must also invest in infrastructure, restore manufacturing efficiency and service delivery. The state underwriting all risks for which individuals have to take responsibility has to be reconsidered, since public services absorb too large a proportion of the total economy, with the result that the EU is becoming structurally uncompetitive. The EU, "more generally Europe, can be characterised as lacking in capital preservation, being short on labour determination and technological innovation, making its chances of long term economic domination slim indeed".[12] The key will lie in competitiveness, innovation, investment and research in knowledge-based industries like nanotechnology, biotechnology and green engineering.

Many nations have enjoyed rising living standards despite budget deficits (Japan, Italy and South Korea); appreciating currencies (Germany, Switzerland); high interest rates (Italy and South Korea) high wages with periods of labour shortage (Germany, Sweden and Switzerland) and limited natural resources (Germany, Japan, Italy, Switzerland and South Korea), which shows that the stock of factors[13] at any one time is less important than the way in which the factors are created, upgraded and deployed. To achieve competitive status, European firms must demonstrate energy efficiency by recycling water and reusing heat generated in the production process, and either reduce costs or identify differentiated products that command premium prices. Competitive advantage may lie in narrowly defined industries or industrial segments. Innovation and improvement in logistics, methods and technology are central, as is domestic demand, local competition and the presence of supplier and related industries. Signs of an upgrading economy are when areas of traditional manufacture are vacated and less productive jobs are moved to other countries through foreign investment and foreign outsourcing.

Encouraging local domestic suppliers sustains competitive advantage and so domestic rivalry is a national asset. A supportive services industry requires a corps of specialised, skilled professional and technical personnel, and opening service industries to both domestic and international competition spurs productivity. The role of government, whether in Brussels or in member countries, is important for determining national economic agendas, subsidies, policies for capital markets, education including an apprentice system, shaping local demand, tax policies and anti-trust laws. Government procurement can be an upgrading force by seeking new products and services, pushing local suppliers into new areas, demanding stringent product specifications, seeking sophisticated products, setting specifications with an eye to what the most advanced markets value and generating competition by being accessible to foreign suppliers.

Protection in Europe

G-20, with 85 per cent of the world economy, has still fallen short of agreeing to a standstill on all trade and capital barriers so that countries could not raise tariffs or non-tariff barriers even where permitted by the WTO. As tariffs have decreased, NTBs have increased, with quantitative restrictions, price controls, regulatory barriers, import quotas, voluntary export restraints, discretionary licensing, anti-dumping duties, health, safety and environment protection. The EU market has significant areas of protection. There are onerous technical and food safety standards. The anti-dumping duties are prone to abuse while the EU services market has even higher protection than trade in goods. In the WTO, the EU with its CAP is a major stumbling block in liberating agriculture. It should open its healthcare and education to foreign workers on short contracts, overhaul its anti-dumping regulations and replace them with competition rules, and make food safety measures less burdensome and more transparent.

It is a hard choice pitting the commitment to open markets against protecting national economies. EU concerns about Asian NTBs include intellectual property rights, governmental intervention and investment restrictions, but unduly focusing on labour costs ignores the substantially higher productivity in developed countries. The EU's attempts to restrict Chinese exports of textiles and shoes caused China to respond, saying. Europe advocates free trade but when its interests are affected, it fails to make itself competitive and instead resorts to protection, disregarding the WTO.

Demography, Immigration

The EU's population will drop from 500 million to 444 million by 2050.[14] The EU's fertility rate is expected to continue falling with a drop in working age population, and by 2040 the average GDP growth is likely to be around 1.25 per cent, with low growth in total factor productivity. The European Union's share of world GDP is expected to fall from about 30 per cent to 15 per cent by 2050. No member country has the 2.1 birth-rate per woman that is needed to keep the population stable and one third of the population will be 65 or over by 2050. Contrary to much current public opinion in Europe, a strategically calculated enlargement programme including Turkey, more legal immigration, and increased flexibility in the workplace including fewer holidays and increasing the retirement age, may prove essential for future economic competitiveness.

The labour pool in the Arab world will increase by several tens of millions by 2020, and that of sub-Saharan Africa by several millions more. The consequences of these demographics rightly cause great concern to Europe, though it will need a measure of controlled immigration to enhance its economic productivity, and research is needed on how to reconcile the increasingly securitised EU immigration policy with the need to refresh the aging European labour market, and not only at the top end. Highly skilled and fee-paying students are still usually welcomed, but many migrant communities in Europe remain marginalised, and despite the rousing speeches of politicians extolling the virtues of tolerance, they are considered a burden rather than making a positive contribution. The problem basically concerns the authority of the secular state and its impact on religious minorities in general and Muslims in particular, who already number over forty million or well over five per cent of the EU's population. Perhaps only a new settlement between the member states and religion can successfully incorporate the growing religious minorities in Europe. The EU has to define and refine its attitude to Islam, the Arab world and Muslim immigration, since Islam has become Europe's second largest religion.

The EU with an ancient culture (like China and Japan) makes immigrant absorption difficult but the EU must open their borders to immigrants in order to sustain its standards of living and consumption. Europe has less experience in living with people whose religion, skin colour and cultural identity are different from its own. There is no single phenomenon called migration that makes sense in practical analytical terms. There are highly skilled, lesser skilled, seasonal, family and asylum seekers, all with different relationships to the host country and the Information Technology sector is strongly international. Debates in the EU about labor migration have climbed the political ladder because of pressures on the welfare state, labour market shortage, unemployment, values, entitlements, identity and belonging, low fertility rates and aging populations.

European nations do not see themselves as immigrant societies. Therefore conservative self-perceptions and other cultural barriers still play an important role despite the economic need for further immigration. The EU controls and restrains migration from Asia rather than facilitates it. International migration, human rights for migrants and European security and economic concerns are often contradictory. This discussion has become securitised in Europe and in the process, the migrants' rights have often been eroded.

Migration is regarded in Europe as individually motivated and a temporary and socially marginal phenomenon. Nations in Europe impede the development of any pro-active migration policy. But migration is in the interest of both the sending and receiving party; it resembles trade and investment where state involvement is considered normal, and is as much a part of the global economy as trade and investment. Terror threats have hardened even previously hard borders, and the migration and integration of migrant communities have become politicised.

The EU requires a labour stream and the emerging Asian countries are able to supply skilled and semi-skilled labour. Second generation Asians are customarily better educated and socialised in western societies. China and Philippines actively encourage emigration because of inward remittances, and their migrants are expected by the sending state to be successful. In the Asian emerging economies, it must be noted that international migration is only small fraction of domestic migration from rural to urban areas, and the number of migrants within Asia itself is far greater than to Europe.

There are different types of migration and the reasons for them should be better known to evolve a policy. By and large, Asian migrants in Europe are socially and culturally invisible and emerge only in times of crisis. Accurate numbers are difficult to come by because of their economic self-sufficiency based on private entrepreneurship. Sending countries like India want to cultivate their diasporic communities to help its economy, and at times that will increase the visibility of its communities abroad.

A new transnational cosmopolitan class is emerging. A large labour force will arise in the developing world from its improving living standards that would need acquiring skills, improving infrastructure, better health care and external migration. International cooperation can be tried and experimented with in this field. The EU's present policy is to limit legal and reduce illegal migration. The legitimate areas are asylum, family reunion, short term contracts, recruitment of high skilled labour and students. But there are too many illegal, semi-legal, forced and not-accepted asylum seekers. Ideas of multicultural societies have stopped in this century and integration and politicisation have become the norm. Multiculturalism now collides with liberalism, privacy and national security. Assimilation has failed in France, as did segregation in Germany and multiculturism in Netherlands and Britain. Europe is looking for an integration policy that works, when its own population is aging, Christianity declining and secularism and Islam are rising.

Islam

If the newcomers are Muslim, established cultures will often have to bend their conventions to accommodate this different culture and religion.

European resistance to outsiders on its periphery makes Europe's internal problems more intractable. In the mid 20th century, there were almost no Muslims in Europe. Now the number is over 40 million, over five per cent of the population. There are five million in France, four in Germany, and three in Britain. Muslims constitute the majority of immigrants in Europe. France has the largest percentage—7 to 10 per cent of its population. By 2025 the Muslim population in Europe will double.

The most difficult mutual recognition challenge is Europe and Islam and the management of increasingly conspicuous cultural and economic differences like freedom of speech against sacred symbols. If Europe wants people to integrate, it has to recognise the validity of some of their habits and social rules from home. "The EU's historic neglect of the Islamic dimension ... is indicative of the struggle of secular Europeans to understand religious non-western societies, to take account of non-western beliefs and cultures and to respond positively to their desire for recognition."[15] Muslims cannot be expected to buy into the European fondness for blasphemy. Europe has to internalise the interests and beliefs of others as a condition for freedom of movement on one side, and freedom of speech on the other. Muslims for their part must acknowledge that Europeans hold the right to express disrespect for religion. Just how free should the limits of freedom be? Who determines its frontiers? The EU should enact laws which deter their citizens from abusing their freedom to insult the sensibility of nations that are non-Christian.

The history of Christian-Muslim hostility and recent radical Islam have made people in Europe fearful. Not so long ago the citizens of the west had their own unquestioned symbols of collective faith and identity. These have changed due to globalisation, integration and loss of faith. Lives are freer than ever before; the continent is secular, liberal and disenchanted. Only three EU countries, Greece, UK and Denmark have established churches. Priests do not tell people what to do, and if they did, they would be ignored. Europe is paying for having departed from its spiritual foundations when it exchanged Christian culture for aggressive secularism that embraced atheism, and this may be the last chance when it still can do something about it. The European state is unable to regulate, or society to integrate. Asylum and family reunification are abused. Some of the first generation immigrants have migrated specially to carry on jihad, while some in the second generation have owed no allegiance to European societies, were opposed to assimilation and any idea of nationality, are downwardly mobile and anti-West. Generally, Europe with an instinctive compassion for minorities, shrinks from strong legislative and security measures.

Can Islamic traditions accommodate European values, however they are defined? Can European cultures accommodate Islam? The Muslim presence looms larger in the European imagination than in the reality. If the candidate states in the Balkans are added, the total number rises to still less than ten per cent. To European secular liberals, Muslims seem bigoted, misogynist, anti-democratic, fanatical and threatening. The image is that Muslims are opposed to gay rights, gender equality, freedom of opinion and speech and permissive individualism; all the hard won freedoms of the post-war period. Questions of faith are alien to secular societies; it is usually sectarian absolutism versus secular absolutism, and of late, after the *Charlie Hebdo* killings, freedom of expression absolutism. After 9/11 and manifestations of radical Islam in the west, perhaps Islam provides declining Christianity with a much-needed imagined enemy.

Islam believes it has an answer to the political, social, moral and identity crises of society. Western models and ideologies and globalisation are seen as part of the secular assault. Muslims see Islam as a solution, relief, and positive asset to counter corruption, secular and western values, which are viewed as mistaken and immoral. They assert the dominance of religion over politics and claim that Islam provides different norms and sources of inspiration and different ways of organising politics, economics and social relations. Several mechanisms contribute to the growing influence of Islam—the increasing religiosity of Muslims, state-controlled Islamisation, financial support for Islamic groups by Iran and Saudi Arabia and other countries, construction of parallel social and economic structures, and provision of public goods in impoverished societies. The EU has not found a way to tackle this unconventional foreign policy challenge. It focuses negatively on elements like Iran, Hamas, Hezbollah, the Islamic State, Boko Haram, and terrorism, but without any policy on the broader societal and religious changes, grass root movements, or transnational networks of the Islamic resurgence. The Islamic assertion is religious and cultural and cannot be contained in security terms. The EU attempt to export western norms and values to Muslim countries is a failure and conventional foreign policy approaches will not work.

Among the emerging Asian economies, Indonesia is a Muslim-majority country with a reputation for a liberal and non-fundamental attitude to society. Democratic India has a higher percentage of Muslims than any EU state other than united Cyprus. If both assimilation and multiculturalism have failed in Europe, perhaps the Indian example is one that could be emulated. It is far from perfect, being incomplete and subject to strenuous debate, but as a generalisation, the Indian state with over 80 per cent observing to a greater or lesser extent the Hindu faith, has accommodated the Muslim, Christian, Buddhist, Jewish and atheist/ rationalist minorities comparatively successfully.

NOTES

1. Balveer Arora in I.P. Khosla, *India and the New Europe*, 5.
2. Liz Mohn, *Cultures in Globalization*, 76.
3. Bernard Wasserstein, *Barbarism and Civilization.*
4. www.europaeum.org/files/publications/.../Spring2007_Zielonka.pdfý
5. ASEM is the acronym for Asia-Europe Meeting and comprises 51 countries
6. http://www.other-news.info/2012/10/what-remains-on-the-european-union/
7. The IMF forecast (Jan 2015) for the eurozone for 2013 is contraction, 0.8 per cent in 2014; 2015 is 1.2 per cent and in 2016, 1.4 per cent. For the EU the forecast is 1.7per cent for 2015 and 1.9 per cent in 2016.
8. David Marsh, *The Euro*, 264.
9. David Marsh, *The Euro*, 276.
10. Slovenia (2007), Cyprus (2008), Malta (2008), Slovakia (2009), Estonia (2011), Latvia (2014) and Lithuania (2015).
11. Michael Snyder, *The Economic Collapse blog*, 16 July 2015. The six eurozone nations are in the list of 24 most vulnerable countries.
12. Dambisa Moyo, *How the West was Lost*, 191.
13. Total Factor Productivity means the best possible use of capital, technology and labour. Other relevant factors would be any or all of geography, weather, rule of law, human rights, property rights and innovation.
14. Dambisa Moyo, *How the West was Lost*, 169.
15. S. Keukeleire and J. MacNaughtan, *The Foreign Policy of the EU*, 325.

5

Europe's Engagement with Emerging Asia

Globalisation

The concept and momentum of globalisation are of western origin; it is considered a western homogenising force in modern times. Hence, there is a presumption among the people in Asia that they are victims of globalisation and never its proponent. The relationship between the Occident and Orient seems formulated always between donor and recipient, active and passive, emerged and emerging. The EU speaks of inclusiveness but is apprehensive about giving ground to the new emerging Asian nations. This is the imperial paradigm and western mind-set of the Europe-Asian engagement.

The West will have to accept that western dominance is no longer the natural order. It cannot be assumed that there will be a single world culture. The next decades are likely to shape the future. Western leaders can be midwives rather than abortionists of a new world order of several competing, interacting, broadly equal civilisations. There can be no further attempt to graft western institutions on non-receptive countries, and the value-system based on western history and experience may not be universalised but be confined to the West.

The developed world dealt with economic growth for 100 years, then politics for 100 years, and now is focused on social issues, the environment and human rights. The Asian emerging economies have to confront all of them at the same time. The feature of the post-western world will be the rising powers contesting the western monopoly on defining modernity, and a non-English speaking, non-western, non-democratic state will dominate the global economic order for the first time in centuries as the world's biggest economy. In the coming order of international relations, some new players may not want to cooperate under the old rules, and the old divides – East-West, North-South, capitalist-communist, developed-developing, first and third world, are becoming irrelevant. At the same time, no former power is prepared to face decline while some new and old powers are cultivating those whose very influence they are trying to check.

China and India show more dynamism and consistent growth than the former USSR was capable of. The emerging Asian economies are calling for more responsibility but still within existing structures, and the demands of the emerging Asians for more weight in decision-making must be satisfied to provide legitimacy in the world order. And the emerging economies for their part must contribute to the provision of public goods. In any case, it was the present system that enabled these powers to emerge with world trade rules and economic openness, though they may seek their own symbols of modernity – the Olympic Games, moon landings, the bullet train, and other projects that are questionable from the cost-benefit viewpoint.

The West has become dogmatic, self-confident and parochial. Europe never had to adapt to foreign norms. There may have been some concepts taken up, such as Arabic numbers, but western cultures never experienced the loss of a significant part of their cultural DNA, as did the Asians to adopt western norms. Today, debates in Europe about immigration and the end of the welfare state portend a long and arduous process of revising loyalties and long-held convictions.

There is no strategic architecture or understanding between the EU and China or the EU and India. There is a good trade and economic relationship, but Europe cannot continue to assert that the trade relationship is totally divorced from any strategic relationship. The two are intertwined and part of the whole. Will the EU be willing to invest time and resources for a closer partnership with Asia, to work with Asians to strengthen multilateralism, to solve global problems, shape the world destiny, and show alternative ways for the world order? For this, a pre-condition is that culture-specific notions, different world views and values have to be studied and appreciated to promote tolerance and peaceful interaction. The EU has usually been perceived from the outside as inward looking and lacking strategic vision—a supermarket rather than a superpower[1]—divided and self-absorbed at the same time. Turning to the Asian viewpoint, are they ready to accept the Europeans as equal partners, to accept dialogue? Must cultural differences and diversity be considered as obstacles to common goals and actions, or can they be effectively harnessed and exploited? There is no need for an *a priori* anti-American bias, but for a common approach to prevent global injustice and imperial arrogance.

Trade Relations

In the next few decades, intra-Asian trade will resemble the volumes of the North America-Europe and North America-Pacific exchanges of the 20th century. As economic gravity shifts, so will trade flows, finance, investment, movements of labour and global consumption. In terms of purchasing power parity, three of the world's top four economies are already in Asia; namely China, Japan and India. In 1980, in terms of purchasing power parity, America had a 25 per cent share of the world economy while China had 2.2 per cent. By 2016, America's share will slide to 17.6 per cent while China's will grow to 18 per cent. More open trade with Asia would not only keep European prices down but encourage reforms in the labour market and employment.

India's share of the world product should rise from 8 per cent today to nearly 15 per cent in 2025 and China's from 12 per cent to 20 per cent, and these gains will be mainly at the expense of Europe and Japan, Japan's share declining due to its working age population that will drop by 40 per cent before mid-century.

EU-Asian trade will be a central plank of the 21st century global economy. China is the EU's second trade partner and the EU is China and India's premier trade partner. For South Korea, the EU is its new export destination, and it constitutes the EU's eighth market. EU investment to emerging Asia is growing strongly. Now a liberalisation of the European internal market and a more liberal trade policy is needed.

EU acts as one in trade policy. In fact, foreign policy for the EU in Asia is very much based on trade policy. The EU, China and Taiwan have bound nearly all their tariffs in WTO schedules, and Korea and Indonesia at 90 per cent, Singapore is a free port with zero tariff. China's applied tariff is 10 per cent, Korea's is a bit higher, and India's much higher. Most countries have a higher tariff for agriculture than manufactures: Korea and India very high, and China around 15 per cent. Europe has a FTA with South Korea (despite being hard to negotiate and ratify due to fears of the EU's car manufacturers) and a draft one with Singapore despite also being hard to negotiate and ratify, and one being negotiated, again with great difficulty, with India. But EU-Asia trade relations need a degree of strategic thinking beyond FTAs which place multilateralism under pressure. Stronger bilateral frameworks of cooperation are needed. Apart from seeking preferential access for selected sectors in Asia, EU requires to enhance its own internal market reforms to have an open door for imports and inward investment. Meunier and Nicolaidis have described the European Union as a "conflicted trade power".[2] Faced with the challenges from the emerging economies in Asia, Europe's high cost economies need to adapt if they are to grow. In 2010 an advisory EU panel had warned that if eurozone members did not coordinate economic policy, ensure greater mobility of labour and boost investment in R&D, they would be the losers. In its FTA policy, the EU attitudes are essentially discriminatory and power-related. It is good to reciprocally open markets in goods, services and investment, underpinned by competition-inducing rules, but the EU must not export its costly regulations—such as labour standards, environment and intellectual property—to Asian emerging economies whose only advantage lies in low costs. The EU's complex rules of origin need to be simplified and harmonised, and extraneous political objectives like human rights and democracy should be kept out of negotiations.

China

EU rhetoric against China on a wide variety of issues is shrill, but is still less strident than that of the Americans. The Europeans should work for a genuine strategic partnership with China. China now sees its emergence as legitimate revenge on history, and Europe's goal should be to integrate China in the global community as much as possible. China is needed by Europe, though it can also be considered by some a threat. With China, Europe must delicately combine partnership, cooperation and deterrence. This may need some coordination with USA, Japan and India; not to confront China, but to seek expanded areas of convergence.

Though China is the second biggest trade partner for the EU after the USA and the EU is China's biggest one, and the daily turnover is more than one billion euros, there is friction in trade and economic cooperation which is the fundamental connection at present with no consensus on complementarity and mutually supportive policies. China has to spell out how it sees the European relationship and what role, if any, it wants the EU to play in global governance. Official joint statements lack well-defined common interests or objectives, and bilateral issues outweigh international questions in bilateral discussions. How the West manages Asia's future will have profound implications for Europe. China is seen as an economic phenomenon and any strategic thinking is an afterthought. But the rise of China and emerging Asia are both an economic and a strategic event, challenging the current order in economy, business, investment and the environment. It is a shift in the global centre of gravity of historic proportions.

China has legitimate aspirations as having been through a century or more of western humiliation imposed by imperial powers. This is writ large in the political consciousness of the Chinese, who see their rise as a reflection of their search for national sovereignty. Europe has so far been missing from this debate though it can help shape the emergence of a common security understanding across Asia. Europe is introspective and so preoccupied with the internal problems of its economy and the eurozone that it runs the risk of global economic and political marginalisation. It has fundamental strengths to help the rest of the world, but these are not to be seen at present.

Europe and the Asian Rise

The EU dwarfs all its individual Asian partners in GDP, *per capita* income, trade in goods and services, and FDI. It is a facilitator but not the source of any new world order; its choice is for a multilateral and soft approach that in a way counter-balances the self-interest of the USA. Europe needs predictable and sustainable relations with emerging Asia. Defining and applying a common foreign and security policy would help unify Europe and make it more influential. The EU has no counterpart in Asia, and Asia has no specific roadmap for Europe. The EU undertakes so many complex tasks that it seems to have an overloaded agenda: are EU meetings with Asian nations project-driven or simply meetings-driven? The EU needs to build common data, expertise and analyses on Asian political, economic and strategic issues: it can leave high-end hard security and military strategy to the USA and deal with other issues, which may be welcome to Asia. Contributing to security, and enlarging relations with new and emerging democracies would enhance influence, leverage and image, but will be difficult, and the arms embargo on China and the market economy status debates show how hard this would be. Basically, the EU cannot contribute to Asian crisis resolution such as on Korea when it is so tied to US foreign policy.

The world is still in a transitional phase with the end of bipolarity, the rise of new powers and the growing strength of economic forces and civil society. The global order is being rebalanced. Simultaneously both over-and under-estimated, the EU is one of the leading global actors, but while the world landscape has changed over the years, the EU's rhetoric has not. With the US unipolar moment peaking, the EU may be better placed to impact the world discourse on justice and sustainable economic development, but it may have only up to 15 years to make its impress felt, though this time is a particularly bad period for the EU internally. If we rule out, as the EU often itself professes, old notions of the deployment of classical power, we have the alternative course of legitimacy, persuasion and diplomacy. Will these empower Europe, or are they just another product and pitfall of wishful thinking? The path ahead may lie in the belief in the power of reason and the emergence and sustainability of international society. For these, Europe will need partnerships among the emerging powers in Asia.

There also needs to be a redefinition of terms. How can the EU have a 'strategic partnership' with both China and Japan, who each define their strategy in terms of a degree of hostility to each other? How does the EU promote democracy when it deals even handedly with India, which is a 68 year democracy, with Pakistan, where the unaccountable military pulls all the strings? Perhaps the EU mistakenly assumes that a would-be European superpower can simultaneously have partnerships with everyone.

Asian economies, despite their dynamism and considerable size, are still termed as 'emerging economies', while the economies of the West, however embattled, have apparently already 'emerged'. This is possibly why in books without number on European foreign policy, there is hardly a mention of China or India, in other words, 40 per cent of the world's population, let alone the smaller but also emerging Asian economies. But then, there was no mention of the EU in recent US presidential debates either, which provides a perspective and places relative strengths in context. Oswald Spengler in *The Decline of the West* had foreseen that "the innumerable hands of the coloured races, at least as clever and far less exigent, will shatter the economic organisation of the whites," and Bernie Ecclestone, the supremo of Formula One, in 2012 told the Spanish paper *Marca*, "Europe is finished. It will be a good place for tourism but little else. Europe is a thing of the past."[3] Some statistics seem to bear him out. In 1992, the only Grand Prix venue in Asia was Japan; twenty years later, there were eight, and European venues had dropped from ten to two.

The Asian rise is the defining feature of the 21st century, and this has implications for people everywhere. It has already changed the global economy, the financial markets, society and the environment. This means the world is entering a new transformative period. Asia will not only be the largest producer of goods and services, but the world's biggest consumer of them. It is the most populous region of the world and will be home to the majority of the middle class. A wealthy and mobile middle class will demand diverse goods and services from health and aged care to education, household goods, tourism, banking and financial services. Europe will need closer educational and cultural ties with emerging Asia and closer people-to-people links. The EU needs to make a serious connection with local Asian intellectual traditions and local history in an effort to explore non-west traditions to make a better case for the West. It should make studies of Asia a part of the school curriculum, giving students an opportunity to learn an Asian language and making business more Asia-literate.

Any policy of containment of China will not work. Nor will American-style 'congagement' (that is, containment plus engagement), implying greater trade and economic connectivity, while Washington's 'rebalance' to Asia checks China's rise as a global power. Europe will have to balance defence and security ties with the USA while strongly backing the Asian rise, including its growing military strength. The Asian century must be regarded as an opportunity as the global centre of gravity shifts. Trade with Asian emerging economies has risen sharply, and financial, political and cultural ties have deepened. Friendships must be cultivated across the region. The long history of Europe-Asia engagement must concentrate on past positives, with exchanges at government, political, business, union, academic, sports and student levels. Europe must show it has a lot to offer Asia with its world class institutions, multicultural environment, skilled workforce, acceptance of skilled and semi-skilled Asian immigrants, and a productive and open economy ready to transfer technology.

Critical will be European reform and investment across the areas of productivity, involving innovation, infrastructure and reform, investing in people through skills and education, science and technology, with adaptability and resilience, creativity and design-based thinking. The understanding of Asian cultures and languages must be deepened. Europe has to work to build trust and cooperation, including by supporting a greater role for Asia in the regional and global world. There must be more intensive diplomacy and social and cultural contact. Europe can contribute to, and equally learn from emerging Asia. Europe cannot build this transformation overnight, but a start has to be made with a definite programme, and careful planning and monitored implementation.

Within a few years, Europe's trade with Asia has risen dramatically. China's new patents have increased 25 times since 1995. Three of the top ten Fortune companies are Chinese. China has bought European sovereign debt and bolstered the euro value against the dollar. It is the biggest world market for cars. It invests 50 per cent of its GDP compared to 20 per cent in Europe. It uses 46 per cent of global coal. It commands 25 per cent of the global luxury goods market. In a cash-starved and shrinking export environment, its foreign exchange reserve is over $3.8 trillion,[4] its sovereign wealth fund has assets of $200 billion and in one month it invested $2.5 billion strategically in 75 countries abroad. It has so far invested more in Europe than in North America. It can inject liquidity into the global system and provide a safety net for the OECD economies. It would invest in eurobonds if they were guaranteed by Europe as a whole.

China said it was ready to work with the international community to promote stability in the international financial market, and will not be bystanders in the eurozone crisis, but it would not shoulder the same responsibilities as those directly responsible for the crisis, the same attitude as it takes for climate change.

Between 1980 and 2008, Indian productivity grew faster than South Korea's. Despite large scale poverty and low *per capita* income, India commands some respect and global influence because it is a big economy. China and India will account for two thirds of the increase in the middle class by 2030, and both are essential for absorbing the marketing surpluses of the industrialised economies. According to the ADB, Asia could account for 45 per cent of world GDP in purchasing power parity by 2020, 66 per cent of foreign exchange reserves and 50 per cent of the middle class, along with a shift in goods production and boom in consumer demand. With doubts about a strong US long-term rebound, the importance of China is paramount and its growth essential for European recovery. If a European business firm is not represented in China and India, it will not be considered global. If Europe does not engage constructively with Asia, it will be consigned to the periphery of international affairs. Asian economies protect Europe from higher prices and from a hard-landing from the global slowdown. To restart growth, Europe will need bigger net exports to emerging Asian economies, and increased investment from Asia would create jobs and growth.

The Asian emerging economies are at the heart of modern re-balancing; individualism is breaking out with economic freedom emerging and expanding in tradition-bound societies. This individual awakening is still embedded in the family unit. Hong Kong, the most capitalist area in the world, remains a family-based tradition-bound society. The Asians will probably avoid the atomisation of dissolving social glue by modernising without westernising. Europe in Asia is not a superior civilisation in a place that cannot possibly attain western accomplishments, and apart from retaining some cultural idiosyncrasies, would evolve in the direction of emulating the political and economic arrangements of the West. Although the modernisation theory of Seymour Lipset holds that all societies head towards democracy and Thomas Friedman claims that no two countries with MacDonald outlets have ever fought a war,[5] the world is not that flat.

In most respects, the world of 2050 will be a far less western world. Our globe is in a period of transition to a new cultural, economic, technological and geopolitical era. The world is still far from being post-American, but there is already more multipolarity and uncertainty in the global order. The United States is no longer able to maintain global stability, while new centres of power are not yet ready. It is still unclear whether the major Asian states, as they rise to world power, will project their own values in order to reshape the new international order. It would seem logical to expect them to do so, and to contest the past western monopoly of defining modernity, but since their rise has been so closely bound up so far with the process of modernisation along western lines, it is difficult to anticipate at this stage what changes they may favour.

The new Asian leaders must offer dynamism, optimism and growth, but thus far, too domestically preoccupied, the Asians have not evidenced any leadership role on the international stage, though they have tested their power of negation and it is clear from the climate change negotiations and the WTO that their consent will be needed to find solutions. Instead of feeling insecure and clinging to the old order of privilege, it is important for Europe to make an imprint on emerging Asia while the latter deliberates and evolves its own approach to the world system, drawing from historical experience and classical traditions. Europe needs to have predictable and sustainable partnerships with emerging Asia, and perhaps a couple of decades in which to forge them before Asian strategic settings become entrenched and the emerging countries become active participants in the full range of global institutions with new conceptual and policy frameworks.

Of course it will be by no means easy. With the largest concentration of the world's population, concerns over the sources and causes of terrorism, proliferation of weapons of mass destruction, seemingly unsolvable inter-state and would-be state problems and imminent conflicts, stresses of abject poverty, food shortages and climate change, the phrase 'Asian century' is a misnomer. In institutional terms, Asia is much less clearly defined than Europe, and the concept of Asia is an artificial construct. Historically speaking it was created by Europeans who contrasted their own modern nation state with the Asian societies that they viewed as backward, stagnant, absolutist and tradition-bound. The concept of Asia was created artificially within Asia as well, by figures like Sun Yat-sen, Rabindranath Tagore and Maulana Azad along with some pre-World War II thinkers in Japan, who called for Asia as a concept to provide a political and psychological arena for resisting colonialism. Today, learning about Asia is to trace the diverse strands of Asian thought that have originated in different regional, national, and local traditions, but which have become intertwined with global life in this century.

Asia is a continent that enjoys neither political nor commercial unity; nor any common security agenda. Its multilateral structures are very weak and systems of governance vary from dystopia and communism to liberal democracy. China, Japan and India give no leadership for greater integration. Nevertheless, the new international landscape will have to take account of the spectacular economic growth over the past decades in certain parts of Asia, with the benefits of low cost labour, vast territory and resources, and rapidly growing infrastructure and technology.

The emerging Asian nations have regarded international society which developed under western tutelage in the 18th to 20th centuries as not being just or neutral, and themselves as being targeted by interventionist strategies. These Asian countries have blamed the western world order for denying them their share of status and authority, and strongly resist external interference, let alone intrusion or intervention. There will be shifts in perceptions of global security needs, and on who should and could police the world, and how. There are past examples of countries, like Japan and Canada, with a strong economic base, that have deliberately chosen to refrain from exercising influence in world affairs, but Asian countries may not show similar self-restraint. They have displayed, and will prove, that opening their economies can be married to a strong assertion of national sovereignty. Because of its huge stake in the US economy, China in particular will no longer be a consumer of whatever international order the West chooses to dispense. Indeed, as the North Korean nuclear crisis has demonstrated, the international community cannot operate in Asia without China's support. No Asian nation will be in a position to challenge the United States militarily for the foreseeable future, but they are likely to become increasingly assertive and less deferential whether the West likes it or not. Indifference to emerging Asia was sufficient for the European boom, but it will not suffice when times are less bright.[6]

Towards a New Asia Strategy

Despite its long familiarity with the Asian continent, Europe was a late starter in Asia. Apart from Japan, Europe was slow to take Asia seriously after World War II. Asia was left out of the Lome Convention (1975 to 2000) and EU's enlargement with new members did not significantly expand its interest in Asia. Europe's first 'Asia strategy' document was in 1994. But there were no common perceptions about European influence in Asia or about Asia in Europe. After decolonisation, the predominantly bilateral ties between Europe and Asian nations did not touch on security issues or the US presence in both continents. New security issues like terror, migration, nuclear proliferation, climate change and pandemics, however, called for a broader and multilateral approach. Only in the 1990s did the EU give attention to emerging Asian economies because producers put pressure on governments to control imports from new industrialising countries like South Korea. In return the EU sought access to the Korean market for alcohol and cars, and pressed for IPR and NTBs. The EU's inhibitions were due to the predominance of the USA in the Asian region and negative experiences such as Tiananmen, human rights violations, trade imbalances with Japan, and the aggressive export policies of South Korea in shipbuilding and steel. Some Asians looked to Europe to avoid too much dependency on Japan and USA for their economic growth, while the US and EU wanted the developing countries to lower tariffs on environmental goods, and facilitation measures to ease customs rules. From Maastricht in 1993 until 2006, only eight per cent of CFSP decisions dealt with Asia—mainly Myanmar, Indonesia and Afghanistan.

This does not include 'declarations' which are often one-off short-term reactions without further involvement. Asia hardly figured in the 2003 European Security Strategy (ESS), and relations with Asia were not pushed by any important member.

In the 1997 Asian financial crisis, EU was either absent or echoing only the IMF doctrines of painful reform, while China provided currency stability and trade concessions to the affected countries. But Europe did not want to be left behind after APEC came into existence in 1993, though it was still perceived as a weak political actor in Asia. The Asians decried EU bureaucratic rigidity, rules over consensus, absence of give and take, and the tendency to preach and give lessons, using social rights and issues as a cloak for protection. ASEM objectives were always left vague and given little priority either in Asia or in the EU. ASEM has a long way to go and has not dealt with any specific problem: it lacks instruments and capabilities and was nearly torpedoed by Myanmar's presence as a member of ASEM to which the EU objected.

The EU initially regarded China's rise as no threat and India's emergence as benign, presenting an opportunity for growth of demand for goods and services. China, in the opinion of the EU, is the easier of the two to understand, whereas India's social fabric is complicated. China certainly takes the EU more seriously while India needs to be persuaded that the EU has any merit. EU has invested considerable resources in China, as a permanent member of the UNSC and the largest donor to several developing countries. China is regarded by the EU as global; India as only South Asian. Many more policy papers and appraisals are prepared by the EU on China compared to India. China has no hesitation in dialoguing with EU—40 to 50 issues are being discussed and there is dense bilateral traffic at the European commissioner level. As a result, China is said to understand the EU better than the Europeans themselves, while other Asian governments are generally deeply perplexed about EU power-sharing arrangements. Differences between EU states meant they had to be lobbied bilaterally and separately, its big members possessing stronger leverages, and the Asians have to go through a tough learning process to act as equal partners. With agreement with member states as the key to any agreement with the EU as a whole, two layers of negotiation become complicated but unavoidable.

China demands engagement, while India is not competitive or aggressive. There is also a capacity problem in India, which has too few officials in its system to engage with the hydra-headed European Commission. For the EU, a strategic partnership, such as the one with India, is little more than a business plan. For China, such a description means a security relationship with strong political ties, but that cannot be realised when Europe's strategic policy is subordinated to the USA. Therefore the EU is regarded as a distant power with limited strategic interests in Asia. The EU is still to develop an operational strategy and to use its resources for effective policy making, which has made Asia lower its expectations.

But now emerging Asia is the fastest growing market for EU goods and also for its FDI. The compelling priority both for emerging Asia and the EU is jobs, growth, environment, energy and social equity. These are internal objectives, but both sides need to support these in the other and strengthen the relationship. Trade dominates in EU-Asia ties, and political and security issues have been secondary, while culture has ranked even lower. The effectiveness of the EU as a problem-solver in Asia is ambiguous or negligible, while Asia is seen as secondary for the EU compared to the USA, the Middle East and North Africa. No one seems to have the calendar open at the correct page. Engagement on new terms between the European Union, with its goal of standard-setting, and emerging Asia would be highly desirable. The Asian emerging powers attach greater importance than the EU to preserving sovereignty and space for domestic policy discretion. If Asian influence grows, many institutions could be brought back to the original ideas that animated them and enrich the received forms of political and economic thinking that have proliferated since the fall of the Berlin Wall. The EU needs to seek closer engagement, cooperation and dialogue, and an EU-Asia meeting of minds would help resolve many world problems. The new emerging Asian economies are seeking a place at the high table in the existing international arrangement. Without that, they will not share in the burdens of change like climate, energy or proliferation. A system redesign is therefore needed of global governance to forge a more inclusive multilateralism. The EU must accept that it is legitimate for Asia to have a stronger say in the international community, which is no longer the exclusive expression of western interests. European colonialism has diminished the moral authority of the former colonisers, and the new system must run on universal values rather than on the interests of any one group and the new economies of Asia must have a stake based on their own civilisational traditions. In return, the Asians must be encouraged to enhance the existing order through their policy actions, even when their interests are not at stake, as responsible global stakeholders.

Comprehending Asia is not an exotic luxury but a matter of necessity. Asian emerging nations are an accumulation of historical experiences, perceptions and achievements. To understand the modern language, politics and economics of the emerging economies, it is necessary to know the historiographies of the ancient continuing civilisations, which are an essential element in understanding modern China, Indonesia, South Korea and India. They are profoundly shaped by historical experience and still searching in classical traditions on how they may navigate the future in this world.

An initiative for a EU dialogue with emerging Asia should be a starting point. The EU should seek this dialogue on the premise of power-sharing, to pursue common understandings on global governance. Diplomacy has to invent a mechanism, perhaps a back-channel, informal but authoritative, on the lines of Jean Monnet's 1955 Action Committee on Europe, but on a trans-continental scale. It should start with work on cultural issues before proceeding to climate change and global trade. Bilateral matters must come last. This EU-emerging Asia dialogue should commence at an informal level to start with. It is not a given that the Asian side will agree on everything, but nor will the EU members. Such a grouping probably makes more sense than the G-8, where Europe is over-represented, and than the G-20, comprising 5 Europeans out of 20. Asia could put its views across on climate change and global trade. They feel it unfair that the USA, that has contributed a bigger share of greenhouse gas emissions than any other country, should ask poor countries in Asia to limit emissions. They believe that the US should pay an economic price for its contribution to this stock of greenhouse gas and make a commitment to reduce its future emissions. On global trade, there was an understanding at the end of the Uruguay Round that USA and Europe would reduce their agricultural subsidies as part of a comprehensive deal in the Doha Round. These commitments were not fulfilled, and now with fiscal deficits in EU, the subsidies are not sustainable. Such a meeting could perhaps make some progress on this issue. On the Islamic world, the Asians can offer helpful advice, and even on the questions of migration, Iran and Pakistan. And perhaps on Tibet and the Dalai Lama, once several encounters have built up a modicum of trust. It will have to be a discussion for the long haul. The US will probably be aggrieved to be excluded, but a discussion behind closed doors will be easier without USA, Japan and Russia. Other Asian countries might also be aggrieved, but the larger the group, the fewer the results are likely to be.

NOTES

1. Yeo Lay Hwee, *Dimensions of Asia Europe Cooperation*, 2004.
2. S. Meunier, & K. Nicolaidis, 'The European Union as a Conflicted Trade Power', *Journal of European Public Policy*, 2006, 13(6), 906-25.
3. www.google.com/.../ALeqM5hUv5QVJNSkq8u1Xy2_xmBwNPJDDw?...
4. *Financial Times*, 11 April 2013.
5. Thomas Friedman, *The Lexus and the Olive Tree*.
6. David Marquand, *The End of the West*.

6

THE EU AND CHINA

The way China turns out is to an extent based on how it is treated. To treat it as a threat may be self-fulfilling. To contain and thwart it would provoke an onrush of nationalism. Treating it as a partner and enveloping it into multilateral institutions will be the better way to define common understandings on identity, interests and security. The US can lead the world but will not dominate, even if it gives up unilateralism, military supremacy and pre-emptive war. The majority of the world's population cannot be governed by a system to suit the interests of Europe and USA.

By 2030, almost certainly by 2040, China's GDP will be the biggest in the world. It is already the world's biggest exporter and nearly the biggest importer of commodities. The belief that the private sector and free market are more efficient than public ownership and regulation has consequently been challenged. The shift in power and wealth from west to east is similar to the shift from Europe to the USA that happened in the 19th and 20th centuries, but this shift will be faster than any in earlier history. The implications of this are not clear; it could be less smooth than the shift from Europe to the United States for institutional and cultural reasons, but it is better for both Europe and Asia to prepare for it as a challenge and an opportunity.

Diplomatic relations between China and the European Commission date back to 1975. There was a Trade and Cooperation Agreement in

1985, and in 1995 came the first EU document on China, with annual EU-China summits after 1998. The EU along with the USA played an active role in facilitating China's admission to the WTO in 2001. In September 2003, a EU-China comprehensive strategic partnership started with the EU's *A Maturing Partnership: Shared Interests and Challenges* and in October 2003, China replied with China's EU Policy Paper, the first such document from the Chinese on any group or country, which noted that the EU would play an increasingly important role in regional and global matters.

The EU needs to anticipate that China will be richer and more powerful, and must strive to make it realise that adherence to global rules and norms is not incompatible with this process, but will enhance and make it sustainable. Increase in Chinese investments in Europe would help the EU's economy, create jobs and growth and support China's external profile. The EU negotiators have to ensure that China does not compete unfairly by using pirated intellectual property or take undue advantage of government support. The EU must encourage internal competitive neutrality: if China expects its growing intellectual property to be respected abroad, it must protect foreign intellectual property at home, including in state-owned enterprises and the provinces. There has to be dialogue on food and product safety, exchanges of scientists on the environment, clean water and climate change, and bringing together Chinese and EU provincial and municipal leaders.

China has so far combined authoritarian government with a partially privatised economy. Since the financial crisis, the Chinese have regarded their model as an alternative to democracy, but the model is culturally specific and few developing countries can emulate it. Export driven growth and top-down decision making may not yield good results for ever. The guiding ideal of the Communist Party is equality, but the society has growing inequality, and most recent waves of technology innovation benefit the best talents and best educated and create divisions.

China has bought European sovereign debt in a big way and bolstered the euro value against the dollar. The EU is the biggest importer for China at €292.5 billion in 2011, and exports from the EU to China were at €136.2 billion, the second biggest market after USA. China said it would continue investing in eurozone government bonds and bonds of the EFSF, support a stable euro and would not reduce its holdings of eurobonds. Europe welcomed Chinese hints to prop up the euro on top of the $500 billion it holds in EU bonds. The world must accept the idea that China may be a cheaper and more flexible source of capital than many alternatives because Chinese banks offer financing at attractive terms for foreigners to buy Chinese goods. The next phase is likely to see China's industrial giants starting to look overseas for new markets and new expertise. That will be controversial because most of them are controlled by the CPC. In areas like telecommunications and energy, they could provoke trade rows in the west.

China regards its EU ties not as a matter of expediency but as a long term strategic policy, and hoped to enlist the EU as a pole to foster a multipolar environment and limit US unilateral attitudes. Chinese saw the relationship as reducing contradictions, and the EU as about building consensus. In fact, China affects Europe's world far more than Europe can affect China's world. Europe is hedging its bets because Sinophiles and Sinophobes there go hand in hand. On one hand, they may assert that China is a 'partner', and on the other they think it may be a security problem due to fears of lost jobs and markets flooded with Chinese goods. China's exporters boosted western living standards by selling cheaper manufactures, but killed off many European manufacturers. China's surplus meant European deficits, and huge global increases in food prices, energy and commodities.

The 'Strategic Partnership' of 2003 was backed by an agreement on space and satellite navigation cooperation. For China, such a partnership meant a security relationship with strong political ties, but that could not be realised when Europe's strategic policy is subordinated to the USA. Therefore the EU is regarded as a distant power with limited strategic interests in Asia. A High Level Economic and Trade Dialogue began in 2008. EU's agenda was to deny preferences, use instruments like anti-dumping and safeguards, and obstruct compensation through WTO's trade dispute mechanism. Its complaints were that China undervalued its currency, did not comply with the WTO, restricted access to public procurement, had social and environment conditions that were NTBs, gave subsides to national industries and placed restrictions on the export of some key raw materials. Seven out of ten European businesses say they are victims of Chinese violations of IPR and 73 per cent of all counterfeit seized in EU in 2011 was from China. China, of course, had its own list of grievances: EU security scrutiny of investments, European sunset industries demanding protection, the EU arms embargo, denial of market economy status, the Nobel prize to a jailed activist, meetings of politicians with the Dalai Lama, European actions on copyright, trademarks and IPR, lack of transparency in regulations and anti-dumping. There are empty threats on both sides to close the market.

The EU has struggled to form a response while China eroded US influence in East Asia, forged ahead with almost 100 per cent literacy and life expectancy nearly at developed country level, promotes its language and culture through Confucius Institutes, has 300,000 students abroad and is taking steps towards oil self-sufficiency with its offer of $15 billion, approved by the Canadian government, to take over Canada's energy giant Nexen, which has cutting edge technology in extracting shale oil. China has reputedly large deposits of shale gas—36 trillion cubic metres of accessible reserves, though at present China has to buy the advanced equipment from the west which adds to the extraction costs.

Like USA and China, EU-China trade ties are too big to fail. The EU is China's largest trade partner ahead of US and Japan, and an important source of investment, but many Chinese policies run counter to the EU, especially regarding human rights in Africa. Business is business, the Chinese might say, echoing what the EU itself states in dealing with China. China represents a development model not in line with the EU; one where economic liberalisation need not be accompanied by political liberalisation or western norms. This is appealing to some parts of the world, not only in Asia and Africa, but elsewhere.

The big three in the EU—Germany, France and Britain—have competing and conflicting agendas on China. They, along with Italy, pursue strategies to optimise their own companies' prospects in the Chinese market on the grounds that only through fostering good political relations with China could EU companies get lucrative contracts. There is also intense competition among European countries to attract Chinese investment. Chinese firms have acquired Volvo and signed a rescue package for Saab. China runs a terminal in Greece, wind farms in Romania and an economic zone in Bulgaria. It has a stake in Barclays, oil ventures with Norway and Switzerland, and an average spend of £ 6.5 million per property in London. A Chinese firm will make white goods in Italy that will be the fifth largest in Europe by 2015. Nevertheless, German investment in China is 30 times the Chinese in Germany. The number of EU investment projects in China may be less than that of the USA and Japan but with an average larger value per unit, more high value added and more transfer of technology. EU companies have an interest in selling or transferring advanced EU technology to China despite IPR being an issue at the governmental level.

As the centre of political, economic and strategic gravity moves from the Atlantic to the Pacific and from the US and Europe to Asia and China, the question is whether the collective EU is prepared for this shift. The Chinese are opposed to EU ambitions to westernise and transform China, but China will have priority for the EU because of its political influence, economic potential, higher economic stakes and trade, which define the degree of interest the EU takes in other countries also. Will China accept the culture, norms and structure of the postwar order? This is the biggest core question. It would help if Europe's engagement was a considered, consistent one, driven by organising principles and not a series of one-off reactions to occasional events. It is not certain that China possesses either the will, intention or capacity to shape tomorrow's world. China's internal debate is still fluid and there is a window of opportunity before final strategic settings become entrenched. But this is a time when the EU itself is in deep distress. Both the EU and USA are getting disengaged and insular in regard to the rise of China, when policy needs to be sophisticated and acute. There must be a significant diplomatic engagement with China from the West or there will be a new global order by default, perhaps inimical to western interests and values. But this will need more intellectual effort, diplomatic coordination, political will and open and candid engagement with Asia than has so far been the case. The relationship needs to evolve from a trade partnership to an equal partnership on global issues because future geopolitical and economic realities require a working relationship. The goals should be mutual confidence building, military transparency, common responses to disaster management and challenges like terrorism, disarmament and climate change, commitments to open economies and sustainable development, and a new Asia Pacific order that could translate into a wider peace, because, for the moment, China is not seeking to oust USA from Asia. The EU should refrain from linking non-trade goals such as democracy and human rights, cultural diversity, environment and sustainable development with economic matters. This makes EU look preachy, pandering to its anti-market non-governmental organisations (NGOs) and other European lobbies, and arouses Asian resistance.

Market Economy Status

At first the EU exported capital or technology-intensive goods and China exported labour-intensive low technology goods. But now China is a competitor in low cost high skill production due to the rapid upgrade of its industrial structure, and is challenging the competitiveness of both the old and new EU member states. Upon joining the WTO China accepted non-market economy status until 2016 but from 2003 has been asking the EU to amend this policy. So market economy status (MES) in the WTO becomes sensitive, and the EU's refusal to give China full market economy status is a weapon cherished by European manufacturers of lower cost goods. In its effect, it enables the EU to raise tariffs on Chinese goods, and in the absence of MES the anti-dumping rules are easier to apply. EU has the record number of anti-dumping cases at the WTO against China, and levies prohibitive duties against items like Chinese bicycles and solar panels.

China complains that the EU does not recognise China as a modern, open market-oriented economy that would give it tariff advantages. EU has fallen back on 5 technical arguments, though some members give various assurances and different excuses to the Chinese on an individual basis. According to the EU, China fulfills only one out of five requirements; less government influence on business and finance, lack of market access for EU firms, non-transparent legal framework, non-transparent laws on corporate governance, property rights and bankruptcy. According to the EU, the Chinese have made too few concessions on human rights and have difficulties in implementing WTO decisions on IPR, market access or sector-based trade agreements. This is a clear case of discrimination by the EU compared to Russia—a European country that has this status, whereas EU-China bilateral trade of €430 billion in 2011 is vital to both sides and has quadrupled in the past 10 years.

The EU's task is to appease its protectionists and because EU companies have access difficulties in the Chinese market. This tough line by the EU Council is however not congruent with the more flexible approach practiced by many member states individually.

Arms Embargo

The arms embargo sustained against China by the EU since the Tiananmen Square incidents in 1989 is held by the Chinese to show the EU's inability to escape from the Cold War mentality. The European Parliament is very vocal against lifting the embargo. In fact, the EU arms ban was a Council declaration, vaguely defined and not binding, and is thus the result of a series of national embargoes, supplemented by the EU's dual use regulation, which is binding. Chinese Premier Wen Jiabao in September 2012 urged the EU once again to lift its arms embargo which has been pending for one decade, and for which the Chinese have been pressing since 2002. The ban limits high technology and dual use sales at a time when China wants to diversify its sources of purchase from Russia which is its main supplier.

The EU has been considering lifting the arms ban since 2005. France, Italy and Germany are opposed to the arms embargo, the Nordics and the Dutch want to keep it, and the US' influence retains it in place. The US supports the ban on account of China's human rights record and its relations with Taiwan. What worries the US and its Asian allies like Japan and Taiwan is that the EU should be involved in Asian regional security or in Asia's balance of power, since it lacked any clear political vision, and the US is adamant that advanced defence technology, currently shared with Europe, should not end up in Chinese hands. When considering lifting the arms ban, the EU has bowed to the concerns and threats of the USA which confirmed to China that the US was firmly in command of the major political decisions of the EU.

The ban assumes importance because for 20 years to come, the main demand for arms sales will be from outside the US and European markets, and mainly from big Asian importers. European defence industry suffers more than the American, which has the benefit of a domestic market bigger than the European countries combined.

Galileo Global Positioning System (GPS)

Enhancing science and technology cooperation with the EU has been a long-term priority for China as a strategic goal for modernisation. Links with the EU would lead to China's economic development and modernisation, and accessing advanced technology which was harder to acquire from USA or Japan. The European Global Navigation Satellite System (GNSS) intended for civilian use was the first major EU project with China and to which China pledged €2 billion and paid €230 million. This project was to produce an alternative to the US GPS. The EU invited China (2003) India (2005) and South Korea (2006) to participate in Galileo. With such constructive engagement, the EU aimed to support China's transformation and integration in the world economy and regulatory system. This would also help EU companies to compete on an equal footing in China and foster business interests. Galileo was to show that the EU and China were ready to promote their technological and industrial interests to maintain and enhance global competitiveness in key strategic industrial sectors.

Galileo started in 1994, 20 years after the US GPS. It largely duplicates the US system already in use in Europe and was designed to fuel a hi-tech business boom with customers inventing new services and applications for geographic location technology, and implicitly, to create independence from the USA. Unlike the GPS, Galileo is under civil control. From 2007, it is financed by the EU, as the first and only major infrastructure project managed by the European Commission. It is unlikely to give any return on investment.

Galileo is blighted by nations skewing the project to favour their national companies, and tussles between US proxies like UK and pro-Europeans like France. The US initially opposed it (UK was also once opposed), saying that if Europeans were unable to fulfill their obligations to NATO, why spend on a system replicating a US model? Now there is a truce, with Galileo using a different frequency. The US also opposed the project since it was perceived as increasing EU technological and operational autonomy from USA, and Washington was concerned that

China would use Galileo for military purposes, especially to counter Taiwanese arms systems imported from the USA. The US also saw China as a potential space competitor since China was the third country after the USSR and USA to send a man into space (2008) and could use Galileo to target US's own space assets in future. In 2004, US and the EU agreed to make the two systems interoperable and the frequency compatible—but not with the Chinese system Beido/Compass, which was being developed separately after 2006. It was hard to distinguish between military and civil programmes in China, but the EU undertook to the US that China would not have access to encrypted features of the EU satellite system. In 2007 came the new Guidelines on the EU's Foreign and Security Policy in East Asia which took a more pro-US position due to several factors; leadership changes in France and Germany, a more pro-US EC president, and accession to the EU by pro-US Central and East European member states. In 2008 the European Parliament also infuriated China by awarding the Sakharov Prize to dissident Hu Jia.

In 2008 the EU decided to exclude Chinese contractors from phase 2 of the EU's Galileo GNSS project, the implementation of which was intended to challenge US primacy in hi-tech industrial and defence related sectors. Until that time China was the most important non-EU partner in Galileo. The decision was taken due to IPR issues, the challenge from the Chinese Beido GNSS project using same frequencies, and above all, US pressure. Galileo has meanwhile been hit by EU budget cuts, recession and austerity. It has already cost about $4 billion, three times the original budget, and has only four (2 in 2011, 2 in 2012) of the expected 30 satellites in orbit. Two satellites in 2014 were failures. All 30 are scheduled to be in orbit by 2019. The project needs another $8 billion in funds replenishment.

Nuclear Opportunities

In civil nuclear research, Europe could benefit from opportunities in China. China is building state of the art nuclear facilities while Europe's are aging and some countries will have to close down experimental nuclear reactors. Nuclear power is heading south to the developing world. Radiation and the costs of Fukushima have caused the North to cap their programmes and Europe has reached saturation point for electric power. Germans closed eight reactors and will close the rest by 2022. Switzerland and Spain have banned new reactors, Italians voted against a nuclear programme, and Belgium will phase out nuclear energy by 2015. Mexico will stop construction of ten reactors by switching to natural gas, but South Africa will go ahead and so will other developing countries. Russia, France, USA and Japan will vie with each other to sell reactors, while pro-and anti-nuclear European camps hamper a unified energy approach to Asia.

In nuclear energy, France has more advanced reactors to offer India and China than the US, and its civilian nuclear agreement with India excludes many of the controversial aspects of the Indo-US agreement and provides for transfer of enrichment and reprocessing technologies which the US had initially excluded. France also seems willing to work within the framework of the Indian Nuclear Liability Act which US companies are not. Britain will start to negotiate a civil nuclear agreement with India.

China has supported Germany but not Japan, for the UNSC, and also supported Cadarache in the south of France over Japan to site the first large nuclear experimental fusion plant, a $12 billion project called International Thermal Experimental Nuclear Fusion Reactor (ITER), but that was less due to favour for the EU than due to its opposition to Japan.

Visas

China has announced a 'visa-on-arrival' scheme for the nationals of select foreign countries. Forty five countries have been listed, including entire Europe and North America, Japan, Australia and New Zealand. This list includes the United States as well, which is considering 'rebalancing' its military forces to Asia. In contrast, both India and China have highly restricted access on their national passports. Indians can travel to 52 countries without a visa, and the Chinese to 44 only, which can be contrasted to the British access without visas to 173 countries and the Americans to 172. India rates 76th and China 82nd in the ease of access table.[1]

NOTES

1. Henly and Partners Visa Restrictions Index.

7

THE EU AND INDIA

China and India have been lonely giants,[1] too big to have any close partners, but as they rise, both China and India will have to accept responsibilities for regional if not global security. India may never bestride the global stage like China but neither will it be a mere walk-on soldier in the play.

India and the EU have many similarities. They are the world's two biggest democracies and are unions of a number of linguistic, cultural and ethnically different states. They are both unwieldy, bureaucratic, caution ridden, and slow to decision. But these affinities have not translated into closeness. The Indian Constituent Assembly debates are full of the dangers of excessive federalism and the need for a stronger union, so India is familiar with the debate always engaging Europe. India and the EU have both been dealing with integration and unity in diversity for over six decades. The concept of multiple identities is something Europe and India also have in common, and Europe and India face common threats of fundamentalism, terror, illegal migration and climate change. India's vision of a democratic, multicultural and multipolar world coincides with that of Europe. With a new economic and security landscape evolving in Asia, Europe's future engagement with it must include India. The EU is India's major trade, development and investment partner and Europe is becoming important for investment and acquisitions for Indian companies. These are positive trends. The UK is the biggest investor in India, and receives over 50 per cent of Indian investments in Europe. It also hosts some 40,000 Indian students and has a 1.6 million strong Indian community.

Aggressive nationalism in the world has to be moderated, and India with its tolerant, multireligious, plural complexion and no ideological inhibitions, might emerge one day stronger than a more chauvinistic country like China. A civilisation that accepted the equality of nations may prove stronger than one that rejoiced in either isolation or superiority. Better cooperation between EU and India would give more leverage to both in regard to China and the USA. Europe as India's ally in the west, and India as the EU's strategic partner, would give both more prestige and more geo-political clout, but the two parties are not of one mind. The relationship has been likened to a "loveless arranged marriage... between a well-matched couple but with no spark of chemistry".[2] India needs a 'Look to Europe' policy to supplement its 'Look East' policy.

The EU and India could cooperate in projects in Africa and elsewhere in the world in a triangular and mutually beneficial cooperation. There is also the possibility of maritime cooperation in the Indian Ocean which is a maritime/littoral space of geopolitical, geoeconomic and geostrategic priority. The EU, being reliant on sea-based commerce, is an important stakeholder in maritime security in the Indian Ocean with its multiple choke points, piracy, terrorism, failed states and rogue states, overfishing, military supply routes, undersea cables, drugs and arms trafficking, and the increasing presence of China.

The EU balances social justice with economic modernisation in regional integration in which India and China are interested, and in the search for distinct ways towards a knowledge economy. China, India and the EU also share concerns on radicalism and extremism emanating from Islamic fundamentalism. The EU needs to have strategic engagement with India on global issues and new forms of global governance. Such fields of cooperation could include human security, social development, capacity building, democratic reforms, agriculture and rural development, energy consumption and sub-national governance.

On the one side, Brussels pushes to broaden the EU-India framework from the European point of view (e.g. with respect to the human rights) which in fact is difficult to be met, and on the other, New Delhi would like some specific solutions to current issues (e.g. with respect to counter terrorism) and to leave optimisation of the framework for the future. The EU-India partnership is a top-down, executive-driven partnership complemented by corporate interests. Ties may be more symbolic than real, but the danger for India is that it may underestimate the degree of coherence that exists already within the EU as seen in the free-trade negotiations, where EU is in the lead as negotiator and not the member states, and thus neglect direct relations with EU institutions. As the major power in South Asia, India does not like European interference in its own backyard, but the EU's potential impact on politics in South Asia is small and its democratisation efforts are complex endeavours with unclear outcomes. A growing and more serious issue is how the EU positions itself in regard to the US' renewed focus on Asia in collaborating more with democratic Asian partners. India and other newly emerging powers and regions, such as Indonesia and Southeast Asia, and even Taiwan and Korea, are still neglected in the European media and public discourse.

India established diplomatic relations with the European Economic Community (EEC) in 1962 but it took 32 years for a ministerial level dialogue to start. On the EU's part, as with other Asians apart from Japan, only after 1990 was there a more pro-active policy shown by Brussels. India-EU meetings at the summit level began on a regular basis only in 2000, after the euro currency was launched in 1999.

EU Attitude to India

The EU is a constructive and widely respected global economic actor of a new kind. It wishes to remain a point of reference, a centre of strategic thought, creativity and innovation. It is economically strong though politically weak, does not have commensurate political or military strength, and cannot formulate a coherent foreign policy position. Strong bilateral positions that are expressed and implemented by its members diminish its credibility as a security player, and it also lacks cultural engagement. In the areas of security interest to India, the EU is almost irrelevant. On strategic issues, the EU has no obvious standing or role. Delhi will point out that there is no EU defence ministry, army headquarters or intelligence HQ, and security cooperation is best dealt with bilaterally, whether on global security issues, terror, nuclear proliferation or energy security. The EU is reluctant to confront Pakistan on terror related issues; it wants to balance between India and Pakistan since it is unwilling or unable, due to its competences, to deal with India's strategic concerns. Europe and India do not face shared threats and have different security contexts. While the EU stresses Indo-Pakistan dialogue, India insists on specific references to Pakistan's support for terror across its border. India has made several proposals for greater coordination against terror, but there was a mismatch of expectations: the EU has more non-traditional threats like cyber and human trafficking, whereas for India there are questions of national integrity, border control, insurgencies and separatism. Most EU members do not share the same urgency or interest in security as India. Participation in the Galileo GPS was mooted by India in 2003 but delayed due to some EU members linking India's participation to arms control and dual use technologies. India joined the International Thermonuclear Fusion Experimental Reactor project in 2005, mainly due to American clearance after Washington had started negotiations with India on an escape route from the Non-proliferation Treaty (NPT) in the form of a civil nuclear agreement.

Both India and the EU are open to dialogue on multilateral issues like terror, disarmament, climate change and a rule-based international order, but the EU is unable to take a united stand on India's nuclear status. There is no coherent European policy towards India, no bilateral trading arrangement, no plan to allocate more of the Community's aid funds to India, or even to coordinate the aid given to India bilaterally by EU member-states or for it to be used to buy imports from EU members other than the actual donors.

India ranks the EU low in its priorities; it still sees the EU rather as an experiment than as an efficient structure. It remains puzzled as to whether the EU is a super state, a supranational entity or a post-modern state. India finds the changing priorities of the EU baffling. The EU has a very low profile in India and the EU has scarce time and scarcer political energy for India. In many ways Europe and India have come to be perceived as the sick men of their regions: once full of spirit and vitality, now stagnating and spluttering, struggling to overcome internal divisions and find a proper space for themselves in the global order. To cap it all, the EU does not regard Asia as multi-polar but concentrates attention on China, much to India's chagrin. In the European Commission's giant bureaucracy, when compared to China, there is lack of India expertise.

The EU feels that India is neither entrepreneurial nor proactive enough and complains about lack of engagement with India. It sees India as poor and mired in its own problems. India for its part engages with the EC but not enough; nor with the European Parliament. India's democratic polity does not earn it any points with the EU, which is uneasy about strategic cooperation, high technology and defence cooperation with India. The USA has been more sympathetic to India's rise, whereas the EU is seen by New Delhi as a staunch defender of the existing order. The EU views India as part of the nuclear proliferation problem and is bogged down by legalistic interpretations of non-proliferation. Many EU member states were uneasy with the US-India 2008 nuclear accord.

There are also other differences. There is optimism in Asia, pessimism in Europe, Europe is threatened by a technology gap with USA, and with China taking over European manufacturing and India taking over European services. Europe has to outsource business and insource skilled labour, and India's market is too protected. Europe believes in a post-modern world of norms; emerging Asia believes in power, realism and balance of power, with little belief in collective institutions. Europe is *status quo* and Asia wants changes in international society to reflect its interests. If India wants to rise, and Europe to stay relevant, they have both to exploit their complementarities.

Indian Attitude to the EU

In India, a point of view close to British Euroscepticism is discernible when reflecting on Europe. For historical reasons, Indians perceive the EU primarily through a British lens and historically prefer the bilateral route with key EU states like the UK, France and Germany. Britain is more or less the spokesman for the EU in India, and *vice versa.* The EU seems to India to prefer process rather than outcome, with a plethora of forums producing limited results, though the same criticism could be made of India. The EU's and India's importance as global players remains at least in part derived from expectations of future power potential rather than actual achievements to date. India has found it hard to see value added in the EU as opposed to individual members like the UK and France, and important Indians regard the EU as irrelevant for India's future status in the modern world. India has not seen eye to eye with the EU on Myanmar, UN reform, Sri Lanka, climate change, the Doha Round or non-proliferation. The EU gives Pakistan little priority, but India does not feel it gets any advantage from being a democracy.

Indians, like most others, have an allergy to being lectured to, and Europe is inclined to preach. Former Indian diplomat Eric Gonsalves states, "the European Commission and the EU are a pain in the neck to deal with".[3] As a democracy longer than many EU states, India wants to handle human rights in its own political space. For the EU to insert human rights into a draft free trade agreement as if they were auto emission standards, upsets Indian negotiators. India accepts multilateralism, but is sceptical about many specific issues: the International Criminal Court, R2P, humanitarian interventions and the ban on anti-personnel landmines. In geopolitics, the mindset of the Cold War has not fully changed, and the EU in India's viewpoint has slavishly followed the US lead on many global issues. So there are differences on Ukraine, Syria, Iran and Afghanistan. India and the EU both hesitate between rejection and acceptance of external interventions. India wants to be a pole in a multipolar world, and wants the EU, led by the UK, France and Germany, to recognise its status.

EU-India Problems

The EU's high moral aspirations reflect those of India after independence in the heyday of Nehruvian non-alignment but India has since moved to a realist power-oriented political project. The voting behaviour at the UN General Assembly (UNGA) in the period 2004-2010 is instructive: in the case of full EU cohesion (when all EU member states cast the same vote), the voting cohesion per annual UNGA session between the then 27 EU member states and India varied from 43 per cent to 53 per cent. This means that, overall, on half of the resolutions voted upon during an annual UNGA session, the EU member states and India cast different votes.

If the EU is considered leaderless, India could be expected to be more understanding: its federal system has produced powerful chief ministers in the states and the most powerful politician at one time was Sonia Gandhi, who was only the head of a political party. Both sides, however, are not willing to learn from one another. The nucleus of Indian incomprehension of the EU, however, lies elsewhere; there is no other country worldwide where national sovereignty and use of hard power rank higher as the first priorities.

"Each ..looks to the most powerful poles… rather than towards each other, and spend more time deploring the shortcomings of the other rather than building… the future partnership."[4] This is a dialogue of the deaf; the EU hardly makes a conscious effort to understand India. Europe talks about India's economic labyrinth; India about Pakistan, but Brussels is impervious to Pakistan's behavior. The Indian model of growth with democracy is no longer any counter to the China model: no one will listen to India in the absence of economic prowess, rapid GDP growth and thriving business opportunities. Both sides appear minimally interested in a special relationship and perceive each other fundamentally as associated with the deficiencies third parties attribute to them. The EU is a strong proponent of legally binding commitments as well as powerful international regimes. The EU encourages social protection, respect for the environment and human rights, while India is reluctant to let its economic growth and development be limited by concerns about these issues. India opposes inclusion of core labour standards in WTO negotiations and linking trade with environmental issues, child labour, the rights of Dalits and the death penalty.

India's complaints with the EU are in regard to nuclear issues, climate change, agricultural tariffs, trade related issues, technology transfer restrictions, access for professionals in the services market and the complexity of EU policies. Access to the European market and technology for India is a big challenge, with health and sanitary regulations and quality restrictions. There are disputes on Trade-related Intellectual Property Rights (TRIPS) and access for textiles, spices, automobiles, software and pharmaceuticals. Nor does the EU extend any noteworthy development assistance, though Operation Flood from 1970 to 1996 was at one time the world's biggest food and development programme and made India the world's leading milk producer.

Indians feel they are talked down to with arrogance by the EU about prosperity, stability and human rights, securitised visa regimes and ignorance about other parties' compulsions. India feels slighted when even small and insignificant member states of the EU, such as Denmark and the Nordic countries, deliver sermons to India on relations with neighbours, human rights, nuclear non-proliferation and disarmament. Most of the emerging economies in Asia gave women the equal right to vote before two EU countries—Switzerland and Portugal—and India has been a democratic country longer than a dozen EU member states. The Delegation of the European Commission in Delhi set up in 1983 is almost invisible, only known to some development activists and NGOs, the EU-India summits are not newsworthy, achieve little, and get scant media coverage. The emerging Asian economies generally feel that all European journalists are obsessed by human rights matters to the exclusion of everything else.

India as a weaker but more moderate country than China considers it deserves a proactive and sympathetic EU, especially in South Asia where China will certainly be more influential in future. In contrast with China, India was once juxtaposed as the 'democratic candidate' and found world-wide supporters who wanted it to succeed as an alternative to the China model as representing democracy with religion and the English legal system and language. In the 1960s, Andre Malraux had told India that Europe provided a 'third option' to USA and the USSR. Is the EU a second option for India and emerging Asia now? EU foreign policy seems to be based on the premise of equilibrium between India and Pakistan, terror and non-proliferation notwithstanding. In many trade aspects, India does not get support from the EU because there are doubts whether India genuinely believes in open trade and a free market. India and the EU need to live up to the promise of their potential. On human rights and secularism it is for India to demonstrate that it is accountable, because the EU through its parliaments and civil society has legitimate concerns and deserves to be convinced.

In information and communications technology, giant companies like IBM and Accenture are expanding rapidly in India to benefit from its low-cost high quality labour, and Indian software companies expand in the USA to create the closer customer relations needed to compete in high-end consultancy services. This is not happening in Europe, where there is no cross movement of jobs and labour as firms compete to provide knowledge leadership, breakthroughs and innovation, and India's ICT firms have not established their own 'brands' as vendors and not just as service providers. The sentiment in Europe to outsourcing to India is creating protectionist attitudes while in India the lack of good infrastructure is a handicap.

India was less likely to be affected by the global slowdown due to its lower level of exports than other emerging nations but the eurozone crisis impacts India because the euro weakened against the dollar, and a stronger dollar pulled down the rupee value. Imports got costlier, fuel prices rose, foreign investors pulled out, stock markets fell, Indian exports of semi-manufactures, manufactures and raw materials declined, software earnings were affected and remittances from abroad dropped. Higher imports and lower exports pushed up the current account deficit and depletion of Indian foreign exchange reserves. So any shrinkage in the European economy was, and would be, grim tidings for India.

Cultural Patterns

Modern India has taken an active interest in the West but only after the era of colonisation when the West could no longer be ignored. The tendency was different in Europe, where the search for the origins of western civilisation in India or to contemplate India as the recipient of unpolluted wisdom reached a peak with the Romantics and Schopenhauer. At the same time, the West also nurtured the opposite sentiment; contempt for everything Indian as "dark and irrational ... standing against the light of reason symbolised by Western rationality". Some like Edmund Husserl regarded the europeanisation of the world as a historically predetermined fate.[5]

India has a resilient core culture. Macaulayism had as its objective the creation of a person "Indian in blood and in colour, but English in tastes, opinions, morals and intellect"[6] and to keep India in thrall to the British legacy. There are identity clashes. Both the EU and India are victims of prejudice and stereotyping, with constructed identities of the other. India aspires to be treated as an equal and overreacts when it is not so, and to India's dismay the EU is not reacting fast enough to this belief. For the EU, caste is a repellent aspect of Indian society, and Europe regards India with the superiority complex of a repository of reason. The media could play a role in forming new identities, but there are few pro-India lobbies in the EU and a strong diaspora only in the UK.

Europe believes human satisfaction and goals are personal and individual; India that belonging to a community is a fundamental human need. The cultural divide on how society should perform has found expression in some cases of family separation where it was felt by India that European ideas are not always right. Twins conceived by a surrogate mother in India were not allowed entry to Norway since the law there did not allow surrogate children to be Norwegian nationals. The Indian government took the children's welfare into account and felt that the Norwegian mother, in Norway, was the best parent possible for the twins. Diplomatic tension arose about two children of an Indian couple in Norway placed in a foster-home in 2011 despite repeated official appeals for a sympathetic and speedy resolution. Upon diplomatic interventions, Norway said it could do nothing to interfere with the judicial process. In a case in 2012, a couple was convicted for 'serious child abuse' in dealing with bed-wetting of their seven year old son in Norway. The parents had threatened to return their son to India and the school had reported them to the authorities. The parents were accused of 'threats, violence and other wrongs' and sentenced to 18 and 15 months respectively. They returned to India in 2013. These interventions by the state into the private lives of families are not a part of Indian culture. India feels it has been treated unfairly and insensitively by certain European countries. Denmark's refusal to extradite a person (Kim Davy alias Niels Holck alias Niels Christian) involved with airdropping weapons into India in 1995 due to India's poor jail conditions and human rights record was not well received. The Indian government has also had problems with European NGOs. It took action against local NGOs using foreign money for a people's movement in Tamil Nadu against the peaceful uses of nuclear energy. These funds had been received from US and Swedish sources and were diverted by local NGOs, including church groups, to anti-nuclear protestors.

Strategic Partnership

The EU has strategic partnerships with seven partners, four of them in Asia. The then EU President Herman Van Rompuy summed up the task at hand for the EU, "Until now we had strategic partners. Now we also need a strategy".[7]

The Cooperation Agreement of 1994 laid down the basis of Indo-EU relations.[8] Annual summits have taken place since 2000 and the Strategic Partnership in 2004 is supplemented by a EU-India Security Dialogue. But India is disappointed by the EU's response on Khalistani activities, when Germany, Netherlands and others dragged their feet, and at the anti-Indian influence of Pakistani diaspora voters which inhibits EU cooperation. Indians prefer the bilateral route such as with UK, a long-standing dialogue partner, or France that has helped in India's civil nuclear capability, to the EU as a bloc. In the Indian view, the EU has an obsession with China, and is too equidistant between Pakistan and India.

The strategic partnership is only a kind of honorary degree conferred by the EU on certain favoured nations: there is no definition of what a strategic partnership is. In 2004, India responded with its first ever paper on a foreign entity, notably envisaging a relationship "immune from the vicissitudes of...relationship with a third party", presumably meaning the USA and China. The resulting Action Plan of 2005 was also the first of its kind for India with any entity, but the up-dated joint action plan of 2008 is one that leads mainly to more dialogue rather than any concrete action. The EU struggles to maintain the military resources necessary to match its economic resources, while India's dilemma is that it is a potential global power without ever being able to establish itself as a regional one. It has to break the shackles of South Asia to integrate itself into the East Asian economic system and project its power and influence globally. The EU can contribute little to the first goal and is seen as an obstacle to the second, unlike the USA. India wants to be treated as something more than just a big market, while it is not clear what the EU seeks from India. Although all the formal structures are in place, the EU and India have been unable to identify one or two core issues from a long dialogue list in the Joint Action Plan. European diplomats have expressed frustration at New Delhi's apparently lacklustre efforts to advance India's Strategic Partnership with the EU and conversely, those in the Indian strategic community harbour largely negative perceptions of the importance of the European Union as a security actor in the South Asian region. Civilian power is equated with weakness and the normative approach is seen as soft imperialism. So the prospective security cooperation with the EU as a collective remains in the realm of the conceptual.

Several areas were to be discussed: conflict prevention, terror, weapons of mass destruction, economic partnership through dialogues, development cooperation and intellectual and cultural exchange. Other matters of concern were political cooperation, the EU to be an observer in the South Asian Association for Regional Cooperation (SAARC) and India joining ASEM. For the EU, India-Pakistan reconciliation was the main issue and India rearming would detract from development and modernisation. So the EU emphasised regional cooperation, but Europe was too neglectful of India's exposure to an unfriendly neighbourhood and consequent trans-border terrorism. Most EU countries do not share the same urgency or interest in security as India because they lay stress on values and not on geopolitics.

In the 2004 agreement, India and the EU narrowed their differences on nuclear weapons. India said it abided by the NPT though it would not sign it, and would agree to common efforts to contain proliferation of weapons of mass destruction. The EU was then split on the US-India civil nuclear cooperation agreement; it wanted India to join the NPT and Comprehensive Test Ban Treaty (CTBT). UK, France and Germany were pro-India, but not the Nordic members.

India relies on hard power capabilities and regards multilateral fora as instruments for promoting its national interest. The EU wants to strengthen international organisations and the juridification of international relations. India insists on non-interference, and does not innovate in conflict resolution in its neighbourhood or even outside it, other than participating in UN peacekeeping operations. It does not go in for multilateral approaches or working with non-state actors towards conflict resolution, and so is unlikely to work with the EU in international theatres. It is hard to locate even one example where India and the EU had jointly played a substantial role in resolving any international crisis.

Development Assistance

In its country paper (2007-13) the EU provided €470 million in development aid to India, mainly in health, education, MDGs, culture, civil society and academic exchanges. The EU seeks to impact the Indian reform process and poverty alleviation, but considering the Indian government's own publicly funded welfare programmes, the EU in India is a small donor of aid and traditional ODA is to be phased out after 2013.

The EU-India Free Trade Agreement

A Free Trade Area for the EU means free trade and investment, with allied negotiations on labour and environment standards and human rights. The EU sees India as "an obvious partner for one of the new generation FTAs" but the present position is quite one-sided: the EU is India's biggest trade partner: it had 17 per cent ($52 billion) of Indian exports in 2013-14, and 11 per cent of imports ($50 billion), whereas India's share of the EU market is growing but at present accounts for only 2.5 per cent of EU total trade. Indo-EU trade is balanced at $130 billion and trade in goods increased fivefold in 2000-2014. European investments in India were $198 billion in 2013-14 and represents 21 per cent of India's total FDI inflow. Indian FDI to Europe is 30 per cent of India's outward stock. India was the 15th trading partner of the EU in 2002 but had moved up to 8th in 2011, and is the third most important trade partner for the EU in Asia after China and Japan. The EU obviously cannot be written off by India—it still tops the current IMF ranking with a combined 25.8 per cent share of world GDP.

The India-EU FTA is officially called the Bilateral Trade and Investment Agreement (BTIA) and negotiations started in 2007. There is no agreed interpretation of what constitutes 'substantially all the trade' but the EU view is that 90 per cent of existing trade over 10 years, and the desire to eliminate tariff and quantitive restrictions on 90-95 per cent of the tariff lines will comply with the 'substantially all trade' criterion of the General Agreement on Tariffs and Trade (GATT). Opening the

Indian economy will result in more inward investment, know-how, technology and logistical skills. The FTA has been under negotiation between Europe and India for the past eight years and many deadlines have expired. Both sides know that mere reduction in tariffs will not lead to increased trade unless NTBs are also eliminated, and the EU thinks only a 'deep integration' agreement would be worthwhile to tackle Indian NTBs and regulatory barriers.

The EU is active in seeking a 'deep integration' agreement going beyond trade liberalisation to service sectors like banking and insurance, retail, legal and accountancy services, government procurement, protection of intellectual property and data exclusivity in drugs that go beyond TRIPS. The EU plans to delve deep into several non-trade issues in market access and national treatment in service and investment sectors, environment and human rights. It wants a negative list of sectors that will not be liberalised, whereas India wants a positive list of acceptable investments and has suggested a negative list of 150 agricultural goods and 250 manufactures. There are cases where the EU is pushing India; on tariff reductions, market access, national treatment in services and investment, implementation and dispute settlement which all go beyond just duplicating WTO provisions.

The FTA is supposed to be based on political convergences that are value added to economic ties and enhance their potential. India maintains a substantial tariff and NTBs but a major problem is the EU insistence that social issues like child labour, human rights and climate change be discussed, though India meets the criteria in the EU's Global Europe strategy, including on market potential. India says there are other forums for discussion of these issues which to the EU constitute non-tariff barriers and protectionism. From India's side, there is the demand that the EU cut farm subsidies because EU's CAP mainly benefits big agro-industrial conglomerates which resort to dumping in developing countries. EU insists on food safety standards and India guards its government procurement market. But India could benefit by a putative $9 billion worth of business by this pact and services could benefit both sides.

The EU and India are predominantly service economies with two-thirds of total employment and 70 to 50 per cent of the respective GDPs. Thus, any trade agreement between the two that excludes services would exclude the most important sector. However, there are significant barriers to agreement on services. The services sector's importance as an Indian employer has been growing over time, rising from 20 per cent of total employment in 1995 to about one-third of the total. EU-India bilateral trade in services increased from €17 billion in 2008 to €19.6 billion in 2010. Putting things in perspective, bilateral services trade accounted for 12 per cent of India's global services trade in 2010 but only two per cent of the EU's extra-EU services trade, since 58 per cent of EU trade in services is within EU borders. Yet the EU remains the largest services exporter in the world with about 25 per cent of the total traded.

The Indian services sector is the fastest growing one in the world after the Chinese. India most restrictive policies are in services trading, with limitations on the operation of foreign banks and a relatively closed insurance sector. Sectors like IT and telecom are already significantly liberalised, while others such as construction, health, banking and insurance, education, retail and courier are moderately liberalised, but legal, accountancy and postal services are completely closed. The important issues for India are market access for cross-border services and service professionals, research and development, dental and health related sectors and telephone-based services. Other concerns are the need for huge minimum capital requirements imposed by the EU, residency requirements, restrictions on legal entity and the absence of national treatment. India would press for the mutual recognition of qualifications, avoidance of double taxation on social security benefits of Indian services professionals abroad, visa issues and labour market and economic need tests. Banking sector licenses granted by any EU member should be acceptable across the EU, as the need to apply for separate licenses in each EU member state is among the more cumbersome obstacles.

India has FTAs with several groups and countries: but none is as ambitious in scope as the EU FTA . The existing FTAs consist of shallow integration, no substantial tariff reductions and gradual liberalisation in trade in goods: there is little on investment, services, standards in environment or technical regulations, competition, labour or rules of origin. Both India and the EU realise that the deeper the integration, the greater the benefit, and are keen on an agreement. The negotiations have covered trade in goods, sanitary and phyto-sanitary measures and barriers to trade, trade in services, investment, intellectual property rights, competition policy, customs and trade facilitation, trade defence, government procurement and sustainable development.

The EU calls for removal of equity caps, nationality and residential requirements, mutual recognition of diplomas and professional qualifications, fair and equitable treatment compared to Indian companies, clarity in foreign direct investment rules, and easing administrative hurdles. The EU wants more banking branches—whereas India prefers subsidiaries to branches—and seeks an investment ceiling at 74 per cent and not 49 per cent, and in insurance at 49 per cent from 26 per cent. The EU desires multi-brand retailing, abolishing cargo preference for the Indian flag and liberalisation of accounting, legal and waste and sewage disposal services. It wants tariff cuts on autos, wines, spirits, dairy and a strong IPR.

For India, benefits are to come from the transfer of technology inherent in greenfield start-ups through investment, and ancillary industries, removal of regulatory obstacles to trade, and an environment where mutually advantageous private contracts and market-led arrangements can flourish. India wants the EU ceiling of 40,000 professionals not have any other restrictions like labour market tests and economic necessity tests and free movement within the EU. It also seeks access for its pharma exports, and opposes access to its government procurement (which is estimated at $190 billion to $235 billion annually), and changes to investment policy and competition policy which were removed from Doha Round as not being in touch with development needs, but now are sought by the EU to be introduced through the FTA route.

India conceding market access and higher foreign equity caps in banking and multibrand retail could act against development goals in rural areas. Any FTA would not require parliament ratification but there would be political obstacles even from within government circles. Opening legal services would need parliament approval and there are powerful lobbies who oppose this. Harmonising government procurement could be a problem with the states, and sectors like construction and health are subject to local laws. Freeing agriculture imports will lead to a surge of subsidised EU products into India and affect small and marginal farmers, while the EU keeps tariffs of 650 per cent on dairy products. Business chambers are concerned not only about the BTIA but all FTAs due to their alleged impact on manufacturing, consumer durables and automobile spare parts in particular.

India might dilute its opposition to the increase of FDI limits on insurance, and lower duties on high end cars, wines and spirits (Japan and South Korea had made a similar demand for cars which had been resisted). India has promised Indian industry to protect 77 items belonging to the auto sector that are in the negative list in its FTAs with Korea and Japan by giving no duty concession till 2016. Autos (tariffs between 60 and 75 per cent) and wine and spirits (tariffs at 100-150 per cent) have strong domestic lobbies. Both sides will leave agriculture out of liberalisation and India wants the exclusion also of a range of industrial goods and restrictive rules of origin.

In 2013, the European Commission's list of 20 top destinations for investment in the next five years did not include India. From the EU's viewpoint, India must be prised open to competition, but the EU is unwilling to have more Indian professionals in Europe or permitting services trade through electronic channels. There is no single set of rules for trade in services across all EU member countries, but India wants not only a package for goods trade including agriculture—an area which both sides subsidise heavily—but market access in services including cross-border movement of natural persons. The EU insistence on guaranteed market access to government and public sector contracts is a deal breaker whereas the EU has little to offer India on services. It wants India to go beyond its commitments domestically on intellectual property rights. India for its part may offer some concession on access to central government contracts but not to public sector ones.

Europe has other complaints against India: Indian manufacturers manipulate the clinical trials of generic drugs, Indian policy threatens intellectual property rights like Indian generic production of branded medicines, and induces barriers to trade such as implementation of industrial policies that benefit local industries at the expense of foreign companies, a preferred market access policy that imposes local production requirements on certain foreign technology firms, and India's actions on drugs, whether a fair balance is struck between public health concerns and intellectual property concerns. The EU also has other grievances: multi-brand retail that is off-limits in most states; labour reform and easing FDI inflows as key 'deliverables'. It objects to NTBs like convoluted customs formalities and import licensing, on which Indian attention is needed even without external prompting.

For its part, India is pressing for entry not only for professionals in information technology but others like architects, teachers and chefs; Indian companies to be considered data secure, especially when declared so by USA; removal of local presence and residency rules, and inclusion of medical and other services. India demands that intellectual property rights should not curtail production of cheap generic drugs for the domestic market and exports, pointing out that 92 per cent of patients on antiretrovirals in low and middle income countries are using Indian drugs. In 2003, Novartis (Swiss) lost a seven year battle in the Supreme Court over a patent claim for a cancer drug. India also has 'compulsory licensing' for a Bayer (German) kidney cancer drug that allowed a generic producer to sell at Rs 8,800 p.m. rather than Rs 280,000 p.m. for the patented drug. The IPR conflicts are on HIV, cancer and diabetes drugs, and are now moving to other areas. Novartis has taken Cipla to court for respiratory drugs that Cipla has launched for 1/5th the Novartis price on the grounds that Novartis was importing less than Indian requirements. While Novartis says there is no legal requirement for the drug to be made locally, Cipla contends that patents must pay heed to right to life and health, and also the drug's pricing. This is seen by Europe as arm-twisting patent holders to grant licences to Indian generic firms. As of now, the draft agreement places EU trade interest over human rights, for example on ARV drugs. EU seems nowhere near giving up its insistence on India complying with environmental standards, labour laws, restrictions on movement of professionals or contentious intellectual property rights that may restrict cheap drugs. And enforcement of human rights, environment and social standards will always be a problem for India.

Both the EU and India need foreign investment to close the gap in current account. EU-India relations continue to be hailed as one with great potential but the gap between plans and action have widened over the past years. The BTIA, when concluded, will undoubtedly be the high point, or perhaps the only big achievement, in EU-India relations.

If there was an FTA, investment from the EU could rise by 27 per cent but the Indian boisterous culture of domestic politics will always make agreement difficult. Apart from which, any agreement would require ratification by all member states in the EU, which could take about 2 years.

There could also be some undesirable controversy because civil society lobbies in the EU and India claim[9] that the EU-India BTIA is something that could fundamentally restructure Indian society and impact the lives of hundreds of millions of Indians, but is being negotiated on behalf of the public in secret by politicians and bureaucrats on both sides. Much of the negotiation is being conducted beyond the gaze of the public and the realms of public accountability, and demands for public scrutiny have been dealt a blow by a recent ruling. Following a lawsuit by lobby watchdog Corporate Europe Observatory (CEO), the EU's General Court in Luxembourg concluded that the EC did not violate EU rules when withholding information about the EU-India free trade talks from the public even though it had already shared the information with corporate lobby groups. CEO warned that this decision risked deepening the secrecy around EU trade negotiations and legitimised the EC's practice of granting corporate lobby groups privileged access to its policy-making at the expense of the wider public interest. CEO further argued that the information which the EC had already shared with the business world could not suddenly become confidential when a public interest group asked for it. The group accused the EC of discrimination in favour of corporate lobby groups and violating the EU's access to information rules. CEO trade campaigner Pia Eberhardt said that the result was a trade policy that catered for big business interests but worked against the interests of the bulk of the population in the EU and other parts of the world. CEO believes that the court ruling had potentially serious implications for other trade policies, such as the negotiations in the TTIP between the EU and the USA. Eberhardt stated: "Citizens and parliamentarians are increasingly worried about the risks that the EU's corporate trade agenda poses to food safety, digital rights and environmental protection. Trade negotiations should be conducted in an open and democratically-accountable way, and it is high time that the Commission stops handing over the negotiating agenda to multinational companies. It is disappointing that the court ruling seems to point in exactly the opposite direction."[10]

Such secrecy deepens the suspicion that the EU-India BTIA has little to do with any notion pertaining to the 'public interest' and essentially represents the demands of big business and results from their strategic hegemony over government bureaucracies and politicians. Both in India and the EU, trade unions, farmers' groups, patients' organisations and other civil society groups have repeatedly raised concerns about the potentially devastating impacts of the agreement, particularly on access to medicines and the livelihoods of Indian farmers and street traders. Indian activists argue that India's thousand year old civilisation is being plundered, and with the EU-India BTIA, democracy was being sidelined for the pursuit of an unaccountable corporate-driven agenda. But with western economies in crisis, India represents potential rich pickings for powerful transnational corporations, and the EU is not likely to be deterred.

South Asian Association for Regional Cooperation

Even after decades there is no SAARC progress towards economic or political integration and India is still not much of a market compared to China, Japan, South Korea or ASEAN. In SAARC, the South Asian Free Trade Area as a target FTA was decided from 2010, a customs union by 2015, and economic union by 2020 but these are all unrealistic timetables, as is the goal for a Preferential Trade Area. Apart from the smaller SAARC members, there is no real economic imperative because India comprises 70 per cent of the SAARC market. The export items are too similar, though some complementarities might exist in services, banking and investment.

WTO, the EU and India

India had difficulty with the western agenda in the WTO from the start, and blocked demands for liberalisation in investment and competition policy, tightening of environmental and labour standards, reduction of tariffs on industrial goods without reciprocal reduction of farm subsidies, and protects its interest in services and intellectual property. Therefore its positioning in world trade has tended to be adversarial to Europe, especially when it shows itself ready to defend its positions almost alone. India sides with developing countries in the WTO on agriculture and reduction of subsidies by the North. Anti-dumping measures on Indian products in EU markets and several WTO-plus aspects in the BTIA negotiation with the EU leave the Indian public with a negative impression.

India opted out of the 'early harvest' negotiations pushed by the developed countries for select WTO members for liberalising foreign investment, visa regimes for service sectors and lowering import duties on 357 ICT products and 54 environmental goods. This so-called early harvest scheme would, according to India, impact adversely on India's ability to strike a bargain on farm goods agriculture—where developed countries subsidise—and industrial products. Among the 357 Information Technology products on which customs duties would be removed are washing machines, window air conditioners and refrigerators, that would help China and Taiwan take a further lead in hardware manufacturing. The environmental list was drawn up by APEC, the proposal being to cut the tariff to 5 per cent. India wanted this issue discussed further in the WTO. The early harvest had suggested a standstill on services, but India lost an opportunity of pushing for easing visa rules for professionals. India is also not part of a plurilateral Trade in Services Agreement (TISA) being worked upon for services, saying easier visas for professionals was not on the agenda.

Having registered scant progress since 1995 when the WTO started, or 2001 when the Doha Development Round began, 159 countries met at the Ninth Ministerial meeting at Bali at the end of 2013 with a smaller three point agenda; a Trade Facilitation Agreement to boost trade by enhancing transparency, harmonising and simplifying customs procedures, and improving trade infrastructure, reducing trade distorting subsidies on agriculture, and assistance to least developed countries. Having initially accepted a package that accorded a 'peace clause' whereby the 'Green Box' agricultural subsidies, which were allowed up to 10 per cent of the 1986/7 prices provided there were no exports or internal market and no distortion of trade, would not be challenged until 2017, India then held out for a 'single undertaking' and held the Trade Facilitation Agreement hostage to the permanent removal of the cap on agricultural subsidies, or a change from 1986/7 as base year prices to current market prices, or to index the price to current levels. India's opposition was on the ground that Indian food production was always subject to the vagaries of the monsoon, and it needed some 62 million tonnes of food grains in storage to provide food security for some 820 million people. India claimed that a temporary amnesty was insufficient; the emphasis in the WTO was on pressing ahead with trade facilitation which benefits big exporters like the USA, the EU and China, and the lack of interest in food security was evidenced by 20 meetings since Bali on the former against only two on the latter, which revealed a profound mistrust of the intentions of the developed countries. The subsidy issue had the potential to expose India to a host of challenges on who was regarded as poor, what should be the level of nutritional support to such people, and what should be the quantum of subsidy. India was impervious to the argument that the Trade Facilitation Agreement would add $1 trillion and 21 million jobs to the global economy, and the advanced economies saw India's attitude as a rear-guard defence of its food security programme, which was costly and full of graft. The failure of the WTO would lead to more regional agreements that are inherently exclusive and unfair, since developing economies are not the advanced countries' partners of choice, and the new trade groupings would leave countries like India out in the cold. The conclusion, thanks to an Indo-USA understanding, was that the peace clause of immunity was made indefinite until a new formula was worked out, and the trade facilitation deal was first in the WTO since 1995, and to some extent restored faith in the multilateral system and credibility of the WTO.

Indian agriculture and pharma have flourished under WTO rules, which are India's ally against western pressure on patents. Europe complains that India has rejected patents for some essential drugs while issuing compulsory licences by ignoring patent rights, which flouts norms, cheats patent owners and confers a bonus on Indian producers of cheap substitutes. But WTO allows India freedom to be strict on patents, allows price control and issue of compulsory licensing for drugs deemed critical for national health. India ranks last among 25 countries for patent protection, but is also a victim, since Bollywood and software piracy is rampant.

Indian Diaspora in Europe

Politically and publicly, EU and India ties are still below the horizon; there is lack of overlapping spheres of interest, but also lack of knowledge of each other, unlike with the USA thanks to a highly successful Indian diaspora. And also unlike in the USA, the European Indian diaspora mostly does not comprise the openly ambitious, upwardly mobile representatives of the upper middle classes. The Indian national profile in Europe is low in comparison to other global powers, India struggles with an image problem partly due to the lack of a strong, non-resident Indian lobby and Europe remains largely unknown to Indian professionals. What is left is academic research and tourism, and expertise on contemporary India is rare in the EU. The EU situation in India is not much better: outside a few élite institutions, the EU is not much of a topic, and the sparse reports of Indian media about the 'old' continent are often of poor quality.

Relations have changed substantially in recent years, from that of aid donor and recipient to one of partnership. India's diaspora's educational achievements and economic status can play a significant role and contribute to Europe-India relations. The growing Indian diaspora in Europe is two million strong. From the mid-20th century, instead of South-South migration, a shift can be noticed in migration from the ex-colonial periphery to metropolitan centers in the industrialised north. It was not the previous type of labour migration but the English educated middle class, which had the cultural and linguistic expertise and social contacts to set up collaborations with their home-country counterparts. The second wave following World War II was marked by the emigration of less educated and semi-skilled Indians to English-speaking countries like the US, Britain and Canada; a characteristic of these migrants was their ability to maintain strong cultural and religious ties with their homeland. The third ICT wave was another distinct category within the new Indian diaspora: it moved to multiple destinations in a transnational space along the networks of the companies for work. Europe is India's second largest market for ICT services, but it accounts for only 31 per cent of India's ICT exports (UK with the dominant share of 19 per cent) while the US accounts for 60 per cent. Indian professionals overseas play a leading role in establishing relationships and India has been a major source of global human capital. Multinational companies are looking for cost-effective employees and the UK is the third destination after the Anglophone countries Canada and USA.

The main reasons for issuing residence permits to non-EU citizens in 2009 were family reunification, employment and education. The highest number of permits relating to education were issued to the Chinese and the highest number of permits for employment purposes, including researchers, highly skilled and seasonal workers, to Indian citizens. Among the nationals of non-EU countries, Indians are the largest group to obtain residence permits in the EU for employment (37 per cent) and the UK was the main receiver of Indian citizens in 2009 with 63.2 per cent. The Indian diaspora forms a potential resource and can play a positive role in clearing information and perception deficits, facilitating interactions and increasing mutual knowledge. But it has not yet gained any socio-political power within host nations in Europe, and due to its wide dispersion, its overall influence in Europe is rather limited.

There has been an increased effort to work towards a common European Union migration policy. Labour migration into Europe boosts competitiveness and therefore economic growth. Europe has to become as attractive a migration destination as Australia, Canada and the USA, and to make highly skilled workers change their perception of Europe's labour market as governed by inconsistent admission procedures. All migrants who come to reside and work legally in the EU should enjoy basic, work-related socio-economic rights. The Blue Card Directive, adopted in 2009, would allow the employment of non-Europeans in any country within the EU. Instead of dealing with different national legislations and different visa and work permit requirements, one single permit would be in place. Individual member states can separately decide how many Blue Cards they wish to grant each year and retain the right to refuse candidates. Denmark, the UK and Ireland are those who have opted out. Unlike the Green Card of the USA, the European Blue Card does not give permanent residence and is only valid up to two years, but it is renewable. After five years it leads to permanent residence, but again unlike the US, not to citizenship. After 18 months of legal residence, the holders can move to another member state, but a highly qualified worker has to apply for a second Blue Card as the applicant needs to comply with nationally determined requirements. In that respect, there is little change in comparison to the current situation, and the Blue Card offers no substantial added value.

Indian Defence Ties with Europe

India has the ninth biggest military budget in the world, at $47.4 billion,[11] that it expends on the second largest standing army of 1.18 million soldiers, and a navy and air force in the top five. However its armed forces suffer from a poor teeth to tail ratio with fighting elements outstripped by support units, and 60 per cent of the expenditure is on recurring costs as opposed to capital expenses that deal with modernisation and acquisition of new weapons systems. India's failure to build a strong domestic defence industry base means that it is the world's biggest arms importer with 65 per cent of its hard and software being sourced from abroad. In addition, most of the acquisitions are done in a muddled manner with no long term strategic planning or inter-service prioritisation and long delays have led to huge cost escalations.

The Indian navy is the fifth to have an indigenous aircraft carrier—but with five years to go before commissioning. It also has one nuclear powered submarine, without any strategic missiles, and still to undergo sea trials. So India has miles to go to catch up with China which has 51 diesel electric submarines and five nuclear powered ones and another five with missiles of 7400 km range. India has only 13 diesel submarines, aging and conventional and only half are operational at any one time. It needs at least 3 carriers, 5 nuclear submarines, and the additional Hawk aircraft to be built by Hindustan Aeronautics Limited (HAL). Warning signals abound about all the airforce's three fighter projects: delays in the multirole combat aircraft, the indigenous light combat aircraft and the stealth fifth generation fighter with Russia means that India is down to 34 squadrons which includes aging MiG-21s and MiG 27s, when it needs at least 44 squadrons.

Some EU countries maintain large defence industries despite cutting of military budgets, the absence of domestic orders and perceptions of threat, so export orders become vital. India is the world's biggest importer of arms, and the EU could expect a reasonable share of the $200 billion that India plans to import in the next dozen years. Defence manufacturing is a high cost industry as advanced technology and outlays on research and development (R&D) are required. Exports are needed to achieve economies of scale and amortise the costs of development. All EU countries adhere to technology denial regimes (Nuclear Suppliers Group, Wassenaar Group, the Missile Technology Control Regime and the Australia Group) individually, and some EU coordination exists on this score. On technology transfer they are all restrictive and the latest generation technology is almost impossible to access.

The prospective, though now aborted, merger between BAE Systems of UK and EADS (French-Spanish-German combine that owns Airbus) could be the way of the future to secure Asian markets at a time when European nations are cutting military budgets. There is no synergy between the military sector and security strategy. The UK was worried that the BAE/EADS merger could damage the transatlantic special relationship and the arrangement was eventually vetoed by Germany. Despite the BAE/EADS fiasco, consolidation due to mergers and acquisitions have resulted in economies of scale, helping international competitiveness. As a result, complex defence products are seldom purely 'national'. Although the defence industry is largely privatised, and dealing with individual countries gets diluted, at the political level the commitment of individual governments to the contract can be differentiated. The 'multinational' nature of the European defence industry has facilitated India in its defence procurements.

For India, transfer of technology is limited by the fact that only 26 per cent FDI was permitted in this sector, which has now been raised to 49 per cent. The EU has to contend with an entrenched Russia, and also growing shares in India for Israel and USA, but India's interest is to avoid over-dependence on any country. For defence contracts, some level of geopolitical understanding must exist, and it was noted in New Delhi that France has eschewed sanctions against India and is considered a reliable partner. A commercial nuclear deal with the French nuclear giant Areva for nuclear reactors and fuel supply was signed in 2009. Importantly, the agreement allowed for reprocessing rights over the spent nuclear fuel from French reactors under safeguards and also provided assurance of lifetime supply of nuclear fuel for these reactors. Moreover, it did not bar the transfer of enrichment and reprocessing technologies and allows India the assurance of a long-term relationship unlike the case with the US. India is considering the biggest single arms order initiated in 2011, namely $20 billion for fighter aircraft from the French Rafale for 126 multi-role combat planes, and selected Airbus 330 MRTT (multi role tanker transport) over competitors for mid-air fuelling at $1.6 billion. France has also signed the $3 billion Scorpene deal paving the way for naval cooperation. In July 2011 a $2.4 billion contract was inked with Dassault Aviation and Thales to upgrade 51 Mirage aircrafts. Other projects with France include development of engines for HAL, the Kaveri engine for the Light Combat Aircraft and the Shakti engine for the Dhruv helicopter. France is negotiating a major project of joint development and manufacture of short-range surface to air missiles with India, and India notes that French and British supplies are not limited by intrusive end-use monitoring as in the case of US supplies. France and India are drawing up a plan for long-term cooperation in satellite technology. France has now become the third most important arms supplier to India after the USA and Russia.

In 2003 India ordered 66 Hawk trainer jets from Britain worth $1.7 billion. In July 2010, during the British Prime Minister Cameron‘s visit, India placed an order for an additional 57 Hawk aircraft worth $1.1 billion to be built by HAL.

NOTES

1. Liz Mohn, *Cultures in Globalization*, 59.
2. Gauri Khandekar, *The EU and India: A loveless arranged marriage*, FRIDE policy brief 90, Aug 2011 and Bernd von Muenchow-Pohl, *India and Europe in a multipolar world*, Carnegie paper, May 2012, 1.
3. I.P. Khosla, *India and the New Europe*, 39.
4. David Malone, *Does the Elephant Dance*? 243.
5. Mishra & Argullol, *From the Ganges to the Mediterranean*, 2.
6. www.bbc.co.uk/news/world-asia-india-20637124ý.
7. Bernd von Muenchow-Pohl, *India and Europe in a Multipolar World*, Carnegie Papers, 2012, 15
8. Indo-EU timetable: 1996 Enhanced Partnership, 1998 Indian nuclear tests, 2000 India-EU summit, 2002 Denmark Summit with major differences, 2003 India terminates ODA from smaller EU states, 2004 Strategic Partnership, 2005 Joint Action Plan, 2006 Security Dialogue, 2007-13 EU Country Strategy Paper.
9. www.globalreach.com/the eu india fta
10. www.globalresearch.ca/the-eu-india-free-trade...driven.../5338049?...ý
11. SIPRI, 14 April 2014.

8

Global Issues and World Forums

New Trade Groupings

Transatlantic Trade and Investment Partnership; Trans-Pacific Partnership, Regional Comprehensive Economic Partnership

In 2013, the United States and the European Union began negotiating a Transatlantic Trade and Investment Partnership (TTIP) which they hope to conclude in 2015. The 28 EU members and the US account for 50 per cent of world GDP and 30 per cent of world trade in goods and services.

The Trans-Pacific Partnership (TPP) negotiations among 12 countries including the US, Australia, Brunei, Canada, Mexico, Malaysia, Singapore, Vietnam and recently Japan, have already been under way for over four years and the negotiations are due to conclude soon. These countries contribute around 38 per cent of world GDP and 25 per cent of global trade. China once seemed to observers to be considering membership of the TPP but problems have arisen with China's currency exchange rate, benefits to state owned companies and unfair treatment of foreign investors. There are also issues on intellectual property, market access for agriculture, manufacturing services and government procurement. So in the near term China's membership is an unlikely prospect. China has declared it is open to membership, despite the fact that TPP is a vehicle for US leadership in the Asia-Pacific region, but has meanwhile sponsored the Free Trade Area of the Asia-Pacific (FTAAP) which has been under consideration in the Asia-Pacific Economic Cooperation (APEC) since 2006. In 2014, all 21 members of APEC agreed to set up a working group to move it forward. This would be a China-centric Asia-Pacific initiative to reduce US influence.

In 2013, the ASEAN ten plus six dialogue partners (Australia, China, India, Japan, South Korea and New Zealand) held their first round of negotiations for a Regional Comprehensive Economic Partnership agreement (RCEP) to be concluded by 2015. Covering 45 per cent of the world population and a third of world GDP, this too is a formidable grouping. Australia, Brunei, Japan, Malaysia, New Zealand, Singapore and Vietnam span RCEP and TPP, but the TPP is vastly more ambitious in regard to intellectual property, domestic regulatory reform, environment, labor, government procurement and NTBs such as consumer protection law. RCEP, the grouping of 16 countries including three least developed countries (LDCs), will not be able to match the TPP and TTIP even if the idea is significantly to improve over the FTAs that each of the six partner countries have with ASEAN. Environment and labour standards are not mentioned in the guiding principles, and it can be surmised that on IPRs, RCEP may not go much beyond WTO commitments. RCEP is not a Chinese initiative. It was launched in 2012 by the ASEAN10 plus 6 countries with which ASEAN has FTAs. With many participant countries already bound by FTAs, or with average MFN tariffs already low, there is limited scope for further liberalisation in market access except in sensitive areas previously sheltered from competition like agriculture, textiles, footwear, automobiles, government procurement and services. There would be special and differential treatment for LDCs that is absent in TPP. The US is clear that TPP cannot give any preferential treatment for participating countries except in regard to longer phase-in periods for the poorer partners.

Despite periodical assertions by G-20 summit meetings about the importance of successfully completing Doha, there is growing retraction of political will and energy necessary for an outcome and the new groupings reflect this pessimism. The US has been promoting competitive trade liberalisation through other tracks once it became clear the Doha Round would not include issues like investment, competition policy and government procurement which were dropped from its agenda in 2003 due to opposition from the developing countries led by India. While Doha was a development agenda, domestic interests in the US and other developed countries showed no appetite for concessions, so it was time for the West to demand more value for technology and intellectual property rights, enforcement of higher environment and labour standards, more access for trade and investment and firm commitments about reform.

There are concerns about TPP and TTIP insofar as China and India are concerned, such as going beyond TRIPS commitments, binding commitments on labour and environment standards and others that may severely limit policy options. Major economies could present specific areas in these mega partnerships to be parachuted later into the WTO, or use the new trade pacts to obtain the agreements vetoed earlier by India in WTO, such as free capital flows, tough patent laws and environmental conditions, foreign access to government procurement and investment rights for foreigners. Indian commitments to its Employment Guarantee Scheme and food security might give it pyrrhic victories in the WTO but lock it out of these preferential trade groups.

Human Rights

The EU and China call each other strategic partners but there is no definition of any core interest or objective. The EU and China have limited cooperation in the security field except for anti-piracy activity off Somalia, and in general terms the EU has a negative impression of China's security role. The EU is weak and its member states are competitive in building stronger ties with China for their national companies and contracts. This was seen when EU members adopted different attitudes in the UN Commission on Human Rights (UNCHR) towards rights issues in China. From 1989 till 1998 the EU co-sponsored a resolution against China at the UNCHR, but desisted when France, Italy, Germany, Greece and Spain urged a halt, and set up a bilateral human rights dialogue with China instead. Any breakthroughs on human rights in China are now attributed to US involvement and initatives.

China has refused to sign up to the UN Covenant on Civil and Political Rights, abolition of death penalty, involvement of children in armed conflict, the International Criminal Court (ICC), CTBT and prohibition of anti-personnel landmines. It may eventually export its own structures and rules as other countries actively seek ties with it. While the EU keeps dialoguing, its agenda does not change, covering human rights, political and religious freedoms, Tibet, Taiwan, the anti-secession law, capital punishment, freedom of press and Internet. But the EU has no leverage except its trade assets, and at the same time, all this is a major source of annoyance for China. So the EU is in a dilemma, whether to raise these points, or gain more political capital and economic advantage with China. It has adopted an uneasy mix. Despite occasional criticism from the European Parliament and smaller EU members like the Nordics led by Denmark and Sweden, who are less concerned about company contracts, and some NGOs, because the EU and China do not share political cultures that parallel their commercial ties, there has emerged a trade-off between business and the liberal-democratic values dear to the Europeans, reflecting the internal divisions between hardliners on human rights and the more accommodating.

India is, like Indonesia, Taiwan and South Korea, a democracy, but this does not mean any subservience to western campaigns, unlike West Europe to the USA after World War II. China's priorities are growth, integrity and stability, and not democracy, and there is little the EU could do to change Chinese society. Asians differ on the priority given to human rights, the R2P, sovereignty and effective multilateralism. In spite of a semblance of commonality in principle, differences exist on concepts of civil liberties, democracy, tradition, mentalities, priorities, tactics, and negotiating styles. Often the Asian response to the EU is outright rejection or rhetorical imitation. The Asian emerging economies react badly to criticisms of lack of governance and human rights allegations, and China responds annually since 1998. In 2012, China issued a 9000 word, 11 closely typed pages report on human rights abuses in the USA, in obvious pique at constant criticisms of human rights violations in China by USA.

The US criticizes European conciliatory and non-confrontational stances, and it has not helped that the Europeans have not developed any special relationships with any Asian democracies. The recent EU strategy was in the China Country Strategy paper 2007-13 with funding for seven years at €224 million, comprising micro projects and a programme to fund NGOs and educational institutions. But Chinese condemn this as an attempt to "westernise ... and disintegrate China". A similar hostile reaction followed the Nobel Peace prize to dissident Liu Xiaobo in 2010.

In Asia, strong versions of sovereignty doctrine prevail. When this is non-democratic, EU must dialogue without the assumption of superiority of possessing liberal universalism. The EU will have to settle for a conclusion that its closest partners in Asia can continue to be nudged to embrace pluralism and tolerance, equal rights and equal opportunities—which are not considered exclusively western but universal values.

Reserve Currency

US current account requirements are about $3 billion a day, which it meets in its own currency. With the steady exit of funds to other currencies, the dollar is losing its seigniorage as the sole reserve currency and the economic hegemony it implies. 2/3rds of world foreign exchange reserves are held in Asia, but financial decision making remains in the hands of the West. China wants to replace the dominant dollar but both the US and the EU have brushed aside the idea. China's proposal for a new reserve currency is due to its concern about US inflation eroding the value of its reserves. This shows Beijing's concern about US financial management and unease at its own large holdings of US government bonds.

China has proposed a currency made from a basket of currencies including the yuan controlled by the IMF and disconnected from individual nations in keeping with the weight the yuan now exerts in international goods and services. China protects itself from any devaluation of the dollar by using the yuan for access to raw materials from Latin America and Russia. It expressed a commitment to make the yuan convertible and stated that yuan settlement could be made for trade in

Shanghai, cities in Guangdong and for currency swaps with several countries like Belarus, Russia, Malaysia, Vietnam, South Korea, Indonesia, Hong Kong, Jamaica and Argentina. There are bilateral deals between China and trade partners to promote the wider use of the yuan. Brazil and China in 2009 agreed to use their own currencies in trade transactions, with Brazil paying in reals and China in yuan. By 2015, roughly 30 per cent of China's cross-border trade will be settled in yuan. Since April 2012 the yuan can float up to 1per cent either side of a daily price set by the China central bank which tripled the amount that international funds can invest to $80 billion. If the experiment is successful the intention is that the yuan will be made fully convertible for investment as well as business, though China will not hasten to open capital and financial markets.

Europe's difficulties mean that there is no chance that the euro can soon take over the dollar's preponderant role. The euro share of the world foreign exchange reserve was around 26 per cent in recent years against 60 per cent for the dollar. The spectre of a global slowdown has meant the world relies more heavily on the dollar. The dominance of the dollar will continue because the preconditions are an open capital account and acceptability to the private sector which needs the confidence that the economy of the concerned country can withstand shocks. Having heavily invested in the dollar, pulling out for China is not an option. For all the talk of flexibility, the yuan is likely to be controlled by Beijing, and with the wariness that China is regarded in many parts of Asia, the market may not buy into it soon. A yuan standard is nowhere in sight as China maintains currency and capital market controls.

The Special Drawing Rights (SDR) are also a long way from being the world currency, and can hardly dent the dominance of the dollar in liquidity or reserves. Major powers will not agree to a new currency anchored in gold and no country will give the IMF the right to money creation. One day, when the yuan and rupee become fully convertible, they could at best join the list of reserve currencies, which may diminish the dominance of the dollar. According to the Indian chief economic adviser, China by 2030 will have sufficient reserves to see the yuan replace the dollar as the global reserve currency, while Klaus Regling, chief executive of the European Financial Stability Facility, gave his view in 2012 that in general terms, Asian currency, especially the Chinese, will show faster growth in official holdings, and the world was moving towards a multi-polar reserve currency system from a system where a single currency dominated. The multi-polar system will have currencies including the dollar, the euro, the yuan and possibly the rupee. Since the euro currency has a relatively limited role in Asian exchange, it may be prudent to keep an open mind about a new global currency disconnected from individual countries to replace the dollar, and as to how the SDRs are valued.

Genetically Modified Organisms (GMOs) and Climate Change

Aspirations to promote development, human rights and sustainability in Europe's foreign policy are understood, but a gap exists between the EU's espousal of universal norms and the reality of international action due to competing normative aspirations and different domestic interests. For example, agriculture circumscribes the EU's normative leadership in the WTO and Doha Round, while the EU itself drags its feet on agricultural and fisheries reform. The pursuit of universal values by the EU is actually the export of EU standards and models in fields like food and biosafety. Whether EU standards are in the best interest of other countries is an empirical question.

EU legislation in energy efficiency, recycling, biosafety and eco-labeling is among most developed worldwide, and there are efforts to evaluate comprehensively up to 30,000 chemicals. Growing resistance from business circles, however, shifted the ground to a more deregulatory outlook when expansion of chemicals regulation was opposed by business interests, though coalitions of environmental pressure groups and environmentally-conscious member states pushed for regulatory export. This occurs when sustainable development competes with economic freedom and trade liberalisation.

In the EU, industrial, agricultural, environmental and consumer interest groups all stake a claim. There are two basic conflicting interests; economic competitiveness, and human health and the environment. For example, agricultural biotechnology came to be seen as risky, but medical uses of genetic engineering enjoyed a high level of support and the backing of industry. When faced with demands by developing countries to regulate

GM exports, the EU retained the distinction between GMOs as food and as medicines. Ever present in the EU thinking was the need to catch up with GM industry leaders USA and Japan. It was in 1996 that EU agreed to a biosafety treaty that stressed ecological protection over the trade interest, though it still objected to the inclusion of medicines, because pharmaceutical companies had successfully lobbied hard against their inclusion. This is a case that reveals the gap between values and implementation that always seems to beset the EU's actions.

In another case, in 2013, the European Parliament limited the amount of food crops used to produce biofuel. Biofuels were seen as a way to cut fossil fuel use, but using food crops can displace food production. So Europe limited biofuels from crops like corn to six per cent of fuel used by 2020 and advanced biofuels sourced from seaweed or waste to make at least 2.5 per cent. But this compromise has yet to overcome lobbying from biofuel groups and needs to be approved by all the 28 states.

Energy and Climate Change in Asia

The scramble for resources in this century will lead to a form of neo-mercantilism in the quest for monopoly access to raw materials and products of nature like water sources. Environmental conflicts are likely first to arise in the poor developing world as a result of reduced agricultural production, economic decline and population displacement, compounded by river water-sharing problems, mass migrations and ethnic and racial strife.

The rapid expansion of the Asian economies means the driving force of the new energy order is in Asia. China and India account for 70 per cent of the increase in global energy demand, and the two countries are projected to double their energy consumption by 2030: this will mean fiercer competition for scarcer crude. China became the biggest consumer of energy in 2009 and its oil imports will triple by 2030. It is the largest consumer of coal and steel in world. China expects global warming will cause 5 to 10 per cent reduction in agriculture output by 2030, and India's will fall by 30-40 per cent by 2080. Climate change will seriously hurt both countries.

Per capita emissions in India are 1.2 tonnes p.a., one of the least, compared to the USA which is 20 times higher. On climate change,

India supports some reduction in the intensity of growth of emissions—the carbon released per unit of economic output—and measures to mitigate global warming, but will not agree to legally binding emission cuts since these are not in line with the Kyoto principle of 'common but differentiated responsibility' for global warming by developed and developing countries. Two interests have to be reconciled; the global good of a healthy environment across the world, and defending India's right to develop and emerge from poverty which requires energy, which in turn produces emissions.

The core issue remains that developed countries were burning the bulk of fossil fuels three decades ago when the UN Climate Change talks started, but that is less the case now and they refuse to be the only ones delivering emission cuts. But developing countries argue that their *per capita* emissions remain lower and the developed must do more to mitigate their emissions while assuming responsibility for historic pollution. This creates the impasse. Between 1850 and 2100 the world can emit 3,000 billion tonnes of carbon dioxide to stay below plus 2 degree C this century, but by 2012, it has emitted 2,000 already, and by 2030 900 billion more tonnes will be emitted—with China at 30 per cent, US 10 per cent and EU 6.5 per cent, which leaves little more for the rest. In 2013, China was greatest emitter of greenhouse gas (GHG) at 28 per cent, US at 14 per cent, EU at 10 per cent and India at 7 per cent. *Per capita* India is least of the four at below 2 tonnes of carbon dioxide per person; China is at 6 tonnes, and US is most at 18. Europe is a leader in climate change because Germany, UK and France made the costly decision to shift from coal to nuclear and natural gas in the late 1980s just before the world was aware that carbon emissions cause climate change.

The USA and China have now caught up with the EU to make deep cuts in GHG cuts by 2025-30. US will reduce emissions by 26-28 per cent below 2005 levels by 2025, which will mean doubling its pace of curbing emissions, and China will peak and increase the share of non-fossil energy to 20 per cent by 2030. But India says it expected greater action before China's peaking year of 2030, and experts say all this is not enough to avert a 2 degree rise in global temperature this century. GHG needs to be cut between 40 per cent and 70 per cent below the 2010 level by 2050 for this purpose.

As far as India is concerned, it may seem rather odd that India with 17 per cent of the world population and 4 per cent of emissions should ally on climate change with China with 18 per cent of the population and 20 per cent of emissions.[1] Phasing out subsidies on fossil fuels is not acceptable to India—but subsidies such as those on diesel cars can be withdrawn. Leaving aside agriculture, Indian emissions to GDP intensity declined in 1994-2007 by 25 per cent and will do so by another 20-25 per cent by 2020 compared to 2005.

China is the largest GHG emitter, which is a blowback from its consumerism, and its rapid industrialisation and the building boom saw China close the gap with the US as the world's biggest emitter. Of the world's most polluted cities, half are in China. Each year this causes 500,000 to 750,000 premature deaths and 95,000 are reckoned by the WHO to die every year from polluted water. Beijing's argument is that its pollution is comparable to Europe during its industrialisation, and *per capita* emissions are still below those of the West. So it resists mandatory targets on emissions because it refuses external controls, and wants to be free to grow. This means that China must be central to any future agreements on climate change. China has led in adapting to low carbon energy sources, but burns increasing quantities of coal. It has refused to limit greenhouse gas emissions, preferring like India to cut carbon intensity by 20-25 per cent by 2020 compared to 2005. But with its economy growing so fast, and China relying on coal for up to 70 per cent of its energy needs, GHG emissions will still rise by 60 per cent from their present level even if the carbon intensity target is met.

The *Living Planet Report* for 2008 suggests that humankind is using 30 per cent more resources than the earth can replenish each year, and that if there is no remedial change, we shall need two planets to sustain our existing life-style. This argues for a new international mechanism to regulate the use of our global commons. Can the EU give a lead in this, with more ambitious commitments to cuts in carbon emissions than 20 per cent below 1990 levels by 2020, and to pioneer new and effective carbon trading models beyond the Clean Development Mechanism?

The South, even large polluters like China and India, still sees climate change as largely a northern agenda to retard their progress and this has become a source of continuous friction between India and the EU. Therefore there will have to be a search for lower-cost ways of controlling carbon emissions other than by restricting economic growth. Without nuclear power, it is difficult to reduce greenhouse gases even as people's needs are met, and to generate sufficient energy from renewables.

Environmental policies are difficult to enforce so import restrictions may be the only tool, but the best way of having a level playing field is to have coordination in environment policies. But no big country wants to reduce carbon emissions. Oil accounts for 35 per cent of world energy consumption; coal for 25 per cent, the same for gas. Nuclear energy at 7 per cent is the safest and cleanest. India is at the 3 per cent level; France at 80 per cent. World energy use will grow by 50 per cent by 2030 and at present rates of consumption, oil can last only 20 years, gas 30 and coal 150. The dominance of fossil fuels that has lasted 300 years is coming to an end.

Climate Change Conferences

Copenhagen 2009, COP 17 Durban December 2011, Rio+20 June 2012, COP 18 Doha December 2012, COP 19 Warsaw November 2013, COP 20 Lima December 2014, COP 21 Paris November 2015.

Prior to Copenhagen

Industrial countries accounted for 72 per cent of total CO_2 emissions between 1950 and 2005 but now China is the biggest emitter with the US second and India fourth. Scientists believe that a plus 2 degree C rise in global temperature would lead to catastrophe. Some questions are; should there be legally binding commitments? What about voluntary actions by developing countries to limit emissions? How much finance would developed countries make available to the developing to enable them to adapt? The ideal was for a 40 per cent cut from 1990 levels, but that was never really on the cards. Kyoto had called for a 5 per cent reduction of emissions for 37 developed countries before 2012, but many had actually increased, such as USA and Canada. Before Copenhagen, the US agreed to 80 per cent reduction in emissions by 2050 and back to 1990 levels by 2020. Vulnerable islands called for temperature rise to be below 1.5 degree C and emissions scaled back by 85 per cent by 2050.

Saudi Arabia wanted compensation if there was a decision to limit the use of oil.

The EU's approach on climate change is closely connected with the political economy of energy production, manufacturing and consumption in Europe. The EU as a whole achieved a 8 per cent reduction from 1990 to 2012, but members like Denmark, Italy, Spain, Poland and Estonia did not. The EU had played a central role in creating the climate change regime and promoting sustainable development. It is committed to global environmental norms and promotes green normative power in environmental diplomacy and biosafety regulation. The American rejection of the Kyoto Treaty provided the EU with an opportunity to take the leadership, and looking to make a difference and find a big issue, the EU put forward a climate and energy package in 2007: the main components were a 20 per cent saving in energy consumption, 20 per cent increase in renewables, and 10 times increase in biofuels, all by 2020, along with new technologies to reduce emissions. The EU wanted to lead the global debate and hoped its soft power, in the form of its leadership of an international movement against global warming, would be acknowledged.

The Copenhagen Conference, 2009

EU officials undertook a global package of post Kyoto commitments to prepare for the 15th UN Copenhagen Climate Change Conference in 2009 with an agenda to replace the Kyoto Protocol. Emerging Asia had not participated in Kyoto, was wary of any commitments on energy use at this stage in its modernisation, and saw them as EU-US threats to sovereignty and economic development. India was silent behind China but its reservations were well-known. The Copenhagen conference was not good for the EU; its strategy was to place pressure on India and China as well as the USA, but the difference between its key member states was so deep that to keep the negotiation going proved difficult, and its own bargaining strategies were not up to the task. EU can claim rightly to have done more to combat climate change than the USA, China or India, but at the conference, significant achievements and good intentions cut no ice. Environment and climate change were shared competencies, which meant that the EU had a common negotiating mandate, but member states were also at the table, and the Swedish EU presidency proved unable to reconfigure key negotiating issues on the spot because of the member states' divisions. Finally, Britain, Germany and France, and not the EU, spoke for Europe and the EU was absent in the conference's final dealings. All this showed up the EU's false optimism about global multilateralism on complex issues, and also showed that multilateralism might work within the EU but not in the global arena where there were sharp national interests even between its members. EU had no political leverage and this collective confederation will have to introspect and find some painful answers. The allocation of pain will be a political matter, raising questions of distributive justice, obligations of the present generation, balance between poor and rich nations, and between human and other species. These are global questions which need global answers, but the EU cannot opt out of the search for them, for which they will need one voice.

The Copenhagen Accord was agreed to by 48 developing and developed countries accounting for 80 per cent of the global emissions. The target of a 80 per cent cut in CO_2 by 2050 was dropped. The EU seemed bent on playing its trump card of moving from a 20 to a 30 per cent cut by 2020, relying on the horse trading that has been plaguing climate change negotiation for years. The accord endorsed the 2 degree C warming benchmark for global progress. Measurement, reporting and verification were also agreed upon, and $10 billion finance was to be committed by 2012 for adaptation. Every major economy has agreed to identify specific domestic goals and commitments. It is now well understood that in the absence of any global accord, the most effective actions have been, and would be, taken at the national and local levels. These would include most of Europe and South Korea. Sweden became in 2009 the first advanced country to decide to phase out fossil fuels, build modern nuclear plants on 10 existing sites, and emphasise wind and hydro power generation with a view to reducing greenhouse gas emissions to zero by 2050.

After Copenhagen, most countries agreed to reduce emissions, the rich to mobilise $100 billion p.a. by 2020 to help the vulnerable to adapt, to create a system to verify emission cuts and programmes to stop deforestation. The USA, Russia, Canada and Japan did not agree to extend the Kyoto treaty, though Australia and the EU did. The UNEP noted it was unlikely that the stated goal of global temperature below 2 degree C rise would be met.

Both China and USA are 20 per cent plus emitters and no agreement is possible without their participation. The EU is a 10 per cent + emitter but has an excess of contradictory leaders. Five per cent + nations are Russia and Japan—but no one looked to them for their support at Copenhagen. Instead, India (5 per cent+), S Africa (2 per cent+) and Brazil (2 per cent+), namely the BASIC group, was needed by China to add weight to its efforts. This seems to be the formula for future weightage for international trade and finance as well, where the decisive factor is always the US/China relationship. It may be noted, however, that apart from discussions at global fora, the EU and emerging Asia are in dialogue on climate change partnerships, though relations are competitive multilaterally due to divergences on core and concrete issues.

Rio+20, June 2012

The same divisions between India and the EU appeared at the subsequent climate change conferences at Rio, Doha, Warsaw and Lima, where the EU continued to press in vain for legally binding pledges with timelines.

In 1992, the challenges were new, the Cold War was just over, and the Rio Treaty produced a legally binding treaty on biodiversity, an agreement on climate change that led to the Kyoto protocol, and the first initiative on protecting the remaining forests. It also established the principle of 'common but differentiated responsibility', which meant that the responsibility of the developed countries was greater, and that the standards for developed countries might be inappropriate for developing countries since they entailed higher economic and social costs. Since Rio+1, greenhouse gases have increased by 48 per cent in past 20 years, three million square kilometers of forest lost, and the population has grown by 1.6 billion, but even so, there is now less sense of urgency.

In contrast to the previous conference Rio+0, few top leaders bothered to turn up at Rio+20. Now the rich and poor are far apart, and politicians do not like being linked to lost causes. At the Rio+20 conference the EU wanted a time-bound plan for countries to shift to costlier and cleaner modes of production, including renewable energy targets. Another debate was on green accounting—which according to developing countries, "intrudes into our development space that impacts human rights". A plan to stop the destruction of the oceans was blocked by the US, Canada and Russia: the text only says countries should do more to prevent over-fishing and ocean acidification. A call to end subsidies for fossil fuel was removed. Fundamental changes in the societies which consume and produce are indispensable for sustainable development, but no one specified what those changes should be.

Yet Rio+20 was not a complete step backwards. The developing countries showed unity; the developed countries challenged the right to development as a human right and the importance of poverty eradication, and tried to shift the responsibility to developing countries. They asked emerging economies to help fellow developing countries with finance, and rejected technology transfer except on commercial terms. Now the task is to formulate global sustainable development goals, especially for energy, consumption and lifestyle. The problem is not with the rising living standards of the developing but the unsustainable lifestyle in affluent societies. Poverty eradication is seen as enabling protection of the environment, because development yields the resources for this.

Doha Conference of the Parties (COP 18), Nov/Dec 2012

At the UN climate talks at the COP 18, at Doha in 2012 the proposal that rich countries should assume moral responsibility and compensate poor nations for losses due to climate change again initially found the EU position not well defined. The affected poor nations were bitter that the US was dragging its feet over the promise made at Copenhagen to mobilise $100 billion a year by 2020 to help them access clean energy and adapt to climate change, and only a handful of countries had made concrete financial pledges for adaptation assistance. They claimed that the original sum was too low anyway in the light of President Obama's request to Congress for $60 billion to deal with Hurricane Sandy's damages and Britain's bid to raise £200 billion for clean energy by 2020. Finally, this general principle was approved, and the Kyoto Treaty of 1997, which covers only Europe and Australia whose total share of greenhouse gas emissions is only 15 per cent, was extended to 2020, with a new treaty to be cobbled together by 2015, to be valid after 2020, and include all countries. All this again will depend on USA, India and China.

The Doha meeting took no steps for mitigation and raised no new finance, and Europe came under criticism for not raising its promised cuts from 20 per cent to 30 or even 40 per cent. The EU has always been held back by Poland, which insists on its right to burn its huge coal reserves. At Doha, the US opposed the idea of rich nations having to compensate poor nations for losses due to climate change, stating such costs could be without any ceiling limit. EU's position was not well defined but suggested it could live with the text. This became a point of principle for developing countries because it was questionable how much extra money the Loss and Damage Mechanism would bring in. In the end the US agreed when the proposal was placed in the context of existing pledges to raise $100 billion p.a. for adaptation.

At this COP 18, the EU took the view that pledges must be legally binding with timelines, but USA and India both resisted the idea of any legally binding obligations. In the end, a compromise by Brazil that a deal must have 'legal force' was accepted. A roadmap was proposed by the EU, the LDCs and AOSIS (Alliance of Small Island States), but BASIC opposed any tight timetable or legally binding character. A management framework was agreed for the Green Climate Fund to disburse $100 billion p.a.

The EU and the developing countries also clashed when the EU suggested that sustainable development goals be decided by the UN Secretary General. The G-77 countered that the SDGs could not be focused only on green issues but should be balanced against social and economic requirements for development. G-77 suggested this could be done only by the UNGA in an inter-governmental process with the participation of all regional blocs. Eradicating poverty had to have the highest priority and could not be subservient to creating a green economy. Developing countries also opposed upgrading the UN Environment Programme to a specialised monitoring agency because they wanted environment issues integrated into development and not isolated.

At the COP 19 at Warsaw, the word 'contributions' was used instead of 'commitments' since China claimed that only the developed countries had commitments. There was debate on a new body to calculate loss and damage from high emissions, different from the costs of adaptation. The developed countries wanted this new institution to be under the United Nations Framework Convention on Climate Change (UNFCCC)'s Green Climate Change Fund. The intention was to mobilise $100 billion annually by 2020, and $10 billion a year until then, for adaptation and reduction by poor countries.

Lima Conference of the Parties (COP 20) December 2014

At the Lima COP 20 in 2014, India opposed any international review of Intended Nationally Determined Contributions (INDC) which are due by March 2015 to curb GHG, claiming they were to be nationally determined and include mitigation (emission cuts), adaptation, finance, technology and capacity building. The EU however claims informal deadlines make no sense unless they allowed others to review each other's plans.

India plans to raise solar power to 20,000 MW by 2022 and then to 100,000 MW and drop emissions by 25 per cent by 2020. Its challenge is to reconcile targets like growth, manufacture, jobs and sufficient energy for all with controlling emissions. It wished the world to give developing countries equitable 'carbon space' to achieve sustainable development and eradicate poverty. It wants to concentrate on solar and growing forests and could do more if finance and technology from developed countries were forthcoming without setting a price on IPR. India is emphasising two aspects; that clean energy technology must be given free and there should be no intellectual property rights restrictions or royalty costs attached.

NGOs say India's stand does not guarantee fairness or adequacy and it may be noted that India's position may also come under criticism from vulnerable countries in the developing world for not declaring robust targets. Lima COP 20 failed to agree to cut emissions in the period 2015-2020. However, domestic climate change legislation is advancing rapidly; since Kyoto in 1997 about 200 domestic climate change laws have been passed, covering about 90 per cent of global emissions. At the end of the day, locally driven emissions curbs will be more effective than any top-down global targets.

Intergovernmental Panel on Climate Change (IPCC) September 2013

The latest IPCC report prepared by 300 scientists from 115 nations states that the earth is warming under human influence. The average sea rise since 1901 is 19 cm. Increase in surface temperature from 1880 to 2012 is 0.85°C. 1983 to 2012 was the warmest period in 1400 years, and Arctic snow melt is up 11.7 per cent per decade, due mainly to atmospheric concentration of CO_2 more than other gases. CO_2 emissions have increased 40 times since pre-industrial times, mainly from fossil fuel emissions and land use change such as deforestation. The world's leading climate scientists for the first time set out in detail the most comprehensive assessment yet of our knowledge of climate change and how much more carbon dioxide humans can pour into the atmosphere without triggering dangerous levels of climate change, and concluded that more than half of that global allowance has been used up. If people continued to emit greenhouse gases at current rates, the accumulation of carbon in the atmosphere could mean that within as little as two to three decades the world would face warming of more than 2°C, resulting in rising sea levels, heat waves, droughts and more extreme weather.

The proportion of the global population experiencing water scarcity and affected by river floods is expected to increase with the level of warming in this century. Coastal and low-lying areas will experience submergence, flooding and erosion due to sea-level rise. Land and fresh water species face the risk of extinction, fish and marine animals will shift their habitats causing invasion of high latitude seas by low-latitude species and extinctions of species in the tropics. Ocean acidification poses risks to marine ecosystems at the poles and coral reefs. As for food crops, global warming without adaptation will negatively affect production.

This calculation of the world's carbon budget was one of the most striking findings of the IPCC. The 2,000-plus page report, written by 209 lead authors, found it was unequivocal that global warming was happening as a result of human actions, and that without substantial and sustained reductions in greenhouse gas emissions, we would breach the symbolic threshold of 2°C of warming, which governments around the world had pledged not to do. The scientists found that to hold warming to 2°C, total emissions could not exceed 1,000 gigatons of carbon. Yet by 2011, more than half of that total allowance of 531 gigatons had already been emitted, and between 2000 and 2010 greenhouse gas emissions had grown at 2.2 per cent each year, compared to 1.3 per cent a year from 1970 to 2000. To ensure the budget is not exceeded, governments and businesses may have to leave valuable fossil fuel reserves unexploited. "There's a finite amount of carbon you can burn if you don't want to go over 2 degree C," Thomas Stocker, co-chair of the IPCC, said. "That implies if there is more than that [in fossil fuel reserves], you leave some of that carbon in the ground."

This raises key questions of how to allocate the remaining carbon budget fairly among countries, an issue that some climate negotiators fear could wreck the UN climate talks which are supposed to culminate in a global agreement on emissions at the Paris COP 21 in 2015. Their other key findings in the report—the first such assessment since 2007 and only the fifth since 1988—included:

- Atmospheric concentrations of carbon dioxide, methane and nitrous oxide are now at levels unprecedented in at least the last 800,000 years.
- Global temperatures are likely to rise by 3.7°C to 4.8°C by the end of the century depending on how much governments can control carbon emissions.
- Sea levels are expected to rise a further 26-82 cm by 2100. The wide variation in part reflects the difficulty scientists have in predicting sea level rises.
- The oceans have acidified, having absorbed about a third of the carbon dioxide emitted.

The IPCC's executive summary prepared for world policy makers was issued on 13 April 2014 in Berlin, and taking account of rising carbon emissions, urged the world to move rapidly away from carbon-intensive fuels with a shift to renewable energy and natural gas as a bridge to move energy production away from oil and coal. About half of all the carbon released into the atmosphere since 1750 has been emitted in the past 40 years alone, with an increased use of coal since 2000 driven by increase in population and economic activity. To stay below 2°C in this century, emissions need to be 40 per cent lower than 2010 by 2030, 70 per cent lower by 2050, and zero by 2100.The report however suggests that changes in lifestyle and energy technologies could yet avert the most devastating impact of global warming.

There is a strong one to one relationship between economic performance and energy emission; and the greatest emissions in the 21st century are from the developing world. The developed world emitted most of the CO_2 in the 20th century, but today it emits 43 per cent and by 2099 this will be down to 23 per cent. The West has in effect exported most of its emissions to emerging Asia because more of the West's responsibility for CO_2 emissions comes from its imports, mainly from China. The reduction of emissions in Europe from 1990 to 2008 is therefore matched by the increase in CO_2 from imports from China.

In India it was felt that the report tried to shift the focus away from the emissions and 'historical responsibilities' of the industrialised countries in the past and the message sought to be given was to forget the past violations and look only at the future. Thereby, pressure would intensify on the developing world to do more to curb greenhouse emissions. BASIC took the view that on the mitigation front, actions by its countries were more concrete than the developed world, and China stated in August 2014 that around 60 per cent of the cut in emissions had been contributed by the developing countries. The BASIC view was not shared by the EU which said that the statistics showed an opposite picture: the UNEP 2013 report suggested that from 2000 to 2010 developed countries' share in global emissions decreased from 51.8 per cent to 40.9 per cent whereas developing countries' increased from 48.2 per cent to 59.1 per cent. China topped the list of the world's leading carbon emitters, followed by USA and India. The EU reiterated that it was willing to increase its emissions reductions from 20 to 40 per cent by 2030 (compared to 1990) if other major emitting countries would commit their fair share to a global effort.

One piece of good news is that since 2007 renewables have accounted for just over half the new electricity generation added around the world. The answer, apart from voluntary reduction of emissions, is that green energy must be cheaper. Everyone then would switch over, including the Chinese. This needs innovation in green technologies. R&D may hold no guarantees, but it may be better to spend on R&D than continuing the now shown to be futile other efforts for controlling climate change.

Hydrofluorocarbons (HFCs)

A separate but related issue is HFCs, climate damaging refrigerant gases that contribute to global warming and is covered by the Kyoto obligations of the UNFCCC. The matter of phasing out the damaging refrigerant HFCs has become a bilateral matter between India and the USA, which manufactures refrigerants with substitutes more expensive than the HFCs used in India. India wishes the matter to be dealt with by the UNFCCC and not the Montreal Protocol that dealt with ozone depleting gases but not greenhouse gases. India refuses to phase out HFCs unless it gains access to safe and economically viable alternatives—which are at present almost exclusively available with the USA. In other words, India seeks adequate financial support from developed countries for switching over from HFCs to properly tested environment-friendly technology. It was the developed countries that gave technology and finance to developing nations to adopt alternatives to ozone-depleting chlorofluorocarbons (CFCs). The developing world had switched to HFC alternatives as result of the Montreal Protocol, but now had to phase out HFCs as well, while the developed wanted to keep the IPRs and patents of new technology to themselves. Yet another issue is Nitrous Oxide N20, that has 300 times the damaging effect of CO_2. It is the third most potent greenhouse gas and most ozone depleting emission, but is not covered by the Montreal Protocol unlike CFCs and hydrochlorofluorocarbons (HCFCs).

UN Security Council

Asia and Europe must work together for an effective and legitimate multilateral system with a functioning United Nations at its core. It is difficult to justify low Asian permanent representation in the Security Council when the EU, with less than half the population of India alone, is already represented by two, and perhaps three members, in any future expansion. There is no Asian consensus on the expansion of the UN Security Council, but the big Asian powers will want to be an active part of the world multilateral system in order to exercise global influence and facilitate a revision of the international order and norms to reflect their interests, concerns and values.

The EU has too many board seats on all international organisations. This is a historical legacy and crowds out new members from the developing world. EU reluctance to relinquish this eccentric power sharing structure to accommodate new realities is a stumbling block to global governance. Europe professes to be open and outward-looking, but that is not how it appears to those outside the EU. In terms of economic or military power, Europe cannot aspire to a major role in shaping world events in this century. Its share of the world's product has declined in the last five years, and it will have to compete in an ever-stiffer competition for raw materials in the coming decades. Its present dependence on energy imports make it vulnerable, and the extent of its self-sufficiency is steeply declining; by 2030 the production of oil and gas within the EU is expected to decline by 73 per cent and 59 per cent respectively, and at least two-thirds of its requirements will thereafter have to be met by imports. The EU's international presence is also disproportionate in *ad hoc* bodies like the G-20 where it has individual members as well as a seat for the EU. In the P5+1 talks with Iran, the P-5 of the UNSC are joined by Germany.[2]

International Monetary Fund/World Bank

The big Asian economies will emerge relatively stronger from the present global recession compared to others. Through most of the Cold War, Asian countries, other than Japan, stood outside, or on the margin, of the western dominated world economy and its Bretton Woods institutions. Now the international and financial architecture constructed after 1944 has to be made relevant with the greater active participation of the Asian economic powers. The International Monetary Fund quotas were set up in 1944 in an agreement that fixes voting rights, financial obligations and entitlement to loans. The criteria are size and stability of the economy, foreign exchange reserves and trade volume. The post-war arrangement left the IMF and World Bank a transatlantic monopoly, and the US Congress in particular is resistant to yielding any space to emerging Asia. The Managing Director of the IMF and the President of the World Bank have always been from Europe and the USA respectively. Peter Doyle, a former top economist in the IMF's European department, has said he was ashamed to have worked there, because of the "fundamental illegitimacy of the selection process" in maintaining the monopoly of Europe for the post of Managing Director of the Fund.

Before 2008 the IMF provided almost no assistance to the EU: now it amounts to about 56 per cent or €110 billion. The problem of sovereign debt once considered exclusive to developing countries has become more serious for the advanced countries themselves; there is credit risk now attached to sovereign debt in many eurozone countries. The distinction between the givers and takers of liquidity in the world economy has changed; USA, Canada and others complain about the shift in resources to the EU when it is Europe that has blocked giving emerging countries a bigger say in IMF decision making, while the BRICS[3] claim that what international financial institutions wish to do is to use BRICS money and retain western hegemony.

China, with the world's second largest economy and largest dollar reserves, has around the same quota and voting rights in the IMF as Italy, Belgium or the Netherlands (3.8 per cent; cf. EU 31 per cent, USA 17 per cent; USA+EU+Japan = 53 per cent)—yet China is essential for injecting liquidity into the global system and providing a safety net for the US economy. India has 2.4 per cent quota and 2.3 per cent voting rights. The EU must relinquish this anachronistic power-sharing structure to accord with the new realities.

The BRICS, comprising 43 per cent of the world population, decided in 2012 to increase their contribution by $75 billion to an IMF crisis intervention emergency fund to help eurozone economies, and have asked for a greater say, including reform of voting power and quota shares. China agreed to $43 billion, India to 13 per cent or $10 billion. South Korea also made a voluntary contribution of $15 billion and Singapore of $4 billion. This makes China the biggest contributor after Japan and Germany to the IMF 'firewall' which has almost doubled to $456 billion. These contributions met the argument that BRICS should be a responsible stakeholder before demanding more rights; China in particular had been accused of having ambitions as a top table power but posing as a poor developing nation when convenient.

In 2012, G-20 had planned to shift five per cent of the IMF quota and three per cent voting power to developing and transition countries, whereas the BRICS had called for seven per cent of the quota in the IMF and six per cent in voting in the World Bank. The World Bank decided to give developing countries an increased say through more voting rights and a $86 billion hike in share capital. USA has 15.2 per cent, Japan 8.9 per cent, Germany 4.4 per cent, France 4.2 per cent, and UK 4.2 per cent. Total voting rights of the developing countries have risen from 44 per cent to 47 per cent and China as the sixth biggest shareholder behind USA and Japan, has gone from 2.77 per cent to 3.26 per cent. India has become the seventh biggest shareholder, and has a voting share increased from 2.77 per cent to 3.09 per cent. Indonesia has also grown while Britain, UK, France, Germany, the Nordics, Benelux, Japan, Australia and Canada have gone down. The extra capital would mean that India could borrow more by $7-10 billion from the bank. It is worth noting that there is resentment among the least developed nations that China and India continue to draw significant resources from the Bank and the International Development Association, the World Bank's soft loan fund for poorer countries.

The reform of the international financial institutions having been stymied by the US Congress since 2010, it was inevitable that emerging powers in the form of the BRICS would contemplate an alternative, and in 2014 this grouping decided to set up a New Development Bank in Shanghai with a capital of $50 billion (ten billion dollars each) and a Contingent Reserve Fund of $500 billion, that will start lending in 2016. Although this new bank will seem a small rival to the World Bank with $223 billion, or the IMF, it is a symbolic remonstrance to the current West-led arrangements, and an anti-dollar alliance that aims at moving the world away from over-reliance on the US dollar in international trade.

NOTES

1. India is the fourth greenhouse gas emitter after China, USA and the EU.
2. P-6= UK, France, Germany, China, Russia, USA.
   G-20= Argentina, Australia, Brazil, Canada, China, European Union, France, Germany, India, Indonesia, Italy, Japan, Mexico, Russia, Saudi Arabia, South Africa, South Korea, Turkey, United Kingdom, United States.
3. BRICS=Brazil, Russia, India, China, South Africa.

9

THE EU, USA AND EMERGING ASIA

In considering Europe's future relationship with emerging Asia, there has to be a third, extraneous, factor that always has to be taken into account. Pessimism regarding the American influence in the world is overdone. It has size and technological base, the biggest corporate business, military commands all over the world, a military budget almost bigger than the rest put together, a \$14 trillion economy, 80 per cent of satellites in the sky, and world centres of learning and research. It leads in biotechnology, medical devices, artificial intelligence, computing and outer space. Its share of global exports is growing from a low of eight per cent, and dependence on foreign energy is falling. It spends 1/3rd of the global funds on research and development for new technologies, innovation and creativity. It has the youngest population in the developed world, a cheap dollar, and is open to people and ideas. It has soft power, creative industries, the English language and the American dream. It leads in the spirit of enquiry and self-examination. No country in the modern era has exercised such influence in politics, economics, science and technology, and in ideas. The applications for emigration to the USA are still the longest. USA may be in decline but it is still the only 3-dimensional power—economics, politics and military—and China is not ready to take its place. It embraces plurality with a constant search for the better ideal. So reports of the US demise are greatly exaggerated.

The US is also known for conspicuous consumption, debts, divorce, racism, deaths by gun violence, drug use, obesity, election lobbying expenses and unbridled freedom of expression. US defence absorbs one in five tax dollars, the second biggest item after pensions. From 2000 to 2009, defence spending increased by nine per cent annually, far outstripping the country's economic growth. The US spends on defence more than five times as much as China, the next biggest spender, and more than the next ten countries put together. This is not for the defence of the US, but designed to control the world by more firepower than that of any conceivable enemy. But US is paying for all this with borrowing from China; in other words, using a Chinese credit card.

There is a fundamental difference between the erstwhile Soviet Union and China. The former was a formidable ideologically aggressive military opponent with whom there were minimal economic or trade links. With China, there is no evidence of the kind of confrontation once practiced by the USSR. China and America's economy are closely interlinked by debt, capital investment and markets, all of which are important to both countries.

Clearly China's ambitions as a rising superstate can clash with those of the West. Competition for global resources and the political and military tensions this could generate are genuine causes of concern. Such struggles, history tells us, have always accompanied the rise of new powers, but to dress up a matter-of-fact economic phenomenon as a preordained clash of civilisations does not help. There are those like author Hugh White in his *The China Choice* who regard the US as set on a collision course with China that could well conclude in war. To avoid a catastrophic conflict, both nations must change course: each country needs to recognise that it cannot dominate Asia alone. Instead, the two need to reach an explicit agreement to share power. Although both China and the US will have to make difficult decisions to reach such an agreement, White places the onus on the US to make the first move. This is not because he regards American primacy as a bad thing. On the contrary, he writes that US leadership in the region has led to a golden age, and that "Asia's success today ranks among the great achievements of the American century". The problem with this thesis is that the facts have changed. In the next decades, China will probably become the world's largest economy, a position that the USA has held since the 1880s. The age of US primacy is coming to a close but China cannot displace America completely and therein lies the danger. White writes that "any attempt by either Beijing or Washington to dominate will lead to sustained and bitter strategic rivalry, imposing huge economic costs and a real risk of catastrophic war". And since the US has clearly decided to reassert its primacy in Asia and, in effect, to 'contain' China, the conclusion has to be that such a policy is dangerous and needs to be reconsidered.

The arguments against this approach are many; that the Chinese economy will soon run aground, or that political instability will eventually cause China's rise to go into reverse, or that the USA and China are too economically interdependent for conflict to be conceivable. It can be added that Beijing lacks both allies and soft power, and that its army is not yet even close to challenging the American military machine, although US dominance of the Pacific Ocean is based on aircraft carriers that will be increasingly vulnerable to a new generation of Chinese weapons. The Chinese military budget is only about 13 per cent of what the US spends each year, so the US outspends China by a factor of 8 to 1.

While there is a case for both the inevitability and the danger of increased rivalry, the concept of any condominium is highly unlikely. There are ideological and political reasons why it is improbable that the US will ever accept that its unique brand of leadership is no longer viable. It also seems unlikely that if and when China has an economy that is notably larger than that of the US, Beijing will tamely accept that its nation has to share leadership in Asia with distant America. And the division of the world into two spheres of influence is not likely to subsist in a world of noisy public opinion, social media and satellite television.

The crises over Ukraine, Iraq, Palestine, Syria and Afghanistan have found the USA diminished and losing conviction about its moral mission though no other country has yet come to join the US at the top. China is uncertain as the Chinese communists will have to decide whether and how to allow other political forces to emerge. India's economic progress has faltered. The EU has imploded. Russia does not have the economic or military appetite for confrontation except perhaps in its 'near-abroad'.

NATO remains the pivot in European security, with the EU dependent on the USA for strategic leadership though it does not want entanglement in US geopolitics. NATO is suffering an identity crisis, with USA frustrated in its ambitions to turn the organisation into a global security actor for burden sharing and 'coalition of the willing' purposes. A thoroughly debellicised Europe's disinclination for war is cultural and the pacification of Europe considered irreversible. The US tries unsuccessfully to reignite Europe's martial spirit and NATO into power projection but there is no common transatlantic thinking on this and underlying conceptual and aspirational differences have not been resolved.

There was hope that the combined strength of Europe would see the emergence of a common EU foreign policy, which would provide a wholesome balance to the abrasive facets of United States foreign policy. But it is hardly likely that the EU can formulate any policy independent from the USA when the latter remains the provider of geopolitical security. Therefore US military engagement must be sensibly embraced. Europeans lack the will to challenge USA, while America is less and less able to translate its military and economic power into influence and leadership. The EU's CFSP (1992) and European Security and Defence Policy (ESDP, 1999) were attempts to achieve a degree of independence from Washington and also a response to US demands that Europe be more self-sufficient. Many Europeans would question the wisdom of facing multipolarity handcuffed to the USA, and attempts by the USA to politicise regional groupings such as APEC on issues like the war on terror have led to disenchantment in Asia. The US has understood this and is working to set up a network of bilateral Asian partners to maintain its primacy. Europe is no longer the main strategic preoccupation of the Americans. Europe's foreign minister Catherine Ashton has warned that the US would turn away from Europe unless the EU became more influential in Asia, and the EU had to boost relations with China to remain relevant on the world stage. The outcome is a balancing act for Europe that will become more and more difficult.

The USA is the non-resident power in East Asia. It harbours a deep ideological conviction that democracy represents the future and communism the past. This may be wishful thinking. The US is seen by Asia as economically demanding in terms of trade liberalisation and politically fickle in its strategic choices and partners. To some sceptical nations in Asia, Europe will have to show that it is 'not America'. The

EU knows that some Asian countries feel that the EU and Asia should make common cause to prevent the imperial arrogance shown during the unipolar era of US dominance, but this will hardly enhance Europe's position in Washington. A new transatlantic alliance based on dual responsibility might be the best route to follow, but is nowhere in sight, while a serious transatlantic rift would be injurious to Europe as well as the USA. Germany is the only country in Europe where there is some semblance of a public debate on the advisability of instinctively following the Washington line in foreign policy.

Other questions arise: can there be a Europe-Emerging Asia dialogue without the domineering presence of USA? Do both parties want to try to influence the US through joint efforts? Also to shape their own destiny and show alternative ways for the new world order, not as a countervailing force but as strengthening the multilateral framework? And yet Europe's future in Asia depends to an extent on implicitly balancing the power of the USA, which is likely in this century to be a Pacific and not an Atlantic power. To be an independent actor on the Asian stage will mean obvious de-coupling from the default American standpoint. But neither the big economies of Asia nor Europe should consider the other as a factor in checking the USA.

In its 're-balancing' of forces, the United States will be stationing 60 per cent of its naval strength with consequential support facilities in the Pacific. China regards this as evidence of US efforts to contain and impede its rise as an alternative power centre. Washington thought economic interdependence would create 'responsible stakeholdership' in China, while China feels the USA assumes an arrogant responsibility to shape the world and prevent the rise of another superpower, and the US-led security system, established for containment, should accommodate Asian legitimate security interests and a growing role in world politics. China is hardly likely to knuckle down to a United States policy of containment. So the US attempts a difficult dual policy of engagement and containment; or 'congagement'. The justification for this American 'pivot' to Asia is to reinforce the balancing reactions of regional states to shape the environment in a way that encourages responsible Chinese behaviour. Washington realised that it could not forge an anti-China alliance since even its allies wanted good relations with both China and the USA, and it would have needlessly ensured future enmity with China. What the US is seeking is to fall short of containment as a strategy, but for China to accept the legitimacy of American presence in the West Pacific.

The US has spoken candidly to China about upholding international law and respecting the human rights of the Chinese people. But this begs the question that living standards have been raised throughout Asia; where people once lived on the edge of starvation, rising living standards have often been given the highest priority. And China has made a contribution to peace and to prosperity worldwide by the strength of its economy and by the stability and reasonableness with which that economy has been managed. American-Chinese conflicts are on human rights, exchange rates, IPR, investment rules and standards, and mirror the EU's complaints. Both the West and China complain about each other in the WTO settlement mechanism. Mutual interests created by globalisation have not dissolved differences, softened the possibility of friction, or blunted territorial disputes in Asia, in all of which China and the USA are both involved directly or indirectly.

The EU, the world's leading civilian power, is an aggregate not of primary powers but of secondary nations pursuing primary status through collective agency. Even if the EU eventually developed an autonomous capacity for international relations, it would not be as a pole but as a subordinate subset in a hierarchical transatlantic order. This implies that the EU may lose any leverage over its strategic relationships. Issues where the EU and USA have been at odds are: Iraq, national missile defence, the Kyoto protocol, ban on landmines, the ICC, genetically modified foods, regulation of the financial sector, the death penalty and the challenge to Google, Microsoft and GE. Negotiations on the TTIP have not been uniformly smooth. Some distancing of the EU position from the US world view would be of advantage to Europe in terms of credibility in Asia. With the US reasserting its command and control, the challenge remains for the EU to engage positively with China and at same time, accommodate the trans-Atlantic alliance.

On the disputes in the East and South China Seas, it remains to be seen if Europe will have the political will and military strength to attempt to counter the Chinese in their home waters even in support of the USA. More congruence would exist in softer security matters such as piracy in the Indian Ocean and freedom of navigation outside the Chinese maritime periphery. China and the United States have an equal interest in preserving the freedom of the seas, but it also worth recalling that China has ratified the Law of the Sea, while the United States has not.

There will be some countries in Europe such as the UK, Poland and the Baltic states, that will always endorse the American interest, making consensus for a line independent from the USA impossible to achieve. This was particularly marked in the issues of a European satellite navigation system—the Galileo project – that was seen as a rival to the American GPS, the non-conferment of 'market economy status' to China, and the embargo against arms sales to China after the Tiananmen Square killings of 1989. It can also happen that the US has on occasion a strategic interest in taking sides with an emerging country rather than with Europe, such as with China at the Copenhagen Climate Change conference. As Hubert Vedrine, former French foreign minister, sardonically put it: "The multipolar world is a multipolar scuffle, pitting everyone against everyone".[1]

In 2006, the European Commission set out new conditions for strengthening relations with China and lifting the arms ban—and these included human rights, cross-Taiwan Strait relations and transparency in military spending. This showed an increased tilt of the EU towards the US and its Asian allies. The Foreign and Security Policy in East Asia adopted by the EU Council in 2007 then effectively aligned policy to the position of USA, Taiwan and Japan. The EU had evidently come to the conclusion that there could on occasion be anti-US coalitions on trade and environment but not on security. So the EU stands behind US security leadership in the region and visits like that of the Swedish prime minister to Pyongyang which took place in 2001 are not likely to be repeated.

North Korea: a Common Problem

On North Korea, still the biggest flashpoint in Asia, the USA and China have agreed to build a 'new model of major power relationship' reflecting Xi Jinping's formula based on mutual respect for core interests and win-win cooperation. The site of North Korean testing is only a few hundred miles from its borders with China, Russia and South Korea, so any mistake or technical failure could be disastrous. Both the USA and China agreed that North Korea has to denuclearise, that neither country would accept North Korea as a nuclear-armed state, and that they would work together to deepen cooperation and dialogue to achieve this denuclearisation.

China's stance continues to be fundamentally the same as before, namely, that the nuclear issue should be resolved through the six-party talks[2] and that this requires more all-round engagement and interactions with North Korea. If North Korea becomes fully nuclear weaponised, it would have a domino effect on South Korea and Japan. China does not like North Korea's regime but likes a reunified Korea even less, and particularly if this new Korea hosted US troops on its soil. China takes the view that the problem is one between North Korea and USA, North Korea and the International Atomic Energy Agency, and North Korea and South Korea, that North Korea's security concerns need to be addressed, and that Pyongyang's real objective is to be taken seriously by the USA and to conclude an agreement with Washington.

South and East China Seas

There is less concurrence on China's claims to sovereignty over the South China Sea or Japan's control of what Beijing calls the Diaoyu and what Tokyo regards as the Senkakus. The US has pledged to defend the Senkakus under the provisions of the US-Japan security treaty. Another looming problem is the China-Japan contested Ryukyu Island chain in which Okinawa is located. The big question for China is whether the US can ever bring itself round to accepting an equal partnership, not only with China but with any country, ally and foe alike. While China may be keen on a paradigm shift, the US mindset still seems fixed on a purely transactional partnership.

NOTES

1. www.csmonitor.com/World/Europe/2010/0127/...Vedrine-on...a.../3 Jan 27, 2010
2. At first there were 4-party talks from 1997 (DPRK, ROK, China, USA) and later 3-party talks in 2003 and then 6-party talks from 2003 (China, Russia, DPRK, ROK, USA and Japan).

10

COLONIAL PERCEPTIONS

Any examination of why Europe and Emerging Asia are important for each other has to consider the inheritance of disadvantage that both suffer from. Around a hundred of today's nations were colonies of four European countries, Britain, France, Spain and Portugal. To which list we can add imperialists like Denmark, Germany, Italy and Belgium. The emancipation of South Asia is still within living memory, the Portuguese colonies in India were liberated *de jure* only in 1975, and with the handover of Hong Kong in 1997 and Macau in 1999, the colonial era of Europe in China came to an end only recently. There is yet unexplored a huge degree of anti-colonial thought that shapes much of the post-western world in which we live.

The residual overhang of colonialism and imperialism affects the perception of Europe, because Europe is seen as following a single cultural script—colonialism that was described by Roger Casement as "greedy, brutal and insatiable when it came to food, drink, women, animals, skins, ivory; in short, everything that could be stolen, eaten, drunk, sold, or fornicated with, or enslaved, tortured, maimed or murdered".[1] And it affects the whole of post-European Asia, though for some like Korea and Taiwan, the bitter memories of Japan's Co-prosperity Zone experiment are more poignant than those of European colonialism. This historical experience is an essential component of Asian nationalism. The memory of European imperialism, "despotism with theft as its final object" according to George Orwell, remains a live political factor everywhere and contemporary diplomacy will fail if it does not take this into account.

The Opium War and its aftermath have cast a shadow on Sino-West relations, both sides tampering with the historical record for their own purposes. In China there continue to be antagonisms, misunderstandings and distortions that the Opium Wars had generated, not least that the West seeks to frustrate its rise, whether by military alliances, restrictive trade measures or the imposition of alien value systems. China's ambitions as a rising super state can clash with those of the West: competition for global resources and the political and military tensions this could generate are genuine causes for concern, for such struggles in the past have accompanied the rise of new powers. But to interpret this historical precedent as an inevitable clash is more a reflection of a continued European fixation with Chinese xenophobia and China's alleged determination to wish the West ill.

The great taxonomist Linneaus had classified the Asians as *Homo Luridus*, which may have given rise a couple of hundred years later to nomenclature like 'The Yellow Peril'. James Matheson, a Scottish pillar of the opium smuggling community in Canton, called the Chinese: "a people characterised by a marvelous degree of imbecility, avarice, conceit and obstinacy...[who] shroud themselves...in mystery impenetrable...and exclusiveness on a grand scale".[2] The addiction to opium was presented as a defining characteristic of China "immured in darkness...intrinsically an immoral and sensual nation". Wherever the overseas Chinese settled abroad, they were accused of vice, violence, and mutiny, and of being alien, secretive and xenophobic. After 1910, the fictional Dr Fu Manchu came on the scene with his global conspiracies against the West: "that awful being", the "incarnate essence of eastern subtlety". In the late 19th century the morbid fear of Chinese dastardliness had become a staple in western fiction. Matthew Shiel's *The Yellow Danger* in 1898 popularised the term 'Yellow Peril', the Boxer rebellion authenticated and pushed the phobia to new levels of hatred, and in every decade since its invention, the Yellow Peril has featured in European consciousness up to the time of Ian Fleming, regardless of the awkward reality of China's political, social or economic incapacity to pose any threat. If the Chinese regard their emergence to great power status as legitimate revenge on history, perhaps they have good reason to think so.

In the Chinese view, their modern history in the 18th to 20th centuries is the story of the 'century of humiliation', of Chinese suffering from and resisting imperialist aggression beginning with the "shameless and filthy" Opium Wars, a plot to "enslave our people, steal our wealth and turn a great nation that had been independent for thousands of years into a semi-feudal semi-colony.." In any trouble with China, the old fears resurface. From the Chinese viewpoint, any problem with Europe turns out to be a black imperialist scheme to enslave a heroic united China. China's misery was imposed by western countries; western misperceptions fuelled China's national myths and these myths have moulded China's interactions with Europe. Relations are still troubled by a highly politicised historical memory, where the West is "infantile, savage and destructive, while China is civilised".[3] China has also been accused by the West of polluting the world—now described as the Green (environmental) Peril—whereas western consumers are the market for Chinese manufactures while China's natural environment absorbs much of the damage of industrial production and its consequences. The survival of the Yellow Peril school of thought indicates the resilience of self-justifying ideas and arguments.

The colonised Indians also get a bad press. Europe took it for granted that its value systems were the predestined victors in the race for ideological and moral superiority and a model for humanity. James Mill, without setting foot on India, opined that "it was a land cursed from one end to the other by the vice, ignorance, oppression, despotism, barbarous and cruel customs that have been the growth of ages under every description of Asiatic misrule", and Thomas Babington Macaulay, the education representative in the East India Company government in 1835, wrote "a single shelf of a good European library was worth the whole native literature of India and Arabia". He also had this to say about the people at the headquarters of the East India Company; "What horns are to the buffalo, deceit is to the Bangalee. Large promises, smooth excuses, chicanery, perjury, forgery are the weapons of the people of the Lower Ganges".[4] William Taylor described the leaders of the Indian mutiny, as "little shriveled skin-dried men, of contemptible appearance and plain manners, holding undisputed sway over a crowd of tailors, butchers and low-born followers of every description...the most excitable, unscrupulous, dangerous and fanatical people that one could well come across".[5] In 1945, just prior to Indian independence from Britain, archaeologist Stuart Piggott in his book *Some Ancient Cities of India* confirmed the view of India as passive and unchanging: "We do not find, and should not look for, an inherent element of progress in Indian history—no organic evolution of institutions to changing human needs, no development of material culture nor the gradual spread of higher standards of living to a constantly increasing proportion of the inhabitants".[6]

The self-perception of the Dutch in their eastern Empire based in Indonesia was also strongly imbued by feelings of ethnic and cultural superiority. *Max Havelaar* by Multatuli, the *nom de plume* of Edward Dekker, was an exposé of 19th century Dutch prejudice and corruption in Java and Sumatra and created a sensation although it was initially disbelieved. It became an inspiration to the later Indonesian nationalist movement. The Dutch were convinced they had a divinely ordained civilising mission to fulfil in Indonesia and this led to Dutch diehard opposition to the nationalist movement. In the three years from 1946 to 1949 there were 100,000 Indonesian deaths. There was no Dutch development assistance to Indonesia from 1951 to 1967. For the Dutch it constitutes a 'collective blind spot in the Dutch psyche' and few Indonesians are now aware of any Dutch historical links; former Justice Minister Yusri Ihza Mahendra, old enough to remember, in 2003 said "I am not against the Netherlands. I am against injustice. Because they are unjust, I hate them."[7]

In Europe, the barbarians were always at the gates to the east: Metternich had declared "Asia begins at the Landstrasse", and one state's civilising mission was the victim's colonial hegemonistic project. If Jews are marked by received memories of the holocaust, Americans of both races by the Civil War, the South Africans by apartheid and devout Muslims by the Caliphate, it can come as no surprise that the Asian personality is imprinted by colonialism and oppression.[8] The EU needs to formulate a plan for bridging the gap that exists between different cultural patterns. It will be necessary to abandon all stereotypical images of Asia and *vice versa*, which derive from historical experiences and the imprint of imperialism.

NOTES

1. Mario Vargas Llosa, *The Dream of the Celt.*
2. Julia Lovell, *The Opium War,* lx.
3. The quotations are from Julia Lovell, *The Opium War.*
4. http://www.thehindubusinessline.com/todays-paper/tp-opinion/of-bengalis-and-books/article1049870.ece
5. The quotations are from Charles Allen, *God's Terrorists.*
6. Anders Andren, *Between Artefacts and Texts,* 59.
7. Krishnan Srinivasan, *The Rise, Decline and Future of the British Commonwealth,* 101.
8. David Marquand, *The End of the West.*

11

VALUES AND NORMS

The EU was meant to be a voluntary association of equal states, each of which is devoted to the principles of democracy, rule of law, human rights, and sacrificing part of their sovereignty for the common good. A united and prosperous Europe, devoted to the principles of an open society, was considered much needed by the world for its ethos. Its brave new world order looked suspiciously like the European Union writ large, a tranquil world of international standard-setting, internet governance, and spreading human rights.

In the 18th and 19th centuries, migrant workers underpinned the industrial revolution in the west. Britain was the first urbanised country and this was a major factor in its eventual world dominance. The West then dominated the world for the next 200 years; French became the language of culture, German of philosophy, English of politics and economy, Italian of music. Liberalism, republicanism, socialism, nationalism and communism were bequeathed to the world by Europe. Because modern history of the past few centuries has been about the rise of western civilisation, it is difficult for many in the west to conceive of a world where multiple civilisations co-exist.[1]

From the French Revolution onwards, the political will and establishment of institutions in Europe fostered the development of international human rights law, and also led to the view that human rights are European or understood only by western people. The biggest success of Europe has been to integrate individual rights into the rule of law, to make protection of human rights the obligation of the state, and through various UN conventions to make human rights legally binding. UN human rights committees continue to be dominated by American and European human rights advocates, experts and NGOs. Values are an overarching and legitimising pillar of the EU's external relations, and the EU likes to be viewed as a uniquely norm-observing actor. Supporters of EU integration highlight the new dimension of no longer following the politics of self-interest and of abandoning the principles of realist power politics. They consider European Union integration an example of new international relations which other powers should follow in order to make the world safer and more peaceful. These pretensions appear hypocritical to many of the EU's non-European partners.

The EU has too many internal divisions to turn into any great Westphalian power. Comparison with US military use led to excessive hopes about the prospects for European soft power. Asian countries like China and India are making global claims by using traditional repertoires and the EU has to find a way to respond to them: virtuous pleas for sacrifices on issues like climate change are unlikely to prevail and Asian emerging nations are unlikely to harken to the EU's lectures about multilateralism and multilevel governance. According to authors such as Mark Leonard in *Why Europe will run the 21st Century*, the European model of community of democracy will prove irresistible. Europe is seen as a transformative power; its social model is prized, with low inequality, energy efficiency, freedom, energy, liberalism, stability and welfare. Europe does not elicit hostility. Other nations "have interests and no values, and the EU has values but no interests". [2] But then, no one at that time was trying to check Europe's rise and the power of Europe's market had made access to it conditional on its *mores.*

The EU will continue to propagate its DNA, moral virtues and historical mission to spread what it considers to be global norms and standards. Human rights, legitimate political authority, multilateralism—these are the foundational ideas of Europe. The EU and USA initiated 80 per cent of the norms and standards that control international trade and regulate global markets and the EU tries to promote standards in labour, environment, free and fair trade, sustainable development, the death penalty, human rights legislation, international law, and multilateral cooperation such as on the ICC, Rights of the Child and the Kyoto Treaty. In this manner, an imperial prescription was propagated globally through norms, trade and trade regulation. "We are fast becoming the institution of reference about governance...a real international authority promoting the rule of law" was the claim.[3]

Contemporary international law is predominantly a creation of West Europe and USA and these two have a strong interest in maintaining and strengthening it and only cautiously altering it. The real divergence comes from the South and Asia. The relevance of shared norms and values has shrunk when China and India are not inclined to provide support to the EU to project its civilising global order. Europeans, and then Americans, had mastery over power, concepts and values for several centuries, which is now at an end. They thought nationalistic colonial forceful policies were over for everyone, and the Berlin Wall's fall gave rise to absurd illusions that there were no global disagreements any longer. But there is no 'international community' yet and power struggles still exist. China is now in a position to say 'no' as at the Copenhagen climate change conference, and the final compromise at the WTO Doha Round was blocked by India. The G-20 was supposed to address imbalances between the producer creditor (China) and the consumer debtor (the USA) but little was achieved because China was unwilling to follow the lead of the developed countries, and the EU's opinion was hardly heard.

Globalisation is often deemed a western cultural homogenising force that has shaped our modern times. This Eurocentricity must now be shifted to what the world demands from the EU, namely discussion on the EU's place in a de-westernising world, tension between universal values and regional interpretations of universality, discrepancy between rhetoric and action, the internal confident self-image and outside perceptions of the EU. Implicit in this discussion is the issue of presumed European moral superiority. The glorification of the supposed virtues of the European people is an argument that has little conceivable appeal to anyone else. Old mega-narratives—the EU for peace and reconciliation, economic prosperity, democracy and stability, and the unique social model—no longer sell in a global setting. In the new world, the inherited assumptions of west and east may have scant purchase. It will be well to abandon the belief that democracy and free discussion are exports of a progressive west to a backward east. The western narrative of global history in which western values enriched the rest of the world may conceal a far more complex truth; that it will not be as easy to set the world agenda as it was one hundred years ago.[4]

If the normative model is not reformed, it is a message that is no longer persuasive. The EU has to face the competition of rising industrial powers along with concerns on how the European way of life can itself be preserved. The EU will have to try to maintain and implement its environmental, food safety and labour norms without forcing global competitors to embrace them. For this purpose, the EU should engage in a dialogue to establish common shared rules of morality and global governance and provide economic incentives for others adopting the norms. It should try to be a model power, not a superpower, and should not be accused of regulatory imperialism. By choosing to act alone, the EU might undermine the concept of a global community. In any case, it can no longer shoulder its obligations alone. The EU too often relies on conditionality as an instrument, with economic and political incentives for compliance. It is the relative power of Europe *vis à vis* a country or region that determines the extent to which the EU emphasises the importance of human rights rather than the gravity of the default. Clearly, this leverage of the EU diminishes the further it travels outside Europe.

With ambitious normative standards, there obviously arise accusations of hypocrisy. Jurgen Habermas pointed out that "our own halfway liberal societies" had vulnerability on this score. He also spoke of "the provinciality of our historical consciousness *vis à vis* the future"; "Our values are universally valid values that all other nations should accept in their own best interests. This pseudo universalism is a kind of universalised ethnocentrism." Human rights policy became a mere fig leaf and vehicle for imposing major power interests: "Today...we encounter this paradox in the concept of 'militant democracy'...in violation of humanitarian international law and [which] justifies this in the name of universal values. This reinforces the suspicion that the programme of human rights consists in its imperialist misuse." On the Responsibility to Protect doctrine, in which the EU countries have enthusiastically followed the US line,

Habermas wrote, "most spectacular...are the humanitarian interventions... in the name of the international community, sometimes even against the will of sovereign governments...these cases...reveal the problematic nature of the attempt to promote a world order which is institutionalised for the present only in fragmentary ways. For what is worse than the failure of legitimate attempts is their ambiguity, which brings the moral standards themselves into disrepute."[5]

From China, leading academician Wang Hui writes, "nothing but its overwhelming hegemony gave Western universalism the appearance of being universal, leading many to believe it was universal."[6] He went on; "The core of Eurocentrism lies in its having established rules according to the demands of Western interests and then having universalised them."[7] Wang Hui again: "Modern European history has produced many unique historical models, such as the nation state and the sovereignty model, market society and its corresponding life values, legal structures and their protective mechanisms, and a strict division of labour and specialisation. The politics, economics and trade models of European capitalism have been spread across the globe through colonialism, which has also disseminated nationalism, cosmopolitanism and other corresponding ideologies to all 'modern societies'. But do the ideas of nation states, market mechanisms, division of labour and even legal mechanisms stem purely from European history? Do other regions not have their own histories? Where was European capitalism actually produced? The hegemony of capitalism is expressed in historiography as Eurocentric and ideological, yet this Eurocentrism is not a purely European phenomenon."[8]

The EU takes the view that any other country's economic rules, the production of products, supervision of firms and training of workers and professionals do not have to be the same as the EU's but need to be compatible with them. EU norms and regulations promote the EU interest even when and if they benefit the target actor. 'Our size fits all' was legitimated by the spread of western culture. What made Europe interesting was a fusion of cosmopolitan ideas of universal rights with the emerging institutional capacity to protect those rights. The deepening of shared values within the EU did not however necessarily mean that such ideas would inform its future international public policy. For example, the priority of human rights in China after Tiananmen proved valid in Europe only for a short time. Normative behavior was conspicuously absent when Germany and Italy pressed for the quick lifting of sanctions for fear that USA and Japan would profit from the European absence.

The EU claims that what is good for Europe is good for the world but there can be competing visions of the good life. As an Australian minister once pointed out, an EU cow receives a subsidy of $2.20 a day—more than what 1.2 billion of the world's poor can live on.[9] The reform of the CAP could move 140 million developing world people out of poverty.[10] The EU faces the perennial problem of seeking justice or establishing order when specific interests are wrapped up as universal values. The EU mistakenly thinks the resolution of its own historical enmities through integration is an experience with universal applicability to be emulated without recognising the moral complexities and dilemmas of international politics. Bringing democracy everywhere is not very different from the approach of colonial powers in the 19th century which cannot work now. Democracy may prevail, but it will not mean that the rest of the world will align with the West. China and other emerging economies will not necessarily share, due to instinct, tradition, historical circumstance and culture, each and every one of the values considered to be liberal and international. Efforts to spread western values will no longer go unopposed by Asian emerging powers who are governed by national interests and not global community values as defined by the EU. In practice, nations do not pursue normative agendas at the expense of their national interests.

The EU often lacks leverage. China may embrace certain aspects of regulation, but will not change its economic policies under EU pressure, nor adopt its normative yardsticks. India opposes the EU's core labour and environment standards in trade relations, and declines to put them on the multilateral agenda. It also opposes rules of competition, investment, and transparency in government procurement. In some respects the EU's norms have to be watered down, such as in environment issues, because of competition from other countries that impose no such constraints, and in energy, labour and finance. Many of the EU's standards were seen by China and India as disguised attempts to protect high-cost producers in highly regulated economies by using welfare standards against cheaper labour in more productive countries. The failure to export the same standards to others may place European firms at a comparative economic disadvantage, but efforts to impose EU norms, where there is little demand for them, is futile.

The debate is still going on in China, which continues to formulate its global interests. It does not seek to articulate any universal values to propagate, at least for now. China started to develop its relationship with the EU when faced with the challenge of Japan and the USA, so that it could continue to expand its economic and military capacity and oppose American unilateralism. But China is wary about the EU goal of westernising and transforming China. It regards the EU's policies to engage China in the international community, support transition to an open society with rule of law and human rights, and support to economic and social reform, all to be a plan to transform the Chinese value system on the model of the EU with the mentality of a savior coming to the rescue of the backward Asians.

The unequal cultural factor is hard to eliminate: "Europe still insists that western culture, value system and social institutions should be the future direction for change in non-western nations." [11] Cultural patterns and values are clearly at variance between the EU and Asia. In Asian emerging economies there is a sense of identity from civilisation rather than from the state. This is combined with a strong work ethic in South and Southeast Asia, where the people have a tendency to work hard and save for future generations. Families in Asia spend up to 50 per cent of their income on children and there is the unshakeable importance of the family as a unit. Hong Kong, the most capitalist area in the world, is a family-based tradition-bound society. Individualism is breaking out with economic freedom emerging and expanding in the middle of tradition-bound societies, but the individual awakening remains embedded in the family unit and family life will probably avoid the atomisation and anomie of the dissolving social glue by moving to modernity without yielding to the western value system.

The EU wants to teach China about human rights, the rule of law and law enforcement, and freedom of expression, association and religion that are sore points which the Chinese see as trying to divide its society with the ultimate goal of pushing China to absorb western ideology. For China, engagement with the world does not mean accepting foreign views of what is good for China. Globalisation, according to Beijing, only means the expansion of the capitalist mode of production all over the world. For China, while it does not openly reject the norms, institutions and processes of globalisation, its relative size and importance allow it to limit the imposition of foreign regulatory standards.

China remains a committed believer in the current global economic institutions while sceptical of liberal governance and freedom of communication. The Chinese are happy to exchange their investment in infrastructure for access to African mineral wealth regardless of the type of government they deal with. Thus when western governments and NGOs are belatedly demanding improvements in African governance, they are undercut by the growing Chinese influence in that continent.

India regards the modern state as founded on and sustained by sovereignty, territoriality and *raison d'état*, whereas the EU is a post-modern construct, with diminishing regard for sovereignty within territorial space, with desire for extra-territoriality in its aspirations and a penchant for interference and intervention. This basic difference in conception explains the inherent mutual discomfort. India thinks the EU is over-institutionalised and over-bureaucraticised, complicated and less attractive than the individual European national capitals.

Any negotiation by the EU must take into account the fact that its knowledge of other societies and cultures is incomplete. It should show impartiality in third party disputes. The legitimate interests of the emerging economies must be acknowledged. In emerging Asia, strong versions of the sovereignty doctrine prevail. When this is non-democratic, the EU must dialogue without any assumption of the superiority of possessing liberal universalism. Wars on account of humanitarian intervention should be totally eschewed unless regime change is both legal and legitimate. Europeans in Asia are not representatives of a superior civilisation battling oppression in a place that cannot possibly attain the levels reached by the West. There is a deep-rooted western assumption that the expansion of freedom and democracy can only do good. The West believes in freedom over discipline, individual rights over community rights, the quality of life over hard work, the individual over the family, media freedom over restraint, ration over religion, that the expansion of democracy in whatever form can only be good for any society, and that western social patterns are valid for all time in all places. Western advocacy of democracy is prescriptive. It took long decades for it to evolve in the West, but non-western countries are supposed to move swiftly towards the western pattern. The selective application of democracy in the past as a tool to target opponents and spare its allies makes the West lose credibility.

The main danger for the EU is in its self-congratulatory and self-centred rhetoric on the lines of Europe being and doing good for the world. But the world is increasingly marginalising Europe in population, economic growth and innovation, and decline in relative power could lead to a decline in normative power as well. The EU has to explain the substance and meaning of such norms better; and to show it has internalised them to a sceptical outside audience. An ethical power seen as hypocritical would be self-defeating. There can be no return to expeditionary ideas of exporting values in the name of liberalism or even worse, civilisation. If the EU is to be seen as a responsible global institution, this implies less agency and activism, and the EU would be better off for it.

The West has a good product to sell in terms of its mature version of democracy; the problem is in its aggressive political salesmanship, relentlessly vaunting its product and pressing it on others. The case of democracy is strong and self-evident but the case is not made if overlaid with geopolitical calculations and aggressive political posturing without regard to human cost. Democracy is plural, not singular; and it is a culture as well as a set of institutions. Good governance can be defined in many ways; it is regarded as potentially valuable and desirable, but democracy can be seen as destabilising if associated with West-backed 'colour revolutions' of doubtful legitimacy that sweep elected governments from power.

In the same way that we now scorn the manner in which imperialists sought to export the virtues of civilisation to colonised people, so there may come a time when the same scorn will be directed to efforts to export the virtues of democracy. Democracy, like civilisation, has its own national and ethnic characteristics and there can be no 'acculturation'. The EU should not assume that apart from retaining some cultural particularities,

Asians would evolve only in the direction of emulating the political and economic arrangements of the West. Many in the non-west think their own systems are more appropriate for their societies. The issue is to balance individual and community rights, and Western-style democracy and capitalism will not abolish the particularities of religion and culture. Abandonment of former empire must be accompanied by revision of notions of national and racial superiority. The central event of the modern era is the intellectual and political awakening of Asia and its emergence. The future will be more cosmopolitan even if there is no eventual total shift of power from west to east.

Old Eurocentric notions of model Europe are bound to fail. We are in a pluralistic, non-European non-western world—one European world among many worlds. It is an illusion to claim centrality in world affairs. The West has aggressively championed the virtues of its patent on capitalism to the rest of the world, so when competitors emerge from India and China, it is paradoxical and upsetting that European workers have to acquire new skills or lose jobs.

The core ideas of the West—enlightenment, secularism, capitalism, democracy—will not inevitably spread to the rest of the world, and the western order as it has evolved since 1945 will not outlast the West's primacy. The Asian emerging nations will not end up by being like Europe, with free elections, free markets, a liberal form of nationalism and the separation of state and religion. The international system is going to progress with each country following own path to modernisation (as in the economic and political transformation of Europe itself), determined by unique historical circumstances and cultural traditions that may or may not result in liberal or democratic principles. There may be communal autocracy, paternal autocracy, tribal or religious autocracy, theocracy and other non-liberal doctrines. Free elections can lead to anti-West leaders. Economic growth does not inevitably and swiftly lead to democratisation. Americans seem to believe that "In this global information age...personal freedom is essential to the greatness of any modern nation,"[12] but it is perfectly feasible that China will be a Communist one-party state even in 2030. The idea that democracies agree on big global issues is not valid—for example, take India on climate change or the Doha Round. A more democratic Turkey and Egypt are more Islamist. A more democratic China may be more prickly, nationalist and belligerent.

In the light of Europe's colonial past and dubious legacy of civilising missions based on moral justifications, the EU has to make its moral arguments based on the foundations of European thinking transparently clear if it wants to win credit in the non-European world. It has to deal with common ideas rather than to prescribe and promote, and be prepared to engage in a two way dialogue. In a Eurocentric world, legitimacy and leadership came naturally; but no longer.

NOTES

1. Ho Kwon Ping, *Back to the Future*, March 2009 Singapore Management University.
2. Mark Leonard, *Why Europe will run the 21st Century*, 19.
3. George Ross, *The EU and its Crises*, 114.
4. David Marquand, *The End of the West.*
5. Quotations are from Jurgen Habermas, *The Crisis of the EU* and *The Divided West.*
6. Wang Hui, *The Politics of Imagining Asia*, 116.
7. Wang Hui, *The Politics of Imagining Asia*, 260.
8. Wang Hui, *The End of the Revolution*, 80.
9. mjperry.blogspot.com/2008/.../farm-subsidies-gone-wild-eu-cows-earn.h...ý
10. Adrian Hyde-Price, *A Tragic Actor?*
11. www.eusa-japan.org/download/eusa_ap/paper_TingWai.pdfý
12. Bill Clinton, quoted by Gideon Rachman 1998.

12

CONCLUSION

By 2025, the United States and the European Union will no longer be the twin colossi bestriding the globe. The world will be shaped towards a far more interactive community, and western universalism may continue in three respects: time, space and language. Time, in respect of the clock, the time-zones, the International Date Line, the calendar and the millennium; space, in terms of the definition and delineation of the borders of continents and countries. The medium of the Internet, air and maritime traffic, and the most common usage in international forums, English, spoken by 1.4 billion people as a first or second language, will be the *lingua franca*.

Henry Kissinger once saw the two major world problems of today as being the movement of the centre of gravity from the Atlantic region to Asia and the impact of a globalised economy on the world order. These are not problems but opportunities. But such opportunities can be seized only through a clear agenda, planning and foresight. There was a moment, during a previous phase of globalisation by way of European expansion in the nineteenth century, when Benjamin Disraeli described the East as 'a career'. It will be so for Europe again, but this time in an entirely different sense. China will become a viable great power on a global scale, probably one of the greatest that the history of our planet has ever seen. The whole of emerging Asia will progress and prosper in the slipstream of Chinese economic growth. India will continue to be a big, muddled, messy, exemplar of pluralism and democracy. It is a safe bet to assume that young persons everywhere in the world today will live to see a very different politically and economically multi-polar planet in which emerging Asia will be a major participant.

BIBLIOGRAPHY

Books

Acemoglu, D. and Robinson, James A., *Why Nations Fail*, Crown, New York, 2012.

Allen, Charles, *God's Terrorists*, Little Brown, London, 2006.

Anderson, Jeffrey G., Ikenberry, John and Risse, Thomas, *The End of the West?* Cornell University Press, 2008.

Andren, Anders, *Between Artifacts and Texts*, Plenum Press, New York, 1998.

Ash, Robert (ed) et al, *China Watching*, Routledge, 2007.

Balme, Richard and Bridges, Brian (eds), *Europe-Asia Relations. Building Multilateralisms*, Palgrave Macmillan, Basingstoke, 2008.

Bickerton, Christopher J., *European Union Foreign Policy*, Palgrave Macmillan, Basingstoke, 2011.

Bolt, Paul J., Changhe, Su and Cross, Sharyl, *The United States, Russia and China*, Praeger Security International, Westport CT, 2008.

Calleo, David P., *Rethinking Europe's Future*, Princeton University Press, 2001.

Cameron, Fraser, *An Introduction to European Foreign Policy*, Routledge, Abingdon, 2012.

Casarini, Nicola, *Remaking Global Order*, Oxford Scholarship Online, February 2010.

Chang, Jung and Halliday, Jon, *Mao, The Untold Story*, Jonathan Cape, London, 2005.

Christiansen, Thomas, Kirchner, Emil and Murray, Philomena, *The Palgrave Handbook of EU-Asia Relations*, Palgrave, Basingstoke, 2013.

da Silva, Jorge Tavares, *Europe giving shape to an idea*, Anthem Press, 2009.

der Harst, Jan van and Swieringa, Pieter C.M. (eds), *China and the EU*, Shaker Publishing BV, Maastricht, 2012.

El-Agraa, Ali M., *The European Union*, CUP, New York, 2011.

Fenby, Jonathan, *Tiger Head, Snake Tails*, Simon and Schuster, London 2012.

Ferguson, Niall, *Civilization*, Penguin, London, 2011.

FPRC Journal. 2013 (1) *India European Union Relations*, E-book. Foreign Policy Research Centre, New Delhi.

Fukuyama, Francis, *The Origins of Political Order*, Profile, London, 2011.

Gandhi, Rajmohan, *Two Revolts*, Penguin Viking, 2009.

Gerth, Karl, *As China Goes, So Does the World*, Hill and Wang, New York, 2010.

Habermas, Jurgen, *The Crisis of the EU,* Polity, Cambridge, 2012.

Habermas, Jurgen, *The Divided West*, Polity, Cambridge, 2006.

Hill, Christopher and Smith, Michael (eds), *International Relations and the European Union*, Oxford University Press, 2011.

Keukeleire, Stephan and MacNaughtan, Jennifer, *The Foreign Policy of the European Union*, Palgrave Macmillan, Basingstoke, 2008.

Khosla, I.P. (ed), *India and the New Europe*, Konark, Delhi, 2004.

Lelieveldt, Herman and Princen, Sebastiaan, *The Politics of the European Union*, CUP, 2011.

Leonard, Mark, *Why Europe will run the 21st century*, Fourth Estate, London, 2005.

Lovell, Julia, *The Opium War*, Picador, Basingstoke, 2011.

Malone, David, *Does the Elephant Dance*? OUP, New Delhi, 2011.

Marquand, David, *The End of the West: The Once and Future Europe*, Princeton University Press, NJ, 2011.

Marsh, David, *The Euro*, Yale University Press, 2011.

Mishra Vidya Nivas and Argullol, Rafael, *From the Ganges to the Mediterranean*, Shubhi Publications, Gurgaon, 2008.

Mishra, Pankaj, *A Great Clamour*, Penguin India, 2013.

Mohn, Liz, *Cultures in Globalization*, Gutersloh, Germany, 2006.

Morris, Ian, *Why the West Rules-for Now*, Farrar, Straus and Giroux, New York. 2011.

Moyo, Dambisa, *How the West was Lost*, Allen Lane, London, 2011.

Peters, Dirk, *Constrained Balancing: the EU's Security Policy*, Palgrave Macmillan, Basingstoke, 2010.

Rajan, K.V., *The Ambassadors Club*, Harper Collins, New Delhi, 2012.

Reid, T.R., *The United States of Europe*, Penguin, 2004

Ross, George, *The European Union and its Crises*, Palgrave Macmillan, Basingstoke, 2011.

Seidelmann, Reimund and Vasilache, Andreas (eds), *European Union and Asia*, Nomos, Baden-Baden, 2009.

Sharma, Ruchir, *Breakout Nations*, Allen Lane, UK, 2012.

Srinivasan, Krishnan, *The Rise, Decline and Future of the British Commonwealth*, Palgrave Macmillan, Basingstoke, 2005.

Thant Myint U, *Where China meets India*, Faber and Faber, London, 2011.

Tharoor, Shashi, *Pax Indica*, Penguin India, 2012.

Thomas, Daniel C., *Making EU Foreign Policy*, Palgrave Macmillan, Basingstoke, 2011.

Toje, Asle, *The European Union as a Small Power*, Palgrave Macmillan, Basingstoke, 2010.

Wang Hui, *The End of the Revolution*, Verso, New York, 2009.

Wang Hui, *The Politics of Imagining Asia*, Harvard, 2011.

Wasserstein, Bernard, *Barbarism and Civilization*, OUP, 2007.

White, Hugh, *The China Choice*, Black Inc, Collingwood, Australia, 2013.

Wong, Rueben and Hill, Christopher, *National and European Foreign Policies*, Routledge, Abingdon, 2011.

Wulbers, Shazia Aziz (ed), *EU-India Relations*, Academic Foundation, New Delhi, 2008.

Journal Articles

Bacevich, Andrew J., "Let Europe be Europe", *Foreign Policy*, Mar/Apr 2010, Issue 178, 1.

Bagchi, Nirmalya, "A Comparative Analysis of the Factors for Fostering Innovation in BRICS from 1995 to 2009", *ASCI Journal of Management* 41 (1): 1-20, 2011.

Baily, Martin Neil and Kirkegaard, Jacob Funk, "Transforming the European Economy", *Institute for International Economics*, Washington, 2004.

Bicchi, Fredrica, "Our size fits all: Normative Power Europe and the Mediterranean", *Journal of European Public Policy*, Mar 2006, Vol 13, Issue 2, 286-303.

Cafruny, Alan W. and Ryner, Magnus, "Monetary Union and the Transatlantic and Social Dimensions of Europe's Crisis", *New Political Economy*, June 2007, 12:2.

Camroux, David, "Asia, Whose Asia? A return to the future of a Sino-Indic Asian Community", *The Pacific Review*, Routledge, 20:4, 551-575.

Conley, Heather A., "The End of the West: the Once and Future Europe", *International Affairs* 87:4 (2011), 975-984.

de Souza, Lucio Vinhas, "A Wider Europe", *Trade Relations between an enlarged Europe and the Russian Federation, Problems of Economic Transition*, Vol 49, No 2, June 2006, 6-33.

Dunne, Tim, "Good Citizen Europe", *International Affairs*, Jan 2008, Vol 84, Issue 1, 13-28A.

Falkner, Robert, "The Political Power of Normative Europe: EU Environmental Leadership in International Biotechnology Regulation", *Journal of European Public Policy*, June 2007, Vol 14, Issue 4, 507-526.

Faust, Jorg and Messner, Dirk, "Europe's New Security Strategy: Challenges for development Policy", *European Journal of Development Research*, Sept 2005, Vol 17, Issue 3, 423-436.

Finon, Dominique, "The EU foreign gas policy of Transit Corridors", *OPEC Energy Review*, March 2011.

Geddes, Andrew, "Europe's Border Relationships and International Migration Relations", *Journal of Common Market Studies*, Nov 2005, Vol 43, Issue 4, 787-806.

Gordon, Phillip H., "The Last Days of Europe: Epitaph for an Old Continent", *Foreign Affairs*, Sep/Oct 2007, Vol 86, Issue 5, 173.

Hartwich, Oliver Marc, "Does Europe Still Matter?," *Policy*. Winter 2009, Vol 25, Issue 2, 35-40.

Hieronymi, Otto, "Rebuilding the International Monetary Order: the responsibility of Europe, Japan and the United States", *Revisita de Economia Mundial*, 2009, Issue 23, 197-225.

Hockenos, Paul, "USA and Europe: partnership of equals", *World Policy Journal* (MIT) Winter 2008, Vol 25, Issue 4, 115-126.

Hyde-Price, Adrian, "A Tragic Actor? A Realist Perspective on ethical power Europe", *International Affairs*, Jan 2008, Vol 84, Issue 1, 29-44.

Icaza, Rosalba, "Global Europe, Guilty!", *Third World Quarterly*, Vol 31, No 1, 123-139.

Jackson, Bruce P., "The Soft War for Europe's East", *Policy Review*. Jun/Jul 2006, Issue 137, 3-14.

Jackson, Bruce Pitcairn, "A Turning Point for Europe's East", *Policy Review*, Apr/May 2010, Issue 160, 49-61

Jain, Rajendra K. and Pandey, Shreya, "The EU in the Eyes of India", *Asia Europe Journal*, Published on line 12 September 2010.

Kaldor, Mary, Martin, Mary and Selchow, Sabine, "Human Security: A New Strategic Narrative for Europe", *International Affairs*, Mar 2007, Vol 83, Issue 2, 273-288.

Karaganov, Sergey and Bordatchev, Timofey, "Towards a New Euro-Atlantic Security Architecture", *RIA Nososti, Russia in Global Affairs,* 21 December 2009.

Krotz, Ulrich, "Momentum and Impediments: Why Europe won't emerge as a full Political Actor on the World Stage soon", *Journal of Common Market Studies*, June 2009. Vol 47, Issue 3, 555-578.

Lane, Philip R. and Milesi-Ferretti, Gian Maria, "Europe and Global Imbalances", *Economic Policy*, July 2007, Vol 22, Issue 51, 519-573.

Lavenex, Sandra and Schimmelfennig, Frank, "Relations with the Wider Europe", *Journal of Common Market Studies*, Sept 2007 Supplement 1, Vol 45, Issue 1, 143-162.

Leiken, Robert S., "Europe's Angry Muslims", *Foreign Affairs*, Jul-Aug 2005, Vol 84, Issue 4, 120-135.

Maull, Hanns W., "Europe and the New Balance of Global Order", *International Affairs*, July 2005, Vol 81, Issue 4, 775-799.

Mayer, Hartmut, "Is it still called Chinese Whispers?", *International Affairs* 84:1 (2008) 61-79.

Mayer, Hartmut, "The Long Legacy of Dorian Gray", *Journal of European Integration*, 2008, 30:1, 7-25.

Meunier, S. and Nicolaidis, K., "The European Union as a Conflicted Trade Power", *Journal of European Public Policy*, 2006, 13(6): 906-25.

Mitzen, Jennifer, "Anchoring Europe's civilizing identity: habits, capabilities and Ontological Security", *Journal of European Public Policy*, Mar 2006, Vol 13, Issue 2, 270-285.

Modwel, Suman and Singh, Surendra, "The EU-India FTA Negotiations", *GEM/Sciences-Po, Paris. ORF Occasional paper* Feb 2012, Observer Research Foundation, New Delhi

Naumann, Michael, "Europe and America: The Ties that Bind", *Social Research*, Winter 2005, Vol 72, Issue 4, 799-806.

Nicolaidis, Kalypso, "Trusting the Poles?", *Journal of European Public Policy*, 14(5), Aug 2007, 682-698.

Petit, Isabelle, "Dispelling a Myth? The fathers of Europe and the Construction of an Euro-identity", *European Law Journal*, Sep 2006, Vol 12, Issue 5, 661-679.

Poettering, Hans-Gert, "Europe as a Global Player", *Harvard International Review*, Spring 2007, Vol 29, Issue 1, 26-29.

Rachman, Gideon, "Think Again: American Decline", *Foreign Policy*, Jan/ Feb 2011.

Reddy, Venugopal Y., "Global Economy: Emerging Issues", 7 September 2011, *Nizam College and ASCI Hyderabad.*

Reddy, Venugopal Y., "New Global Financial Architecture: Approaches and Issues", 25 October 2010. *London School of Economics and ASCI Hyderabad.*

Reddy, Venugopal Y., "Recent International Financial Turmoil", 2010, *ASCI Hyderabad Foundation Day Lecture.*

Reh, Christine, "The Convention on the Future of Europe and the development of Integration Theory: A lasting imprint?", *Journal of European Public Policy*, July 2008, Vol 15, Issue 5, 781-794.

Rydzewska, Joanna, "Beyond the Nation State: New Europe and Discourses of British Identity", *Journal of Contemporary European Studies*, Apr 2009, Vol 17, Issue 1, 91-107.

Sally, Razeen, "Europe and Asia", *Institute of Economic Affairs*, 2008 Blackwell, Oxford.

Sally, Razeen, "Europe, Trade and Globalization", *Economic Affairs*, June 2007, Vol 27, Issue 2, 99-109.

Sally, Razeen, "Liberty Outside the West", June 10 2011, *Hayek Lecture*, Freiburg.

Sally, Razeen, "Looking East: New EU-Asia Trade Negotiations", 3 November 2007, *ECIPE*, Jan Tumlir Policy Essay 03, 2007.

Saltmarsh, Matthew, "EU Asian Relations in the Media", *Asia Europe Journal* (2004) 2:15-18.

Subacchi, Paola, "Reforming Economic Governance in Europe: Exploring the Road to Effective Coordination", *International Affairs*, July 2005, Vol 81, Issue 4, 741-755.

Sweeney, Simon, "Europe, the State and Globalisation," *Public Administration*, Vol 85, No 3, 2007, 857-883

Whitman, Richard G. and Juncos Ana E., "European Union's Relations with the Wider Europe", *Journal of Common Market Studies*, Sept 2009. Supplement 1, Vol 47, 193-212.

Yeo Lay Hwee, "Dimensions of Asia-Europe Cooperation", *Asia Europe Journal* (2004) 2:19-31.

Zielonka, Jan, "Europe as a Global Actor: Empire by Example?", *International Affairs*, May 2008, Vol 2008, Issue 3, 471-484.

Zimmermann, Hubert, "Realist Power Europe?", *Journal of Common Market Studies*, Nov 2007, Vol 45, Issue 4, 813-832.

INDEX